In the Basement
of the Ivory Tower

The Truth
About College

PROFESSOR X

PENGUIN BOOKS

PENGUIN BOOKS

Published by the Penguin Group

Penguin Group (USA) Inc., 375 Hudson Street, New York, New York 10014, U.S.A. • Penguin Group
(Canada), 90 Eglinton Avenue East, Suite 700, Toronto, Ontario, Canada M4P 2Y3 (a division of Pearson
Penguin Canada Inc.) • Penguin Books Ltd, 80 Strand, London WC2R 0RL, England • Penguin Ireland,
25 St. Stephen's Green, Dublin 2, Ireland (a division of Penguin Books Ltd) • Penguin Books Australia
Ltd, 250 Camberwell Road, Camberwell, Victoria 3124, Australia (a division of Pearson Australia Group
Pty Ltd) • Penguin Books India Pvt Ltd, 11 Community Centre, Panchsheel Park, New Delhi – 110 017,
India • Penguin Group (NZ), 67 Apollo Drive, Rosedale, Auckland 0632, New Zealand (a division of
Pearson New Zealand Ltd) • Penguin Books (South Africa) (Pty) Ltd, 24 Sturdee Avenue, Rosebank,
Johannesburg 2196, South Africa

Penguin Books Ltd, Registered Offices: 80 Strand, London WC2R 0RL, England

First published in the United States of America by Viking Penguin,
a member of Penguin Group (USA) Inc. 2011
Published with a new preface in Penguin Books 2012

10 9 8 7 6 5 4 3 2 1

Portions of this book appeared in "In the Basement of the Ivory Tower," *The Atlantic*, June 2008.

Portions of the new preface previously appeared online in *The Atlantic, The Daily Beast, Inside Higher Ed,*
and *The Washington Independent Review of Books.*

Grateful acknowledgment is made for permission to reprint the following copyrighted works:
  "This Is Just to Say" from *The Collected Poems: Volume I, 1909–1939* by William Carlos Williams.
Copyright © 1938 by New Directions Publishing Corp. Reprinted by permission of New Directions
Publishing Corp.
  Excerpt from "Autumn Begins in Martin's Ferry Ohio" from *The Branch Will Not Break* by James
Wright. © 1963 by James Wright. Reprinted by permission of Wesleyan University Press.

THE LIBRARY OF CONGRESS HAS CATALOGED THE HARDCOVER EDITION AS FOLLOWS:
Professor X.
  In the basement of the ivory tower : confessions of an accidental academic / Professor X.
    p. cm.
  ISBN 978-0-670-02256-4 (hc.)
  ISBN 978-0-14-312029-2 (pbk.)
  1. College teachers, Part-time—United States—Social conditions. 2. College teachers, Part-time—
United States—Anecdotes. 3. English teachers—United States—Anecdotes. I. Title.
  LB2331.72.P76 2011
  378.1'2—dc22   2010035383

Printed in the United States of America

Author's Note

THIS BOOK is what we teachers call a quest narrative, touching on the perils of real estate and higher education. It is inhabited not by archetypes or composites but by people, though I have taken great pains to disguise them when necessary to protect their privacy. I have also changed the names of the colleges where I teach, freely added bell towers, parking lots, and quadrangles, and moved lecture halls and gymnasiums around like an architecture student running amok with his models. I write anonymously because I have no desire to single out my institutions; I believe the issues I raise to be universal. I love teaching and I love my colleges. I hope they will continue to have me.

Contents

Preface to the Paperback Edition

S INCE THE APPEARANCE IN the *Atlantic* of my essay "In the Basement of the Ivory Tower" in June 2008, in which I questioned the wisdom of sending seemingly everyone in the United States through the higher education mill, it's become increasingly apparent to me that I'm far from the only one with misgivings about the value of a college education. Indeed, I've discovered to my surprise that, rather than a lone crank, I'm a voice in a growing movement.

I hadn't expected my essay, inspired by the frustrations of teaching students unprepared for the rigors of college-level work, to attract much notice. But the volume and vehemence of the feedback the piece generated was overwhelming. It drew more visitors to *The Atlantic*'s Web site than almost any other article that year and provoked an avalanche of letters to the editor. It even started turning up on the syllabi of college writing classes and the agendas of educational conferences.

In the years since then—and especially after I added to the critical tumult by expanding my arguments into this book—I found myself noticing similar sentiments expressed elsewhere. Start paying attention and you will soon find that more and more Americans are skeptical about the benefits of college. "Some Say Bypassing a Higher Education Is Smarter than Paying for a Degree," reads a recent headline in *The Washington*

Post. The article, which addresses everything from higher education's outsize price tag to its questionable correlation with career success, garnered more than 4,000 Facebook recommendations on the *Post*'s Web site. Last spring the Harvard Graduate School of Education published a study suggesting that (*gasp!*) four-year college is perhaps not for everyone. Rather, for a growing proportion of students, the report contends, internships, apprenticeships, and vocational training would be far more beneficial.

Even for the academically inclined, the value of college in this economic climate is increasingly subject to question. "Is Going to an Elite College Worth the Cost?" asks *New York Times* reporter Jacques Steinberg. He surveys economic studies, peruses labor reports, and interviews economists and sociologists to ascertain whether there's really a significant payoff for choosing a swanky private college over someplace less glamorous. The answer? Inconclusive. Parents, of course, obsess over the Ivy League admissions game, carefully studying up on how to give their kids an edge. *U.S. News & World Report's* annual college breakdown gets as much publicity these days as the Oscar nominations. But are those students fortunate enough to gain admission really getting an education worthy of the fuss? Reports of rampant grade inflation at many of these schools throw even a straight-A transcript from a prestigious university into question. (Some colleges, including Princeton, have taken to imposing limits on how many A's instructors can award in any course, while the University of North Carolina has resorted to including median class grades on students' transcripts so as to make it more readily apparent which A's were earned in easy courses.) A recent book by Andrew Hacker and Claudia Dreifus, *Higher Education?: How Colleges Are Wasting Our Money and Failing Our Kids*, makes the case that students at elite colleges are being left to fend for themselves while their impressively credentialed professors take constant sabbaticals and leave the actual teaching to inexperienced assistants.

Yet despite mounting skepticism, and in the face of the economic downturn, colleges continue to demand ever-higher fees, saddling graduates with crushing debt. In June of last year the Federal Reserve released new figures showing that the nation's total student loan debt now sits at about $830 billion—for the first time surpassing the nation's credit card debt. Student loan debt, it should be noted, is in many respects less forgiving than credit card debt. "These loans typically can't be discharged in bankruptcy," explains the *Wall Street Journal*. "They have different repayment terms, some of which have heavy consequences for borrowers who miss payments." Some commentators have even suggested that the crimp the financial downturn is putting on students' ability to get loans may in fact be doing those students a favor. In a piece titled, "Huge Debt Incurred for College Tuition Just Doesn't Make the Grade," syndicated financial columnist Michelle Singletary writes, "I'll be honest. I think if college students and their parents have a harder time getting loans, that's a good thing. Perhaps now more people will stop and consider the long-term implications of taking on so much of this so-called good debt."

In the past, the unquestioned argument for taking on so much debt has been the "college premium," the increase in earnings over a lifetime that one can expect to get with a college degree. But does such a premium still exist?

A recent report, "The College Payoff," examines the data and not surprisingly answers the question resoundingly in the affirmative. I say "not surprisingly" because the study was sponsored by the Georgetown University Center on Education and the Workforce. What possible economic interest could the folks at Georgetown University have in promoting ever-increasing levels of college attendance? As the authors tell us in their introduction, they "are honored to be partners in [the] mission of promoting postsecondary access and completion for all Americans." They might have wanted to tag this statement with a big SPOILER ALERT.

Some of what the report reveals is obvious. Workers who never finish high school often don't make all that much money. Workers with professional or graduate degrees sometimes make a boatload of it. It's good to be a doctor or a lawyer. And as for the vast swath of jobs in the middle, the ones between janitor and cardiologist, workers with a bachelor's degree will indeed earn more than their less-educated counterparts. A human-resources manager who has not attended college can expect to earn $1.9 million over the course of a working lifetime; throw in a four-year degree, and the figure increases by a cool million. A food-service manager can expect to take home $1.2 million in a forty-year work life; that same manager with a bachelor's can pull in $1.8 million. A college degree will boost the figure for a paralegal or legal assistant from $1.7 million to $2 million, or about $7,500 a year, figuring an employment span of forty years.

OK, so the college premium exists. That doesn't mean it ought to.

Unless you've got an alternate strategy to make money, unless you're the plumber I seem to keep on retainer or the genius who invented the Snuggie or unless you're fortunate enough to manufacture wraparound desks, thirty of which go in every college classroom, college attendance is non-negotiable.

But that doesn't make it right.

What the study reveals inadvertently is most interesting: just how many positions are currently being filled by those who never made it past high school.

Some numbers will come as no surprise: 71 percent of janitors have only high-school degrees. Fully three quarters of all pest control and grounds maintenance workers are in the same situation. A little more than half of barbers and cosmetologists have a high-school diploma or less; the same holds true for 67 percent of tobacco-roasting machine operators.

But did you know that 11 percent of "chief executives and legislators"—the study's categorization—have been only to high school? The figure jumps to 23 percent with an associate's degree or less. Eighteen percent of general and operations managers never attended college. Education administrators—now that might seem a highly educated group, but 5 percent have seen no reason to pass through the gates of higher education, and 14 percent have only some college. Claims adjusters, appraisers, examiners, and investigators—18 percent haven't gone beyond high school, and twice that number don't have a four-year college degree. Fourteen percent of advertising salespeople went to high school and then called it quits. High school only: electrical and electronics engineers, 4 percent; industrial engineers, 8 percent.

Some of these percentages might not be large, but their very existence demonstrates the fact that those without college, or without a completed college degree, can probably do their jobs just fine.

American colleges would have us believe that the skills they purport to teach, the critical thinking and higher levels of reasoning and all that, are crucial to competent performance in the workplace. This is baloney, less a line of reasoning than a sales pitch rooted in academic snobbery—a naked appeal to our intellectual insecurities.

Do we want to extend the argument, and say that those lacking a bachelor's degree are the absolute worst at their jobs? Twelve percent of financial managers have only a high-school education—are they the ones who plunged the country into the recession? Perhaps the 14 percent of human resource managers who didn't go to college are the ones who kept our unemployment rate hovering at 10 percent. The 4 percent of miscellaneous engineers, including nuclear engineers, who didn't get past high school—did we dispatch a delegation of those Homer Simpson–like nincompoops to help set up the safety systems for Tokyo's nuclear reactors? I guess we should blame the bottom 8 percent of securities, commodities, and financial services sales agents for designing all those toxic mortgage instruments.

The surgeon and the rocket scientist require specialized training, but most occupations are not brain surgery and not rocket science. The students I teach as an adjunct are pointed toward midlevel careers. If not for America's lopsided love affair with higher education, none of my students would really require the B.A. or B.S. degrees toward which they labor painfully. High-school literacy and math skills would be quite sufficient. Four years of college are, for them, a waste of time and an economic burden. According to the latest figures from the Project on Student Debt, it's fair to assume that more than 60 percent of them will graduate with student loans, and those debts will average about $25,000.

Unfortunately, America's sense of self-worth is still bound up in its college numbers. To force fewer people into college might be a societal good, but it's hard to imagine Barack Obama gripping the sides of a podium and announcing, "College enrollments fell by almost 9 percent last year, and I couldn't be prouder of the American people." That's not what modern industrialized nations do. We feel we'd be laughed at.

The college premium exists, to be sure, but it's an artificial construct. Colleges have inserted themselves squarely in the occupational world. Industry and academia march hand in hand to a song of credential inflation: young people who aspire to working at anything beyond fast-food assembly better have that sheepskin in hand. Most B.A. degrees say little to employers in terms of specific skills; they are a marker, like a hand stamp that gains one entrance to a nightclub. They point to little more than a willingness to pay college tuition and complete degree requirements. Those lacking higher education find themselves ineligible for promotion, herded to lesser career tracks.

There are more college graduates in the United States than ever before. I ask you: are things running noticeably more smoothly?

A firefighter with a college degree can expect to earn, in his lifetime, $600,000 more than his counterparts without. When my house is burning down, when I'm trapped on an upper floor, I want simply the best firefighter to come to my aid. I want someone brave and true and skilled in the art of rescue. It will be of no help or reassurance to either of us that he once wrote a research paper on Maslow's Hierarchy.

The Autobiography of Malcolm X, "Shooting an Elephant," *Coming of Age in Samoa,* "Hope is the Thing with Feathers," *The Interpretation of Dreams, The Second Sex*—the warhorse texts of college study make fine reading for those who are interested, but are ultimately relevant to very few of us. Let's stop making the American workforce pay for the privilege of experiencing them.

. . .

Since when have colleges become so controversial, anyway? They used to embody humankind at its most elevated; now, they're just another institution to be wary of.

I attended college in the 1970s, when higher education wasn't newsworthy. When you went away to college, you really went away. I checked into a sylvan campus far away from everything, signed up for a meal plan, submerged myself in the library stacks, and essentially disappeared. Society took little note of academia's somnolent doings because there was little to take note of. Student activism on any significant scale was moribund. The Vietnam War was over.

Colleges were viewed, in the main, as a hiatus from the real world. In my cinderblock dormitory, I watched no television and read no newspapers.. We seemed to dwell more in the dusty, monochromatic past than the present, even when we weren't reading Chaucer and Tacitus. I spent four leisurely years imbibing great books and ideas. I could write a good literature paper—it seemed one of the few things I was suited to do—so a degree in English was my destiny. Since college was a lot cheaper in those days, I didn't rack up much debt. I knew my degree wouldn't get me a job, but no one had promised that it would. It wasn't as though the college was hoodwinking me. My pursuit was rather solipsistic and no doubt shortsighted but harmless—a solitary pastime, like collecting penguin figurines or breeding orchids.

Twenty years later, I found myself teaching part-time at a small private college, and I was struck by the extent to which the institution had changed. College wasn't the old place of retreat and meditation that I remembered—a place to quietly condition one's mind with four years of intellectual crunches and sets and reps. It no longer seemed that intellectual a place at all. Now it was a place where students accumulated credits to advance at their jobs. College was very much part of the workaday world. All kinds of people attended because if they wanted a bigger paycheck, they had no choice in the matter. The rolls had expanded dramatically, which seemed initially like a good thing. But I was teaching many students who weren't prepared to do even high school work. I was expected to coax critically reasoned research papers from students who possessed no life of the mind at all: young and not-so-young men and women who didn't read and thought not a whit about ideas.

The task was impossible. I couldn't shake the sense that the college simply wanted to enroll as many students as possible—and that colleges in general had become more focused on the bottom line than in my day. The system had ended up expanding in ways that industry always expands: by jacking up prices, putting money into public relations, and broadening the customer base by marketing even to customers dubiously served by the product.

If my informal observations about the tenor of our national discourse are accurate, however, many of those customers are finally starting to ask some tough questions—chief among them: Is all this higher education really necessary?

And while colleges claim to instill critical thinking skills, I'm not sure they're thrilled to be the focus of so much critical thought.

Preface

M Y WIFE AND I MARKED the turn of the millennium by buying a home that we really couldn't afford. We dreamed of living in an old clapboard house dripping with character, of cheerfully raking our leaves and tending a vegetable garden, of walking hand in hand to the center of town, where we could shop in the markets, or loaf with a newspaper in the library, or sit on the village green and bask in the solemn presence of the churches. We wanted our children to grow up knowing everyone in town.

We got all that, but the cost to our bank accounts and mental health was incalculable. Not long after we closed on the house, we both realized that one of us would have to work a second job in order for us to maintain a middle-class existence. I am the proud possessor of the most useless advanced degree there is—a Master of Fine Arts in Creative Writing, which qualifies me to do very little other than teach introductory-level college English courses. And so I awoke one morning from uneasy dreams and found myself transformed into a part-time instructor of college English.

I spend many of my evenings now away from my family. I finish my job (I labor in a rather dreary corner of the government) and stop home for a quick bite. I don't want the children to realize how much I am away from them, and this time together creates the illusion, I think, that all is normal. I eat a sandwich and we discuss their school day before I push off to ply my nighttime trade.

For a number of years now I have been teaching classes at two schools: a small private college, which I will call Pembrook College, and a two-year community college, which I will call Huron State. Both were desperate for adjuncts, the low-cost part-timers who work without benefits and make up a growing percentage of many college faculties. Never had I imagined that this would be my destiny, to put in a full eight-hour workday and then drive wearily to teach night classes at a bottom-tier institution. While a large part of the world watches *American Idol,* I rattle on about Kafka and Joyce and Gwendolyn Brooks to a classroom of reluctant students. Some are wide-eyed and fidgety with fatigue. I teach expository writing, trying to wring college-level prose from students whose skills may just graze the lower reaches of high school. We assemble and disassemble paragraphs. We hack out useless words—a painful step, that one, for we sometimes find ourselves left with nothing.

On the first night, I ask a few questions. How many of you took this class because of an abiding love of literature? No hands go up, ever—they are honest, I will give them that. How many of you are taking this class only because you have to? Now all hands shoot up, to the accompaniment of some self-conscious laughter. How many of you hate studying literature, and have hated it for as long as you can remember? Many hands, most hands, sometimes all hands go up. Again we laugh. The ice has been broken. How many of you read for pleasure? One hand goes up, sometimes two.

In this simple opening-night meet-and-greet session we come smack against the crux of college life in what I think of as the basement of the ivory tower. College enrollment has expanded wildly over the last thirty years, and more than ever before includes many students who are unprepared for the rigorous demands of higher education. Many of my students have no business being there, and a great many will not graduate. As they freely admit, they are not in my classes because they want to be. The colleges require that all students, no matter what their majors or career objectives, pass English 101 (Introduction to College Writing) and English 102 (Introduction to College Literature). Some of my students don't even want to be in college in the first place, but what choice do they have? For a licensed practical nurse to become a registered nurse requires an associate's degree (awarded after approximately two years in college) in applied science—68 college credits divided equally between nursing and general education. To become a state trooper requires two years of college, and please note that in some states military and/or law enforcement experience does not substitute for the required degree.

A quick look at the classifieds reveals the large number of jobs that either require or discreetly suggest that the applicant have at least some college under his or her belt. A tabloid newspaper is looking for someone to sell legal advertising. Qualifications: high school diploma or equivalent, some college preferred. A wholesaler needs to hire an accounts receivable clerk. Qualifications include a familiarity with Microsoft Office and the ability to assemble billing statements and send them out on a monthly basis, to call past-due accounts, and to process payments; a two-year college accounting degree is also required. Retail giantess Ann Taylor prefers that her district managers have a bachelor's degree. Interested in testing water? High school required, college preferred.

College preferred. What sort of job applicant in the midst of a recession disappoints the supervisor from the start by not satisfying his or her preference?

We are used to getting what we want in the United States, and we have a vague feeling that the world would run more smoothly, more efficiently, more professionally if every worker had some college under his or her belt. But who stops to think of the cost of this worthy aspiration to the taxpayers and to the weary souls who are being sent back to school, often at great expense, for no real reason? There is a sense that our bank tellers should be college educated, and our medical billing techs, our county tax clerks, our child welfare agents, our court officers and sheriffs and federal marshals. We want the police officer who stops the car with the broken taillight to have a nodding acquaintance with great literature. We want that officer to have read *King Lear,* to understand Gloucester's literal blindness as a signpost toward Lear's figurative blindness, and to be aware that the Fool and Cordelia, the two great truth-tellers, never appear onstage together, and were probably doubled by one actor. I suppose that would be nice. Perhaps having read *Invisible Man* or *A Raisin in the Sun* will render a police officer less likely to indulge in racial profiling. I wonder. Will an acquaintance with Steinbeck make the highway patrolman more sympathetic to the plight of the poor, so that he will at least understand the lives of those who simply cannot get it together to get their taillights repaired? Will it benefit the correctional officer to read *The Autobiography of Malcolm X*? The health-care worker *Arrowsmith*? Should the case manager at Child Protective Services read Sylvia Plath's "Daddy"?

America is an idealistic place, and we seem wary of the vocational education track. We won't do anything that might impede the freedom to pursue happiness. Telling someone that college is not right for him seems harsh and classist, vaguely Dickensian, as though we were sentencing him to a life in the coal mines. Telling individuals that they're not "college material" is like telling them that they can't afford the house of their

dreams with the two-car garage and the big spread of land—
that their fate is to stay in the cramped apartment with the
running toilet and the knocking radiators and the bass-playing
neighbor.

This push for universal college enrollment, which at first
glance seems emblematic of American opportunity and class
mobility, is in fact hurting those whom it is meant to help.
Students are leaving two- and four-year colleges with enormous amounts of debt. The latest figures, from 2007–08, put
the percentage of four-year graduates leaving college with debt
at 66 percent. The top 10 percent of those owe $44,500 or more;
50 percent owe at least $20,000.[1] Lower-income students at least
have part of their tab picked up by the taxpayer through such
programs as the federal Pell Grant, but for those of my students
who want to become state troopers or firemen, the unnecessary
cost and the inefficiency of the whole process is staggering.

Community colleges are the cheaper alternative to four-year
schools, but can they really be called cheaper when so many
students do not graduate? Fully 50 percent of community college students drop out before their second year and only 25
percent manage to finish the two-year program in three years.[2]

As my students drift into the classroom each evening, I find
myself feeling sorry for them. Many are in over their heads.
This whole college thing often turns out to be a bust. College
is difficult even for highly motivated students who know how
to write papers and study for exams. My students have no such
abilities. They lack rudimentary study skills; in some cases,
they are not even functionally literate. Many of them are so
dispossessed of context that every bit of new information simply
raises more questions. Some are not ready for high school,
much less college. For many, college is a negative experience.
The classes are more difficult than they could have dreamed,
and there is simply no time to complete all the work.

As an adjunct, I am paid a flat fee for each class that I teach. I receive no benefits, and I am never going to get tenure. Adjunct instruction is a relatively recent innovation, dating, on a significant scale, from about the mid-1980s. It is a growing field. From 1987 to 1999, use of adjuncts grew by 30 percent at four-year institutions.[3]

The increased use of adjunct instructors is a direct result of the explosion in college enrollments, which have expanded dramatically since 1980. In 1940, there were 1.5 million college students in the United States. Twenty years later the figure had doubled, to 2.9 million.[4] In 1980, there were more than 12 million students enrolled in college, and by 2004, we were up to nearly 17.5 million. Census projections for 2016 hover around 21 million.[5] Everybody goes to college now, though not everybody graduates.

Somebody has to teach these twenty-or-so-million students, and hiring adjuncts is the most economical way to do it.

As an adjunct, I am faced with the unenviable job of teaching college classes to students who are quite unprepared for higher education. A number of societal forces have coalesced into a tsunami of difficulty: the happy-talk mantra that anyone can do anything if he or she works hard enough; the sense of college as a universal right and need; the new mania for credentials; financial necessity on the part of both colleges and students. Colleges wish to maintain strict academic standards while admitting everyone who wants to get in, a pool that includes a great many questionable learners. The result is a system rife with contradiction. The conflict between open admissions and basic standards can never be reconciled. Something has got to give.

Sometimes my students piss me off. I could scream when they hand in assignments that don't make any sense. But I can't stay mad at them. They're doing their best. The colleges must bear some responsibility; they, after all, are benefiting from a situation that is, to use current jargon, not sustainable. There seems to be a great gulf between the realm of hype and hard reality. No one is thinking about the larger implications, or even the morality, of admitting so many students to classes they cannot possibly pass. No one has drawn up the flowchart and seen that, while more widespread college admission is a bonanza for the colleges and makes the entire United States of America feel rather pleased with itself, there is one point of irreconcilable conflict in the system, and that is the moment when the adjunct instructor must ink an F on that first writing assignment. The zeitgeist of eternal academic possibility is a great inverted pyramid, and its rather sharp point is poking, uncomfortably, a spot just about midway between my shoulder blades.

I am the man who has to lower the hammer.

We may look mild-mannered, we adjunct instructors, in our eyeglasses and our corduroy jackets, our bald heads and trimmed beards, our peasant skirts and Birkenstocks, our dresses with collars that look almost clerical, but we are nothing less than academic hit men. We are paid by the college to perform the dirty work that no one else wants to do, the wrenching, draining, sorrowful business of teaching and failing the unprepared who often don't even know they are unprepared. We are faceless soldiers culled from the dregs of academe. We operate under cover of darkness. We are not characters out of great academic novels such as *Pnin* or *Lucky Jim*. We have more in common with Anton Chigurh from *No Country for Old Men*. I am John Travolta in *Pulp Fiction* but in a corduroy jacket and bow tie. I feel evil and soiled. I wander the halls of academe like a modern Coriolanus bearing sword and grade book, "a thing of blood, whose every motion / Was timed with dying cries." But what can I do?

. . .

On a snowy Wednesday night in January, I stand before a class of twenty. I have come directly from work. So have the students. Some wear rayon suits and cruel-looking high heels. A few sport medical scrubs in bright purple and aquamarine. Some are very young and some are in their forties or fifties; most are in that awkward middle ground, late twenties to early thirties, when the impulses of youth find themselves crowded out by the vast pressures of adulthood. As I lecture, a few students on tight schedules eat chicken and rice off Styrofoam trays. I feel like Robert Goulet doing dinner theater. We read "Sunday Morning" by Wallace Stevens.

> *Complacencies of the peignoir, and late*
> *Coffee and oranges in a sunny chair,*

The verse gets difficult, and the class grows impatient. Each allusion, each wooly metaphor, seems to lead us astray from the direct path of interpretation. *Why doesn't he just say what he means?* My students put up with poetry, barely. Most are in school to get a better job. They've got no time or inclination to start opening Wallace Stevens's nested boxes of meaning. They need to get where they are going.

Snow is falling. It taps at the classroom windows. My students grow uneasy and restless. They look at their cell phones. Some have long drives home in unreliable vehicles, but unless a daytime blizzard shutters the school completely, there are no mechanisms for canceling or even shortening a night class. Stevens falls flat. Matthew Arnold fares just the smallest bit better. I point out the violence in "Dover Beach," the clashing ignorant armies, the fragments of shale hurled randomly by the waves up the shore, nature molding life into form through acts of apparent chaos. In college, I wrote a paper on "Dover Beach," failing to notice that the whole thing was about Darwin's theory of natural selection, and received a C. My professor's stern marginal comments have traveled down the ages, and now make up the central point of my little lecture.

The final poem of the night comes from the back of the textbook, the section of contemporary poetry. Sometimes I teach poetry in strict chronological order, because I feel that to understand any art you have to understand what came before. Then I get fed up with the rigidity of that approach. I also sense the students paying less attention to the poems themselves than to the dates of composition. They watch the years creep forward. Soon it will be over! I can feel their excitement when we get to modernism. *This must be the end! What is there going to be—something after modernism? There couldn't possibly be postmodernism, could there?* So then I try teaching the poems randomly, scattershot, letting one work lead to another, trying to foster in the students something approaching the joy of discovery. The textbooks don't have a clear idea how to handle this; some years the texts we use (the department mandates them) follow chronology, and other years theme.

We read "I Go Back to May 1937" by Sharon Olds. In this poem, the speaker examines photographs of her mother and father at school. They are innocent college kids, she writes; "they would never hurt anybody." The speaker marvels at her knowledge of what the future holds. She addresses the old images directly: "you are going to do things / you cannot imagine you would ever do." She chronicles her parents' mistakes and suffering—"you are going to want to die"—but, naturally desiring her own existence, wouldn't change history to keep them apart. "Do what you are going to do," she writes with resignation, "and I will tell about it."

Snow drums with force on the windows. Other classes seem

to be calling it a night. We hear the hubbub and nervous laughter of groups filing past the classroom door. I tell my class that they can leave. The speed with which they jump out of their seats is unseemly. Some of the younger students are packed and gone in twenty seconds.

I put away the desktop podium and spend a few minutes sitting amid my books and papers. The Sharon Olds poem blindsided me. I can't get it out of my mind. My wife and I—we were as innocent as those college kids in the photos. Our marriage was a placid one. We seldom argued. And now look at us!

The house we bought, out entrance ticket into the American suburban dream, has soured our life together. We fight bitterly now, in an unfamiliar way, until we are hoarse and spent. Today it was about grout. The bathroom grout. The craziest thing: whether or not all the bathroom grout would need to be replaced. Our quarrels have taken on a weird geometry. A single word (grout, chimney, foundation) or a single small event that under different circumstances might escape notice (the rain pattering on the roof in a new and more vivid way, an unexplainable delay in the arrival of heat in the morning) can spark an oddly bitter argument, one of those great shaking fights that seems to reverberate with a life of its own. Our dirty grout and chimneys in need of repointing start to seem inexorably linked to our massive personality flaws. Afterward we are exhausted and tearful. We move in a hangover of gloom.

The classroom building is very quiet. I don't hear the distant droning of any other adjunct. Everyone must be gone. I find myself reading the Sharon Olds poem over again. There is my life, flapping like laundry strung from the poem's long, taut, artless-seeming lines. My students digested the poem and thought of nothing but the snow and the balding tires on their cars. I want literature to resonate for them, but perhaps the prerequisite for that is the sort of pain I wouldn't wish on anyone.

At the poem's end the speaker achieves a measure of resignation. She would not alter reality, if she could, and stop her parents from coming together. She wants to live, of course; she realizes that the essence of life is suffering, and she might as well be around as the artist documenting their pain. "Do what you are going to do, and I will tell about it," she writes.

I've been sitting at the desk for a long time. The classroom motion detector senses no life, and the lights wink out. It's time to go home.

1

The Adjunct

I ATTENDED COLLEGE in the 1970s. Midsemester of my freshman year I found myself chatting with the girl who sat across from me in a history class. She told me she was studying to be a nurse. She was a sweet girl, with a friendly, square-jawed face and twin plastic bows holding the sides of her hair in place; no doubt she went on to make someone a solid and dependable wife. She asked me what college I was in.

"What college?" I said mockingly. "Silly girl. *This* college. What do you think, I commute to UCLA?"

She gave me the fisheye. She introduced me to the concept that a College of Nursing existed on campus, but that intelligence didn't spur me on to figure out which particular college I was in. I went to class, studied a little, read the campus newspaper's accounts of research labs and internships and sometimes wondered: how in the world do you get involved with something like that? It was another classmate who finally clarified everything for me. Harry, twenty-five years old, was a chronic pot smoker and indolent film major. His checkered academic career had left him highly sensitive to the nuances of school enrollment and academic placement. He'd been cashiered from other colleges; he knew the ins and outs. He ticked off the colleges at our own institution for me. There were colleges of nursing and business and education and performing arts.

"So which do I go to?" I asked. You see how stupid I was? Arts and Sciences, he replied.

"Film seems like a liberal art," I said, my confidence in such matters growing. "You must go there too."

Ah no, said Harry wistfully. He was in the College of General Studies, which was the least prestigious of all the schools. He was hoping to keep up his grades so the administration would allow him to transfer into Arts and Sciences, officially declare his major, and be taught by full-time professors, not just adjuncts.

Harry had truly enlightened me. I began looking at the teachers at our sprawling university in a new way. I took note of the instructors who appeared on campus only at dinnertime, the middle-aged bald guys in trench coats and Florsheim shoes carrying accounting textbooks. I saw them and thought: CGS teachers. Adjuncts.

And then I forgot about these distinctions for about twenty years.

. . .

When I finally finished my master's degree, my wife had a brainstorm. Why didn't I adjunct, maybe a class per semester? It would give us some extra cash for vacations, or maybe for a new car if the need arose. We speculated on how much money adjuncting paid. I thought a grand per course; she thought more like two. She turned out to be right. The money attracted me, but I couldn't get my arms around the idea of actually teaching college. It seemed highly unlikely.

Nevertheless, I made crisp copies of my newly minted MFA degree, retyped my unimpressive resumé, photocopied some writing I had published, and prepared a package to send to nearby Pembrook College. Pembrook was nothing but a name to me, a tidy collection of buildings that I glimpsed on occasion from the highway, a place that sometimes turned up in squibs in the newspaper. I'd never set foot on its campus, and didn't know what its academic strengths were, or if it even had any. I never gave a thought to who made up its student body. I sent the package off.

Normally this would be the place to write ". . . and promptly forgot about it." But I had no time to do any forgetting. A scant week later I got a call from Dr. Ludlow, the chairman of the English department. We set up an interview.

The campus turned out to be lovely, a neat little collection of buildings from various eras nestled on a hillside. The place was a quiet haven of ornate stonework and columns, peaked roofs, stained glass windows, Gothic Revival archways, sweeping quads, and prim Victorian scalloping. Students chatted or examined their cell phones or studied languidly under spreading trees. On the athletic fields, balls clicked faintly against bats. Bells tolled irregularly. I sat in my car and breathed it all in, deeply. I felt an inordinate peace. I had a job interview looming, but I was not nervous. What place could be more tranquil than a college campus? The only thing I felt was a gnawing regret: why hadn't I gotten my Ph.D. and spent my life in such placid surroundings as these? The cares of marriage, of raising children, the crushing monotony and bureaucracy of my full-time job—these all melted away. Could there be a healthier environment than college? A middle-aged professor in a polo shirt and Wallabees—Wallabees!—moseyed abstractedly past the car, open text in hand. He was trim and fit-looking. He exuded calm. What must be the state of his arteries? How unobstructed must they be? In my mind, I could hear the strong rhythms of his sluicing blood.

Dr. Ludlow greeted me warmly. She was a petite woman, a flat five-foot-tall. She was attired exotically in a dark dress with slits through which I glimpsed a crushed red material, like coffin satin. She told me how much she had loved my journalism, and my ego arched with displeasure. I found her use of the term "journalism" just slightly, vexingly inaccurate: my essays had been published in newspapers and magazines, but the first way I would categorize them would not be journalism. Had I written accounts of Zoning Board of Appeals meetings, that would be journalism. But whatever. She was just being nice. She said she had laughed out loud at the humor in some of my pieces. Well, okay then. Now we were talking. She was flattering me. I knew immediately: she wanted me for the job. What they were looking for, she said, was someone to teach freshman English, known as English 101 or Introduction to College Writing, and English 102, Introduction to College Literature, to students in the evening program. She handed me the standard English 102 anthology, a big brick of writing from all eras, and asked me what approach I would take to teaching "Daddy" by Sylvia Plath.

Suddenly, I was very nervous. I paged anxiously through the book, looking rather desperately for the poem. I had to get a grip. "Well, the first thing I would go over is basic study skills— the use of an index and all that, heh, heh." She seemed unmoved by my self-deprecating humor. I finally found the poem and read it through quickly. I had read it in college. In fact, it was during this episode that I formulated the approach that would serve me so well with "Dover Beach." I had gotten a poor grade on a paper about "Daddy" in one of my own freshman English classes because I had neglected to mention Ted Hughes. The simple explanation for this was that I hadn't *known* about Ted Hughes. Never heard of him. Of course, he was mentioned prominently in the little biographical sketch of Plath that introduced her section of poetry in the text, but I hadn't been assigned to read that, had I? But now I talked feverishly and passionately about Plath and Hughes, their symbiotic and consumptive relationship; I talked about the poem's irony, about the way its foursquare rhythm comes at the reader like a drill press; I alluded to its childish rhymes, and of course its edgy metaphorical choices—the Nazis and all. I could see in Dr. Ludlow's face that I was doing well. This is a poem, I said, that simply couldn't be fully understood unmoored from its real-life circumstances. I talked about all I knew about the Hughes/Plath union, which really wasn't much, and then I saw a small darkening of Dr. Ludlow's features. Her brow creased; her mouth made a moue. I had taken my approach too far. I hit the brakes and backpedaled. "But of course, we don't exactly know where the reality ends and the poetry begins," I said. "It would be a mistake to confuse the speaker with Sylvia Plath. And that's one thing I would want the class to be very clear about."

Dr. Ludlow smiled. She liked my answer.

I was astounded at how well the interview was proceeding. I couldn't quite believe that I would be teaching college. I was still frankly in awe of my own college professors. Their lives seemed purposeful and integrated—full of pleasure, and none too strenuous.

A year or two after graduation, I was in the Strand Book Store on Broadway at 12th Street in New York City. I came upon one of my English professors: a woman who taught a class in the "autobiographical acts"—whatever those were—of Mary McCarthy, Edward Dahlberg, Lillian Hellman, and the then-obscure Maya Angelou. The day was terribly rainy; the store smelled of wood and damp—the floor, the shelving, the pasteboard. She stood four rungs up on one of those library ladders, reading from some ancient-looking text with an olive-green cover, completely engrossed. I stood right next to her, enthralled. Her presence before me seemed nothing short of miraculous. She was no more than thirty. She wore a trench coat and a Burberry hat. A drop of rain hung at the tip of her tapering nose. I had enjoyed her class, and had met with her in her office a few times, but now I was too frightened to talk to her. I followed her around the store. I stalked her. She addressed a clerk, and smiled a radiant smile; I looked away, grimacing at my own cowardice, and when I turned back she was gone. She had put down her olive-green book, deciding against purchasing it. It was called *Getting to Know Your Cocker Spaniel*.

Imagine my thrill of recognition to encounter, years later, in my students' English 102 text, "Three Girls" by Joyce Carol Oates, in which a pair of young college poseurs stalk an unglamorous peacoat-wearing hair-braided Marilyn Monroe, not daring to talk to her, in the very same Strand in 1956. (In Oates's story, La Monroe hits the Judaica section, and heads to the checkout counter with *Jews of Eastern Europe*; *The Chosen People: A Complete History of the Jews*; and *Jews of the New World*.)

Some of my college professors dazzled with their erudition. Some I mocked. Some I thought insufferable bores. I thought it criminal that a few of them were allowed to teach. But to all of them I took off my hat. To stand before a class, lecturing for hours at a time, armed with nothing more than the stuff of the mind, able to field any question, no matter how far-flung, seemed impressive.

To teach college seemed a preposterous endeavor, but what I didn't realize was how closely I fit the profile of an adjunct instructor. I had spent my college years mocking premeds and soul-dead accounting majors and psychotic computer science types. They all had the last laugh. I was a classic adjunct type with a master's degree, a failed artistic career, and a need for cash. Men and women of my stripe litter the streets of the metropolis like discarded latte cups, waiting tables or proofreading for law firms or hanging on in their cubicles to the lowest rungs of the publishing industry. But in the exurban heartland where

I live, they are in short supply. Where I live there are the country people, who have been here for generations, rather wealthy transplants, and civil servants, none of whom typically will be found adjuncting.

. . .

Dr. Ludlow knew that she had a live one on the hook. She told me that she couldn't believe how lucky they were to find someone like me. Then she looked away. "There's only one thing," she said. Her body language was alarming. She sat hunched forward in her office chair, her legs entwined beneath her, fingers interlaced. God, what was happening? The woman was all knotted up. "The pay. I don't know what to say. The pay, the salary—it's an embarrassment. I'm embarrassed to offer it to someone of your skills."

"Well, how much is it?" I asked.

She looked to her office door. Her face was in direct profile. Her cowl of hair came to her jawline. High cheekbones, puffy eyes, bit of eyeliner, bit of a beaky nose.

"I can't make myself say it," she said.

"Please don't let it concern you."

She shook her head. "I can't."

We had reached an impasse. I would have to worm it out of her, which was humiliating. I was pretty sure I had the job, so, unafraid of queering the deal, I did what you shouldn't do at a job interview and made a joke.

"Pretty please?" I said.

The tension was broken. Dr. Ludlow pressed her palms to her mouth.

"Nineteen-hundred per course," she said from under her hands.

I wasn't sure what to say. Normally, I would have assured her that the money seemed fine, or some crap like that, but since she thought the money an insult, I couldn't very well contradict her. I didn't want to seem insane (talk about queering the deal), so she and I just sort of hung our heads sadly.

"I think it might get better," she said.

"Okay," I said.

I felt a little irked. This was my first exposure to the peculiar manner in which colleges do business. They consider themselves exempt from traditional market forces, and I suppose that if they think it, they are. Dr. Ludlow's admission that I wouldn't be paid enough for my trouble seemed not honest but smug. I found myself longing for the more traditional business approach, all hypocrisy, in which the capitalists pay nothing but aren't quite so cheerful about it.

Each course, Dr. Ludlow told me, would require 38 hours of instruction. I started doing the calculations in my head: $1,900 \div 38 = $50 per hour, which, as it turns out, didn't sound all that bad. Ah, but I supposed I would have to grade papers as well. How long would that take? I added 7 hours to make it an even 45: $1,900 \div 45 came to exactly $42 per hour.

Compared with Dr. Ludlow, I would be making a pittance. But I'll say this: the pay wasn't at all bad for part-time work.

"Welcome," said Dr. Ludlow. "And if you know anyone else interested in teaching, we'll be happy to talk to them."

I was pleased with myself for getting the job, though I suppose Dr. Ludlow's wondering in passing if I knew any other potential adjuncts was a tip-off that it's not the greatest job on the planet. Do you suppose that when Barack Obama tapped Tim Geithner for Treasury, he asked him if he knew anyone else interesting in becoming a cabinet member?

I took the textbooks with me, sent Dr. Ludlow an official copy of my MFA diploma, and, secure in my conviction that the laws and etiquette of business didn't apply to colleges, blew off the thank-you note for the interview and hire.

. . .

That is how I became an adjunct instructor—or, as they are sometimes known, a "contingent faculty member"—one of those reviled beings whose very existence seems to epitomize What's Wrong With College Today. According to the Modern Language Association, here's one sample yardstick for judging the quality of a school: the fewer adjuncts on the job, the better:

> The Modern Language Association believes that college students have a superior educational experience when they are taught by faculty members who have appropriate institutional support. As a rule, full-time faculty members, especially those holding tenured or tenure-track appointments, teach under conditions that provide clear educational advantages for their students. . . . Part-time faculty members, while they may be fully qualified scholars and teachers, are generally poorly paid, receive substandard office space and other support, and have tenuous institutional standing and little chance to advance professionally. An institution's use of a critical mass of full-time tenured and tenure-track faculty members therefore provides a measure for judging the quality of undergraduate education.[1]

I was a member now of what academic theorists call the "instructorate," as opposed to the "professoriate," which enjoys health care and retirement benefits and where anybody with any sense would rather be. As Michael Murphy, director of college writing at the State University of New York at Oswego and a former adjunct himself, puts it, members of the instructorate "are widely regarded as the great academic unwashed, the grunts, pieceworkers subject to—and even produced by—

the crass economic pressures of the academic marketplace. To most of higher education's regular citizens, part-time instructors are an embarrassment."[2] In the world of college, I was a screwball, a loser, a pretender, a scoundrel, and a scab.

The literature is filled with stories of adjuncts pushed to the brink and going over the edge. Consider the tale of Mary Ann Swissler, a luckless Seton Hall adjunct, who fired off an ill-considered e-mail to her students and, in the words of the administration, "would not be returning":

> After discovering that some of her students had used a public Web site to criticize her teaching abilities, her wardrobe, and other aspects of her appearance . . . Swissler said in her e-mail message to the students that such comments "confirmed to me what I had to keep to myself all semester: that most of you mental midgets are the most immature, sheltered, homophobic, sexist, racist, lying sacks of [excrement] I have ever met in my life." She added, "Seton Hall may be kissing you're [sic] asses now, but out here in the real world, brats like you will be eaten for breakfast."[3]

The academic literature treats adjuncts with a mix of weary condescension and revulsion. Check out this headline from the *Chronicle of Higher Education*: "Keep Adjuncts Away from Intro Courses, Report Says," as though the adjuncts had some manner of contagious disease. Adjuncts will almost never get selected for available full-time positions; to choose an adjunct is, to put it charitably, not a sexy choice. A recent survey of colleges in the Midwest revealed that only three of sixty department chairs said they would be willing to consider adjuncts, even long-term adjuncts, for full-time jobs.[4]

The full-time professor on the tenure track is an endangered species. According to a report by the American Federation of Teachers, only 27.3 percent of faculty fit this description in 2007, a decline from 33.1 percent in 1997. In community colleges, only 17.5 percent are full-time tenured or on the tenure track.[5] Colleges are using more and more graduate students and adjuncts for instruction. The *Tufts Daily* runs an alarmed story: "Some Departments Seeing Rise in Number of Adjunct Professors."[6] "Sharp Rise in Adjunct Professors Has Obvious Downsides" is the headline in an editorial from the *Daily Iowan* bemoaning the fact that the University of Iowa has increased its use of adjuncts by 19 percent over the past five years.[7]

I understood that the use of adjunct instructors like me was probably not good for students. I understood that adjuncts were an exploited class, and that they were, in effect, faculty-union-sanctioned scabs. I didn't think about any of this. I was glad to have the work. I didn't even think the pay seemed that bad. Fired up about my new career, I telephoned a much-educated and highly opinionated friend and, before telling him of my own plans, asked if he had ever thought about adjuncting.

He dismissed the question with an audible yawn. "I would never dream of it," he said.

"Why not?"

"It's too little money. Adjuncts work for the pleasure of feeling important and being called professor. I won't work for mental wages."

2

Writing Hell

THE CLASS LOOKED UP AT ME with curiosity as I tossed my attaché case on the desk with studied casualness. The board was filled with writing; I erased it all and wrote my name, followed by ENGLISH 101—COLLEGE WRITING. I set out my attendance book and a stack of course outlines. I sat on the edge of the desk and cleared my throat. The class snapped to attention. The quiet in the room was petrifying. There was nothing stopping me from beginning. Mounted on the ceiling was a projector; its lens, like a gun muzzle, pointed straight at my heart.

I thought of what Stanley Edgar Hyman, the husband of Shirley Jackson, whose short stories we would soon be reading, said when asked how he went about teaching a college class. "I've been doing it for years, and before every class, I take a piss, I check my fly, I wish I were dead—and I go into the room and begin."

I'd had a three-hour orientation with one other adjunct and one of the deans, whom I will call Dean Truehaft. He was a sixtyish man, spare and trim, with a high forehead and a prim mouth, a man who appeared to be moderate in his habits and well cared for. He wore a boxy suit, but for some reason I kept envisioning him in spandex, like one of the bicyclists who whiz through town on the weekends. He told us some useful things.

He warned us never to be alone with a student, particularly a student of the opposite sex. He told us that it really wasn't acceptable to end class early. "Some instructors do that," he said, with a weary rasp in his voice, "and frankly I am at a loss. It's not ethical, it's not fair to the students, and it can interfere with our accreditation." The other adjunct asked a lot of panicky questions about photocopies and snow chains and whether or not he'd be working in a classroom with a SMART Board, and when he heard the answers he shook his head in despair—really, this wasn't set up very well.

I didn't know anything about teaching in college, but I did know about keeping a job. I knew he wouldn't last. I followed his progress discreetly. He taught for a single semester and split.

I would call the orientation mildly useful, in the way that all training sessions of this sort are. I learned about parking stickers and library hours and how to contact security. As the session wound down, he broached what I would discover to be the most nettlesome, complicated, and foundational issue I would face as an adjunct. He talked about the academic skills of the students, and his voice dropped and deepened into a most patrician sort of groan. I might, he said, find myself tweaking my curricula a bit. The students often needed to brush up on some basic skills. But I was to adhere to the college standards at all costs. "Give them the grades that they deserve," he said. "It's really very simple."

He seemed rather pleased with himself. Because there were only two adjuncts in his training session, he got through it quicker than he expected, and said we could leave 45 minutes early.

I told my class: "Let's go over the syllabus."

They held their papers before them, and looked up at me with great expectations. We went over nuts and bolts. As a somewhat paranoid government employee, I knew enough to put in the stuff that could have legal ramifications: the number of absences that would lower a grade, the policy on absences for religious reasons, the mechanics of the grading system, whether or not a quiz missed because of absence counted, etc. I told them how many essays we'd be writing, and said that they should put their cell phones on vibrate, and they should come to class. My words sounded alien to me. They seemed to be coming from someplace far away. I hadn't yet found my voice as an instructor. It had been a long time since I'd been in a classroom, and even then I had been teaching middle schoolers. I was channeling all the professors I'd ever had, their bemused jokes and muttered asides; I may have ended up sounding like the creased gnome who'd taught me Pascal's *Pensées* in graduate school.

Panic swelled in me. Everything about what I was doing felt wrong, and we'd been in class a grand total of 15 minutes. Why was I doing this—for a little vacation money? It didn't feel right. John Cheever, in "The Bella Lingua," tells of a middle-aged American man in Rome taking Italian lessons from an elderly teacher: "It disturbed his sense of fitness that he, a man of fifty, should be sitting in a cold flat at the edge of Rome, being read a children's tale by a woman of seventy. . . ." That was how I felt. My sense of fitness was disturbed. I was too old for this. All of my life seemed askew.

"Let's see who's here, shall we?" I murmured. *Shall we!* That was my first British Lit teacher.

I took attendance. I asked the students about their majors, about why they were taking the class, and got essentially the same answers that I was to get in every class from then on. Two young men in baseball caps who appeared to be friendly already were getting degrees in criminal justice. Both were planning to make the law enforcement rounds, taking the state trooper exams for several nearby states. Julie, a young woman with a gentle voice, clad in pink scrubs and electric-green clogs, planned to work in pediatric oncology. I told her I thought that sounded like depressing work. (Perched on the edge of my desk, I found myself sliding right into college professor mode, holding forth with instant opinions about everything.) She said that yes, it could be sad, but there was lots of opportunity there, and really, wasn't all nursing quite sad when it wasn't very happy? Julie had a considered philosophy and put me in my place rather nicely. Several teacher's aides were studying to be teachers. One middle-aged woman had a strong Spanish accent; she revealed that this was her first college class, and admitted, with abject deference, that she was very, very nervous. She did look terrified. "We'll try to see that it's not your last," I said, trying to sound warm and vaguely self-deprecating. The class applauded her. "You'll do fine," someone said.

At that moment I marveled at just how good one human being could be to another.

There were a few other students hovering around my own age. One woman wore an oxford cloth shirt and a thin summer cardigan; the sleeves of her shirt were rolled halfway up, revealing tattoos on both forearms. Her children were out of the house, she said, and she was now following her dream of a career in public relations. Next to her was a Saturn mechanic in one of his mechanic's shirts, with his name embroidered in script above the pocket. And there was a hulking building contractor, too big for his desk, who looked like a parent sitting at his kid's school's open-house night.

Oh, that innocent, Edenic first class! For at that moment I felt nothing but affection and admiration for the students. Here was a cross section of the citizenry with one thing in common: the desire to better their situations. How great a country were we living in that such dreams of academic salvation could be realized? On that night, the American sense of possibility seemed our greatest national characteristic. The women's rights movement, the civil rights movement, the seniors' rights movement all had simmered and bubbled and come to a full rolling boil over thirty years, and what was once the exception was now the rule: everyone, it seemed, either went to college or went back to college to fulfill their dreams. I took my hat off to them. They'd been working all day; I knew they were tired. I was tired. The classroom, having been used all day by the full-time students, was a demoralizing mess. Candy wrappers littered the aisles. Julie the nurse ate a tuna and bean sprout sandwich; she perched the wrappings daintily atop a garbage can filled to overflowing. On the blackboard ledges sat small dunes of chalk dust that eddied about when the classroom door was opened; by night's end, I would look as though I had been involved in some sort of toxic cleanup.

. . .

"Let's talk about writing for a moment," I said.

We talked, or rather I talked at them, for an hour. I had a sense that perhaps no one had ever addressed for them the emotional component of writing.

"I'm a writing teacher, yes, but I'm also a writer," I told them, and a case could be made that neither thing was exactly true. I didn't care. "This is not just something I got a degree in. And the first thing to know is that we're all in writing hell. All of us."

What I was about to tell them—how writing was so tied to our weaknesses and lunacies and psychoses—was not covered in our English 101 textbook. I'd been thinking about writing for twenty years, and it all burst out of me in a torrent.

"You sit in front of the blank screen and feel like an idiot," I said, "unable to form a single cogent thought. I sit there and I think to myself: what business have I writing anything, when

I can barely remember how to burp? Breathing itself seems a cognitive struggle. At least the computer cursors don't blink at you anymore. They used to, rhythmically, like the impatient tapping of a foot. Oh, the worry! The anxiety! I've been fighting it for years. I remember working on a typewriter, with the bond paper in the roller and my feeling, as I sat there, of rising panic. *I've got to get something typed or that paper will be hopelessly curled!* And then where would we be?"

I told them: the writer must just start, and write terribly until he can, with any luck, get into a groove. This is not how other endeavors work. The barber would go out of business if the first few haircuts of the day were complete butcheries. The surgeon does not leap into the operation knowing how badly it will all go at first.

Writing is difficult for so many reasons, I said.

It doesn't fit in with our contemporary ethos, in which everything is neat, cleaned, pressed, ordered, and lightly perfumed, with ample backup systems in place. Ours is an age in thrall to perfection. We demand every contingency prepared for, routes planned to the last turn in MapQuest, high definition and great nutrition, stadium seating and mouth-covered sneezes and enormous umbrellas and frequent hand washing, spotless sidewalks, 20/10 vision, a New York City without crime; we demand sobriety, prudence, and good manners. Writing, no matter how disciplined the writer or detailed the outline, is a messy business. No matter how hard the writer works, the writing is never quite complete. The writer is like a kidnap victim: blindfolded, in a sack, in a car trunk, struggling for a glimpse of the light of cogency. Even the most careful and orderly-of-mind writer must fight battles on multiple fronts simultaneously, rendering repairs on the introduction that make paragraph seven entirely redundant, introducing the lightning-brilliant never-before-uttered concept in paragraph two that makes paragraphs three, four, and five seem vaguely sheepish, as though they are pointedly not mentioning this stunningly brilliant idea.

Writing is difficult because, at first blush, most of us have little to say. Even when we think we have an essay in us, even when our passions are inflamed, attempting to order and flesh out our thoughts just makes the reality apparent. The whole thing starts to deflate. Under no circumstances, though, should the writer stop writing at that point, for what we have to say emerges from the craft of writing—our pieces are in some ways a by-product of the endeavor, the way a toned body emerges from exercise, or a fluted and tapering vase emerges from fingers pressing on a spinning mass of clay.

We will not be writing "the college essay," I told them, but rather "the college composition. An essay indicates something tried, something essayed. A composition is built, crafted, worked on, composed. It must be level and plumb, like a bookcase or a coffee table, planed and sanded, all of its nail holes puttied. The composition is not merely an end but a thing."

And now here's a contradiction, I told them—the first of many. Writing is difficult because of its many contradictions. The full, rounded, resonant meaning of prose emerges as it is worked over, but some of those ideas must be present at the outset. On the old television series *The Odd Couple*, Felix the photographer thinks he might like to try his hand at writing, and so follows Oscar the sportswriter around, taking notes on what he does. Oscar sits motionless at the typewriter and looks heavenward. Felix asks him what he is doing. "I'm thinking of stuff to write," Oscar barks with impatience. "Ah!" says Felix, intrigued, and dutifully jots a note to himself: "Think of stuff to write." Now that is a rather profound summary of the process. The thinking part of writing is often overlooked. I would be very pleased to have that as an epitaph: HE THOUGHT OF STUFF TO WRITE.

I had been looking off into the professorial middle distance, strolling around the room and not making eye contact. Now I looked closely at the class. They were with me. They had felt, in some form or another, what I was talking about. My tattooed woman dug into the flesh of her hands with her thumbnails. Her eyes didn't leave me. She wore an expression of wonderment. I felt very powerful.

I pressed on. Writing is difficult because we don't even call it what it is. The writing, the recording, the typing, whatever, is the least crucial part. Writing is thinking and crafting and editing; unfortunately, the writer always desires to make progress, and without constant vigilance may slip out of thinking and crafting mode and into mere progress, which can signal doom.

Writing is difficult because it seems so useless. One cannot imagine one's writing having the smallest impact on the world. And is there any process that calls for more self-discipline to get it right with less potential payoff?

Gore Vidal said it well. "The phrase that sounds in the head changes when it appears on the page. Then I start probing it with a pen, finding new meanings. Sometimes I burst out laughing at what is happening as I twist and turn sentences. Strange business, all in all. One never gets to the end of it. That's why I go on, I suppose. To see what the next sentences I write will be."[1]

E. B. White said that, when writing, he had "occasionally had the exquisite thrill of putting my finger on a little capsule of truth, and heard it give the faint squeak of mortality under my pressure, an antic sound."[2]

Both writers manage to convey how the act of writing can seem like the pastime of a lunatic.

Writing is difficult because sometimes as we write we are forced to confront the shattering reality, about midway through composition, that no part of what we are saying is true. Writing, often inconveniently, reveals truth. The composition of an essay advocating a position may reveal to the writer that he believes the exact opposite. What could be more demoralizing? The honest writer, upon seeing that the piece will not move forward, chucks out everything and begins afresh, which requires copious amounts of moral fiber. Writing assignments require honesty and fortitude in a way that chemistry homework doesn't.

Writing is difficult because it is so fraught; we know that we will be judged as people by the work we present. Math, even badly done math, is more neutral. As a friend of mine said after watching a comedian who failed to amuse him, "You never say, 'Hey, what a bad comedian!' You say, 'Hey, what an asshole!'" Writers are in the same fix. We are judged as human beings by our writing, but how difficult is it for us to convey in writing the depth and subtlety of our minds? How often do we receive an e-mail at work that portrays the writer as completely different (and not in a positive way) from the person we know so well? It's a writing issue. At the wedding, the sozzled best man, normally a considerate chap, manages with his toast to the bride and groom to embarrass every last person in the tent. It's a writing issue. The man disappoints because his prose does.

The reverse, of course, can also be true. On September 11, 2001, when asked how many firefighters New York City had lost, Mayor Rudolph Giuliani would say that he didn't have the figure yet, but it was certain to be "more than we can bear." That morsel of extraordinary diction—the choice of the word "bear"—would help make the mayor the most respected public official in the United States.

I told my class of writers to think of a compressed spring. When expanded, the spring can do nothing; potential energy is only created when the thing is compressed. The most powerful writing is that which has been cut to its essence. The writer must discard much of what he does. Is that the case in any other field of endeavor? Writers know to be suspicious of any seemingly clever turn of phrase. Are accountants told that? Must they, as an old writing teacher of mine liked to put it, knock down their own sand castles? Are medical researchers cautioned to kill their darlings? ("I came up with a cure for cystic fibrosis over the weekend, but I chucked it out. I don't know . . . It just seemed too pat.")

The class was still with me. I could feel their apprehension and sense their resolve. In this class, they thought, they would finally slay their writing demons. College instructors, even newly minted ones, know when they are falling flat and I certainly was not. I had them convinced, at least for the moment, that good writing was the most important thing in the world.

The contradictory instructions, I warned the students, will never stop coming. Exhaust your topic, cover it thoroughly—but at all costs avoid tangents. Stay focused, adhere to your thesis—but illustrate with very detailed examples. Be vivid in your language—but not wordy. Be tightly organized—but remember that some memorable writing results from serendipity.

Writing is difficult because the smallest infelicities—repetition, bits of ambiguity, parallelism out of whack—can harden into speed bumps, slowing the reader down and distracting from the content. Prose must go down like honey. Take another look: "When expanded, the spring can do nothing; potential energy is only created when the thing is compressed." The spring/the thing—is it a rhyme, a typo, a what? The reader will slow down, perhaps by an amount so small as to be immeasurable, but for the duration of that sentence, the rickety girder work of the prose overwhelms the meaning. A careful writer can wrestle with a sentence like that all day, end-ing up in one of those weird positions writing puts you in, wishing that springs had been called something else.

Finally, I told them, writing is hard—and writing courses are hard—because really there is no such thing as college-level good writing. There is no such thing as beginner's-level or intermediate good writing. Writing is either good or it is bad. Good writing has something fine and profound about it. The homeliest classroom assignment, composed well, written with honesty, carefully crafted, can put us in the mind of Thoreau.

And now for the last word, the most demoralizing fact of all. Even when writing is technically without fault, it can be not much good. When I was a young teenager, my sister, eight years older and a marvelously impressive figure, sat down at the huge Smith-Corona she'd gotten for Christmas and began writing a novel. I was speechless with admiration. She wrote a chapter or two and abandoned the project. I asked her what had happened.

She considered a moment and sighed, "It just all seemed so *pedestrian*," she said.

Her phrasing has stayed with me all these years. What better way to describe the dull, weary, stale, flat, and unprofitable way that our own writing often strikes us? Pedestrian. If she had brought that level of inspiration to the actual composition, she'd have written one corking novel! It's all been done before, we think. Why am I even bothering? Some other monkey at some other typewriter has churned all of this stuff out before. Even as I write this now, I can't shake the feeling that, sitting in some dusty back room of the Strand Book Store, there sits a yellowing copy of some other *In the Basement of the Ivory Tower,* all of my thoughts and words out there already, already written by somebody else.

I was practically panting with excitement. Had an adjunct ever had a heart attack on the first night of class? I had forgotten how much I loved thinking about writing, and never before had I had the opportunity to do so at such length. Everything I thought poured out of me, all of my writing worries, my frustrations, my writing demons, coupled with all that I had learned after spending thousands of hours at the keyboard, thousands at the typewriter, thousands hanging over legal pads. God, I thought, I'd written for so long I'd written through multiple ages of technology. And there was more. Already I was filling up with more stuff about writing. Yes, yes—I would have to tell them about balance, about preambles that are too long and rushed conclusions; I would have to tell them about my wife's trick—how she, as the first step in evaluating a page of my writing, would look at the literal shape of it, eyeing it from halfway across the room so that she couldn't actually read the text but could see the paragraphs as mere shapes, like the outlines of continents on a map.

I stepped out into the corridor for a breath of air. I needed to compose myself. First night of class: I noted that most of the other adjuncts had already dismissed their students for the evening. One other teacher, at the far end of the hall, was still going. His rasp was indistinct. I heard not his words but just the rising and falling of his voice, which had a querulous quality to it as he explained some lengthy proposition. A corridor of classrooms at night is a lonely but exciting place. I had to swallow down a rising gorge of exhilaration. I coughed to cover my excitement. A writing cliché to avoid: I felt wondrously alive. Not necessarily particularly happy, but surgically opened, splayed, scalped, vivisected, and mounted. I was my own raw self. This was me, take it or leave it. I felt like I'd been confessing at a meeting, Alcoholics Anonymous, or any of the other sorts of assemblages that take place in empty school buildings.

I stepped back into my classroom.

"And now," I told the class, "we write."

The students, all business, took out notebooks and loose-leaf and folders and pens. Someone piped up with a question: would they be keeping a writing journal? They knew more about what was supposed to go on than I did. Had some of them taken the class before? I would learn in time that, yes, they certainly had. I told them that I didn't believe in journals. When you have that much writing lying around, you don't want to waste it, and so you try to shoehorn that writing into whatever projects happen to come up, and it seldom fits.

"We have to do a base-level writing exercise," I said. "I have to get a feeling of where everybody is." They nodded. They understood they had to participate in such tedious formalities. "Write me an introduction and then three good body paragraphs. Here's the topic: I'm exactly the same person that I was five years ago. Or, if you don't like that one, I'm a completely different person than I was five years ago."

A hand rose: do you want a conclusion?

"No," I said, briskly and with great authority. I had already learned, as a professor, to speak ex cathedra. Never had I given the idea of conclusions any thought, but instantly I apprehended the boundaries of the matter. "Conclusions are childish. Let the reader draw them. You shouldn't have to tell us."

The woman with the tattoos and cardigan ventured a rather nervous comment. "My teacher always told us to turn our introductory paragraphs on their heads. She wanted us to use the same words, but mixed up, for the conclusion."

She was about my age; this was the sort of *McGuffey's Readers* stuff teachers used to spout.

"If the last paragraph is just the first in disguise," I said, "then why even bother with the middle? We haven't progressed even slightly."

The students made notes. They wrote a first draft. They got

up and stretched and wrote a final draft. They worked with great industry and seriousness of purpose. They thought before they wrote. They twisted their bodies as they wrestled with their undoubtedly twisted prose.

My first night of class, it seemed, was an unalloyed triumph. Christ, I thought. How fucking inspirational am I? Look at these people go! I sauntered down the hall, in the direction of the other teacher. I peeked into his room. He was instructing up a storm, teaching some sort of accounting. He was very tall and bulky, in a suit and Rockports and aviator glasses. His classroom had a whiteboard, which was covered with numbers in various colors. He held three colored markers clawlike be-tween the fingers of his left hand. A rhombus of light from the overhead projector shone in the middle of the board. He nod-ded to me and went right on teaching. That man—God knows what his name is—has now been with me for a decade, teach-ing a classroom or two away. We greet each other tentatively when we pass in the hall. We chat while waiting for photocop-ies. We talk of the weather, and jovially complain about the work ethic of our students. We note the passing of time every September, and commiserate over the midsemester doldrums, and laugh together almost giddily when the term is over. We laugh, but it is clear that we both want more classes. I long to ask him: why are you here? Are you, too, under a house? Is it divorce, or gambling debts, or a civil judgment? Did you back your sensible Toyota out of the driveway and over a child?

Class drew to a close. The students handed in their papers. Some hung back, wanting to talk. Some of the older students burned to talk to me. They were nervous. Writing has always been a challenge. They said it various ways: I've got it up here [pointing to head] but I can't get it to come out here [making handwriting motions]. When I write I feel like I'm drunk. I never have enough to write, says a nurse's aide, but my husband can't understand it because he says I never stop talking. Such is the mystique of writing that the biggest men—the building contractor too bulky for his seat, for example—are reduced to jelly by its difficulties. Writing is *so* boring, one said. I want to jump out of my skin, said another; I feel like my body is inhabited by crawling insects of boredom.

I liked that last one. That's not pedestrian at all.

Oh, Dean Truehaft: leave early? Hah! We were twenty minutes over. Has a college class, in the history of higher education, ever been as excited about a curriculum? I was feeling pretty full of myself. I was happy. This wasn't like work. This was undiluted spiritual satisfaction.

"Okay," I said to the class. "Are you happy you signed on?"

"All we want is three credits," someone said.

3

Revelation

E VERYONE AT HOME WAS ASLEEP: the children upstairs, my wife in the downstairs bedroom, scant feet away. Her door was open. I could hear the sound of her light snoring, such a comforting sound, a gentle rasp followed by a pleasing gurgle. Two window air conditioners whirred upstairs. The roof of our Cape Cod house sliced through the bedrooms, not unattractively, in a 1950s sort of way, but since there was no attic, the rooms, pressed against the surface of the roof, were virtually uninhabitable without air-conditioning in the summer.

I put down my mug of coffee. I looked over, for the third and perhaps the fourth time, my stack of baseline essays. I did not then own a cell phone and had never sent or received a text message, but I needed the phrase that would become one of the greatest of electronic clichés.

WTF. What the fuck.

The essays were terrible, but the word "terrible" doesn't begin to convey the state these things were in. My God. Out of about fifteen students, at least ten seemed to have no familiarity with the English language. It seemed that they had never before been asked in school to turn in any sort of writing assignment. I can say that there were words misspelled, rather simple words at that. I can say that there was no overarching structure to the paragraphs, that thoughts and notions were tossed at the reader haphazardly. I can say that there were countless grammatical errors; sentences without verbs; sentences without subjects; commas everywhere, like a spilled dish of chocolate sprinkles, until there were none, for paragraphs at a time; sentences that neither began with a capital letter nor ended with any punctuation whatsoever. I can say that the vocabulary was not at a college level and perhaps not at a high school level. I can say that tenses wandered from present to past to past perfect back to present, suggesting the dissolving self of a schizophrenic consciousness. I can say that some of the mistakes concerned matters of form explained to me by Sister Mary Finbar on—as God is my witness, I can remember this— the very first day of first grade, matters such as the definition "a sentence is a group of words expressing a complete thought" and the requirement that, before nouns and adjectives and adverbs beginning with a vowel, the writer is obligated to use the article "an," not "a." I can say all that, and you may still think to yourself: English teacher. What do you expect? Nitpicking bastard.

Perhaps, dear reader, you think the main issue is the arrogance and superiority of the aforementioned teacher rather than any problem with the students. Perhaps you think of me as Guy Crouchback, the protagonist of Evelyn Waugh's *Men at Arms,* who during World War II censors letters and observes snootily of the writers that some "wrote with wild phonetic misspellings straight from the heart. The rest strung together clichés which he supposed somehow communicated some exchange of affection and need." I could quote broken sentences all day, but I won't. The words banged against each other in unnatural ways, twisted up like mangled bodies. There is something pornographic about viewing such poor work.

I think of a four-line utterance without a verb—the world's

longest sentence fragment—and the old joke about the world's tallest midget comes to mind.

Nothing I can do can really convey—so that you can feel it, as I did, in the cold pit of my stomach—the true abilities of many of these students. Fine-tuning—that's what I had expected to be doing: turning workmanlike prose into something substantial, something rounded, something that occasionally even sang. Instead, that lonely night in my little Cape Cod, I drowned in incoherence. I was submerged in a flood of illogic and solecism and half-baked coinages, this last being a charitable spin on the use of made-up words.

There were exceptions. The older students were better. The woman with the tattoos and cardigan knew what she was doing, in the sense that she didn't make up any words, and she had some sense of having embarked on a piece of construction, something to be fashioned, like a birdhouse or a ladder-backed chair, something that needs to be plumb. To my relief, she had her tenses firmly corralled, her verbs and their auxiliaries lined up in formation like little tin soldiers. There was another competent paper, this one from a woman in her forties. Her fourth child, the last one, was poised to leave the house for college. She was a true minivan mom, the picture of unruffled composure. The personal essays she would hand in that semester portrayed all the complexities of suburban living. She wrote of Brownie troops and uniform swaps and soccer tournaments; she wrote of brokering complex favors with three other mothers so that none of their boys would have to miss an optional T-ball practice; she wrote of the struggle to make and serve dinner around four competing sets of extracurricular activities. With her youngest about to leave, she had gotten a job coordinating training sessions for medical and clerical staff of a hospital. She wrote how nervous she was about it, but I knew she would do fine. Compared to managing a household, taking guff from condescending surgeons and disgruntled X-ray techs would be a breeze.

The tattooed woman and the hospital administrator wrote nice essays, but let's not go crazy. Their essays were organized and cogent, but their writing was small. This was not truly college writing, if we define that animal as writing that manifests the intellect. Their writing was polite and muted and almost Shaker-like in its simplicity and barrenness. It's a gift to be simple, and the artist may rattle on about how difficult it is to achieve simplicity, but shouldn't college writing flex some cognitive muscle? "Indefensible"—that's the sort of word I expect to see in a college student's paper. "Apex." "Trenchant." "Heretical." "Casuistry" (when in doubt, I always worked "casuistry" into my college papers). "Facile." "Unassailable." "Axiomatic." Chewy words. Words that slow the jaw, like jerked beef. My professors no doubt caught the whiff of the undergraduate blowhard in my writing. But we are, after all, in the realm of undergraduates. Isn't it more appropriate for an undergraduate to wrestle with bulky concepts than to not have a notion of their very existence?

It's a good question, but I was facing a bigger one: what to do about the students who not only couldn't write, but who seemed to have no business in a classroom at all. How could I hope to teach them? Where would I begin? It would take me a year just to make up the deficiencies: a year of five-day-a-week meetings and six-hour classes, a year during which there was no expectation that we would actually get to doing college-level work, a year in which we would start again at the very beginning.

The enormity of the task was breathtaking.

I pictured it: "All right, everybody. Listen up. A sentence is a group of words expressing a complete thought."

I read the essays again, drank my coffee, and went to bed.

The next day my wife asked me, rather cheerfully, how my students were.

"Not so hot," I said blandly. Of course, that didn't quite cover it. "Actually, they're kind of terrible. They're bad writers."

The matter dropped. Over the course of the next few days, I thought about their work. Disjointed sentences—sentence fragments, really—swam before my eyes as I mowed our compact patch of grass, fiddled with the downspouts, freshened and fluffed the mulch around the boxy hedges. I may have worked much more industriously than was usual; the pile of bad work in my briefcase filled me with a sort of buzzing nervous energy. I didn't want to think about it. I started to resent the amount of time the students and their bad prose were weighing upon my mind. I watched with alarm as my per-hour teaching rate dropped.

A door had been opened to me, and I found myself surveying a landscape as drawn by M. C. Escher (that old favorite of undergraduates), in which the laws of logic and physical reality ceased to function, the sort of place where circular staircases ascended infinitely and fish transformed into birds and college looked a lot like junior high.

But I sang a happy tune to myself.

"I guess they just need to write the rust off," I told myself gamely. I vowed to get them working at something approaching a college level. I would teach them. I would work hard. We would make a fresh start. I cried the perpetual cry of the instructor: I would succeed where others had failed.

4

Compare and Contrast

THIS WAS ALL NEW TO ME, of course, but Introduction to College Writing, or English 101, as set out in many textbooks, uses the following system, which I have come to think is a good one. Expository composition is broken down into various categories, each of which is designed to accomplish primarily a single goal. The narrative essay tells a story. The descriptive essay uses as much sensory detail and imagery as possible. The compare-contrast essay . . . well, I don't think I have to tell you. Division-and-analysis essays break down a subject into component parts: an essay about whether or not it's worth the trouble to see a ball game at Dodger Stadium, for example, might deal with the convenience of the journey, prices for tickets and parking and concessions, quality of the stadium food, and whether the total experience of the game itself adds something beyond that which could be experienced on television. A process analysis essay explains how some action is to be performed—how something is done—as opposed to a cause-and-effect paper, which explains why something happened. An argument paper takes a stand on a position.

Narrative, description, compare-contrast, division-and-analysis, process analysis, cause-and-effect, argument—these are the seven sacraments of the expository writing program. Instructors of English 101 are intimately familiar with these categories. Theoretically, these seven varieties of writing are required of the student across the curriculum. A process analysis essay, for example, prepares the student to write lab reports. Argument papers are required in nearly every discipline; one hallmark of an educated person is the ability to make persuasive arguments concerning his or her field. In addition to these seven types of essays, there is one more beast lurking in English 101: the dreaded research paper, complete with parenthetical citations and a list of works cited, all in Modern Language Association format.

To break the instruction of writing into these different forms may at first seem artificial. Every decent piece of expository prose uses elements from all the categories. We would start by dissecting Bruce Catton's "Grant and Lee: A Study in Contrasts." This piece is a classic example of a compare–contrast essay, but it also boasts plenty of description, lots of examples, and puts forth a series of arguments about essential differences between the Union and Confederacy. The notion of these different categories of essays struck me as artificial when I first perused the textbook, but I have come to feel that the thrust and focus the system imparts to even the most inexperienced writer can be useful. After all, one of the most troublesome aspects of writing is its breadth of possibility. The writer's palette is the whole world; the great writer looks at all of existence, all of human history, and selects just those elements that will correctly make his point. Writing to the dictates of a category serves as an initial limiter, a helpful boundary setter.

The use of writing models makes intuitive sense to me. My own learning about writing has always started with the impulse to mimic form. When I started writing essays, for example, I had real specifics from the prose of Nora Ephron buzzing in my brain: the seemingly light and anecdotal approach, the glimpses of the author visible briefly even in the most impersonal passages; the passages of high seriousness, often at the essay's payoff, whose meanings resonate after the wisecracks have been forgotten. I try always to keep my language lively, and much of this impulse stems from my reading—hundreds if not thousands of times—a book I received for Christmas when I was in seventh grade: *The Beatles Book*, edited by Edward E. Davis. It is a collection of academic essays about the band, all written around 1967, by a clutch of old-time highbrow academics and pop-culture critics, people like Richard Poirier and Richard Goldstein and Ralph J. Gleason. I remember *Rolling Stone* once dismissing the book as a piece of pretentious crap, but I loved it. The book is a true period piece. It reflects a sense that the Beatles really mattered; they had changed everything, including the polite art of essay writing. The book's prose was amped up, cranked up as though straining to be heard over the din and clang of "Paperback Writer." Even the academic stuff read like New Journalism. I think now that much of my own writing style derives from one essay I practically memorized; it was on the Beatles' films by a woman named Leonore Fleischer. She wrote for *Ramparts*, I think, and went on to a long and I hope profitable career, turning out film novelizations, cowriting books with Marilyn vos Savant, and for many years editing the "Sales and Bargains" section of *New York* magazine. In her Beatles essay "Down the Rabbit Hole," she had an Augie March–like way of juxtaposing high and low diction that I found thrilling, and that has stayed with me always, like those mundane sensory images from seemingly random days in one's childhood that nonetheless remain vivid in the mind forever. She wrote of the old-timey feel of the *Sgt. Pepper* album:

> The home ties are strong, and the compulsion to fantasy even stronger. Paradox is the Beatles' middle name; modernity mixes with nostalgia.

Which just sent me, at thirteen, reeling. She grabbed British-isms (Ringo Starr had a "slightly daft look"; in his screen persona he was "doing the Rita Tushingham bit"; *A Hard Day's Night* was a "lovely" film), and these merry stylistic inflections made her prose hum like a struck tuning fork. I was in love. How does one use words so cleverly and wisely? Leonore Fleischer was in my adolescent dreams a brilliant woman and a charmingly tough broad, and her little essay fed my aspirations for many years. It kept me writing.

Anyway, when I returned to class, frightened as I was by those first-night sample essays, I was determined to make the class a success. We would just proceed slowly and logically. We were to begin with the compare-contrast essay. All I had to do, I believed, was teach the method. The class and I would stroll together through the textbook. Teach the method: slowly, carefully, so that everyone gets it. The textbook must have something worthwhile to say, right? These things are written by experts. Surely if we go through the text in detail, section by section, the students will get the idea. It couldn't hurt, right?

I read aloud to the students from the beginning of the chapter. *In comparing, you point to similar features of the subjects; in contrasting, to different features.*

The contours of the thing are intuitively obvious. The essay's function is to limn the ways in which two or more entities are alike and different. Simple, right? Writing is simple. The ideas are straightforward; the goals, what we want our writing to do, are readily apparent. The theory behind any piece of writing is no more complicated than the theory behind cutting one big diamond into two smaller ones. But the doing of it . . . that's another story. The mood in the room shifted. A small, growling beast of hostility stirred itself awake. In the blink of an eye, the students were discomposed. I elaborated on the text's instruction, but every teacher knows the feeling: my words seemed to die and fall to the ground about a foot from me.

Now my throat was dry.

"Let's look at the actual process," I said brightly, for that was the text's next section. "We have to have a valid reason for considering these two subjects together. Grant and Lee we can compare because they're both Civil War generals. Obviously. But we can't compare Robert E. Lee and Bob Dylan. There's no basis for comparison.

"And once you've got your purpose, it's important to do an outline." I said it so quickly on the heels of my previous statement that the thought occurred to me: can one interrupt oneself? "You've got to make sure that you're comparing the same features of both subjects. If you're comparing your first old clunker of a car to the Lexus you zoom around in now, and you talk about the old junker's ride, gas mileage, and repairs, then you've got to cover the same ground with regard to the Lexus."

I drew a chart on the board. "Now, there are two ways to structure this thing. You can talk about all the features of the first subject, then all the features of the second subject. You can spend the first part of the essay on the clunker, and then the second part on the Lexus."

First you say how they're the same, then how they are different. Or you say how they are different first. Or you mix it up a bit. The pedagogues, of course, have to make things complicated. Here's Professor Shirley Dickson giving us a roundup of the different ways the essay can be organized:

> In the first organizational pattern, named *bipolar* (Gray & Keech, 1980) or *whole-whole* (Raphael & Kirschner, 1985), the writer describes each topic separately, providing all of the features and details of one topic (e.g., Grasslands Native

Americans) in the first set of paragraphs followed by parallel paragraphs about the second topic (e.g., Pacific Northwest Native Americans). The second compare-contrast organizational pattern, *integrated* (Gray & Keech, 1980) or *part-part* (Raphael & Kirschner, 1985), is a point-by-point comparison of two topics. For example, in a composition of the Grasslands and Pacific Northwest Native Americans, the first, second, and third paragraphs might be about the homes, transportation, and foods of each, respectively. The third organizational pattern, *mixed* (Raphael & Kirschner, 1985), is a combination of bipolar (whole-whole) and integrated (part-part). Some paragraphs might be only about the Grasslands or Pacific Northwest Native Americans, whereas other paragraphs might be about the similarities and differences in one feature of both, such as religion.[1]

I admire Raphael and Kirschner, who got there early enough to lay claim to the concept of *mixed*.

A blanket had descended on the classroom, a blanket of gloom trimmed with a border of indignation. Our textbook spent ten pages on the writing of compare-contrast essays; we had gone through all of it, point by laborious point, and were really none the wiser. The shit I was telling them was too easy; really, it would all be blazingly obvious to a dimwitted second grader. The students had been waiting, pens poised above their notebooks, for some great message from on high, some great secret of writing, and I had nothing, it turned out, to give them. My students were unskilled and unpracticed writers, but they weren't stupid; they knew what the point of the comparison essay was. The devil is always in the doing.

My head swam that night as I realized how little help the textbook would offer me. The goals of writing are stark in their simplicity, the methods apparent, the theories nonexistent—

none of which makes writing good instructional fodder for textbooks. The doing of it, the adhering to a logical point that's worth making in the first place, that's troublesome, and requires a vast landscape of practice.

Over the years, I have come to think that the two most crucial ingredients in the mysterious mix that makes a good writer may be (1) having read enough throughout a lifetime to have internalized the rhythms of the written word, and (2) refining the ability to mimic those rhythms. It is very difficult to make up for gaps in a lifetime of reading and practice over the course of a fifteen-week semester. As Mark Richardson, an assistant professor of writing and linguistics at Georgia Southern University, says, "Writing involves abilities we develop over our lifetimes. Some students are more advanced in them when they come to college than are others. Those who are less advanced will not develop to a level comparable to the more-prepared students in one year or even in two, although they may reach adequate levels of ability over time."[2]

All that said, there had to be something to this textbook. It had gone through a half-dozen editions. The authors, in their acknowledgments section, thanked no fewer than forty-one college teachers from all over the country for their input. The book had all the bells and whistles, including a companion Web site, and as the preface informed me, the text featured "realistic treatment of the rhetorical methods," "extensive thematic connections," and "abundant editorial apparatus."

We read and talked about the readings that accompanied the compare-contrast instruction. We diagrammed their form on the board. We read Bruce Catton closely, as tens of thousands of classes have before us (the essay was published in 1956, and is in nearly every writing textbook I have ever seen). Outside of the English 101 curriculum, though, he is something of a forgotten figure. Fifty years ago, his narrative histories were best sellers, and he was as ubiquitous in the popular culture as, say, Doris Kearns Goodwin is today. When I was a kid, his works were well represented on my family's bookshelf. *Banners at Shenandoah* and *A Stillness at Appomattox* were among the books I found so alluring—whose titles were poetry to me—that I vowed to read them when I got old enough to understand them, along with A. J. Cronin's *The Keys of the Kingdom,* Vance Packard's *The Hidden Persuaders,* and an oversize graying book of photographs called *Women Are Here to Stay: The Durable Sex in Its Infinite Variety Through Half a Century of American Life.* Of course, once I got old enough to truly understand things, I never read a single one of them. Such an odd way for Catton's career to play out, with one perfectly crafted essay preserved between the covers of so many textbooks.

We extracted all we could out of Bruce. We had all the side-by-side lists you could want. Lee "might have ridden down from the old age of chivalry, lance in hand, silken banner fluttering over his head." Grant, in contrast, was the "modern man emerging; beyond him, ready to come on the stage, was the great age of steel and machinery, of crowded cities and a restless, burgeoning vitality." We even talked about Catton's occasionally old-fashioned style, with its charming inversions ("Daring and resourcefulness they had, too . . . ") so appropriate for the grandeur of the subject matter.

The students wrote everything down in their notebooks.

We read the whimsical "Neat People vs. Sloppy People" by Suzanne Britt. I find Britt's piece funny, though not as funny as the next piece, "Batting Clean-up and Striking Out" by Dave Barry. Barry's essay wanders off in directions only he can go; his ability to deliver bits of adolescent silliness using the hoariest comic forms—all with a wide-eyed earnestness—and have it all come out actually funny may make him the most singular literary talent of our age. It goes without saying that the class had never heard of Dave Barry. They laughed, a great many of them, rather heartily. Some didn't, perhaps because they simply didn't find him funny or perhaps school had always been so tense for them that they had long ago shut off the receptors that react spontaneously to anything presented in a classroom. This was mere schoolwork, quite divorced from life. I envied the opportunity those who had enjoyed the Barry piece now had: to go out and scarf up everything Dave Barry had ever written. And yet I knew that this was not going to happen.

Finally, we read "The Black and White Truth About Basketball," Jeff Greenfield's famous analysis of black and white styles of basketball play, first published in 1975 in *Esquire*. And now I had a new writing ambition: to write an essay that would be published, edition after edition, in college textbooks for a minimum of twenty-five years.

We'd dredged everything we could out of Barry, Greenfield, et al. We'd looked for examples of thesis statements and topic sentences, which wasn't easy; writers often leave these items unstated, drawing in the reader. And though we could generate some topic sentences where Jeff Greenfield hadn't, my students didn't exactly understand why they had to—which is why using the essays most texts include as models is problematic: the writing is simply too subtle and too idiosyncratic. I would think it a bad bet for anyone to try to imitate Dave Barry: my students, Vladimir Nabokov, me, anyone. The benefits of our reading would, I knew, be small and indirect; reading this handful of essays must be better than reading none, and we were trying to make up, with a small clutch of baby steps, for a lifetime of not reading.

Now it was time for the students to plan their own essays. The textbook had boiled the compare–contrast essay down to a series of steps, with examples and tips and Venn diagrams and checklists. My students had been instructed, by the chirruping text, to develop a plan of organization and stick to it. As we used to say in the old neighborhood: No shit, Sherlock.

We considered the list of topics in the text. "The main characters of two films, novels or stories." "Computers: Macs vs. PCs." "City life and rural life." "Malls and main streets."

"The topic has to come from deep within you," I said. "It has to be a comparison that only you can make. In specificity lies the universal." I repeated that last sentence, and they wrote it down dutifully. "Talk to me as though I were on a barstool beside you, or across the table in the diner at three in the morning. Be that detailed. Give us the comparison that's been eating away at you for years. Give us the whys and wherefores." I was a new teacher of writing, but I knew that much: that the writer must be obsessed by the topic. As Jennifer I. Berne of the University of Illinois says, "Control of topic is essential in writing workshops because the writing student must feel that they have the most knowledge in the room about what they are writing." She quotes Lucy Calkins, who wrote in her book *The Art of Teaching Writing,* "By supplying a topic from my experience and giving it to my students, I indirectly taught them that their lives aren't worth writing about."[3]

The period was over. The students arose, full of determination to succeed at their task. They were nothing short of abuzz. The building contractor said that he had never felt better prepared for a writing assignment in his life. If only, he said with some anger, someone had done this sort of work with him twenty years ago. The entire cast of his life might have been different.

Well, yes, I thought to myself. But at least you encountered me now, before it was completely too late. Professor X can't be everywhere, you know. In a lifetime, how many students can one man lead out of the writing wilderness? (My interior voice was sounding so rich and plummy!) I try my best.

. . .

The following week, they brought their essays to class. Were some of them actually swaggering a little? The mood in the classroom was bubbly. New friendships seemed to have sprouted. I collected the essays, their first drafts, and went off with them to the copy machine. We were going to use the workshop format, with everyone looking at and helping to revise several of the submissions.

I had told them to write from personal experience but warned them that everyone in class would see their work. I also warned them about the pitfalls of writing workshops. "I've taken a boatload of college classes in my time," I said, "and only in writing workshops have I seen people cry."

Not every student's piece would be a success, I knew, but I wanted to share the joy in real time with those students who had made progress.

I returned to the classroom and handed each student a pile of photocopies. "Keep them in order, so we don't get confused," I said crisply. I gave instruction. I had wavered on whether or not to have the students read their essays aloud; I decided not to, for the time being. "Everybody read with a pen or pencil in hand. If great language jumps out at you, note it down. If something is unclear, note it down. If you have questions after reading a paragraph, jot them down. Let's read through the pile and come back and do individual pieces."

I knew what was certain to happen. Inspired by my passion for writing, the students had labored mightily, and turned in the best work of their lives. I would see that they had made small but discernible progress.

How I would love, dear reader, to deliver a different report from what I am about to write. I would love to say how blown away I was by their work. I would love to concede that the grammar was rough, and that as first drafts the essays needed lots of spackling and releveling but that we had tapped into their experiences and the stuff they had written was pretty neat. That's what I thought would happen. I pictured us as being comfortably swaddled in a quilt of narrative. I had worked hard to teach them. They seemed eager to learn. Surely the lot of us would progress *somewhere*. It had to be. We were all playing our roles, as though we had played them thousands of times before.

Our narrative had derailed. The story took an unexpected twist.

The papers were even worse.

Once, after I'd been instructing for a few years, I eavesdropped for the first time on another English 101 class. The instructor was a very experienced woman of about my age who had seen it all. She was rather a classic adjunct type. Slim and intense, unsmiling, she wore a long brown skirt with as much material as a schooner's sail, mustard-colored tights that pilled, naïve-looking flat shoes. She wore no wedding ring. Her voice was throaty, from years of smoking or teaching. I couldn't shake the feeling that she'd had a tough go of it. Her first-night speeches to her class were remarkably similar to mine, but she did have one ringing catchphrase all her own.

"Please do me a favor," she said to the class. "Don't hand in garbage."

I hadn't told my students that. I'm not sure it would have mattered.

For there is no other word but garbage for what my students handed in. My older students did all right, I suppose, but even their work had fallen off. It was bad. When I categorize the lot of assignments as barely literate, that's an average; some papers were not literate at all, and I'd be hard-pressed to say what exactly, in their compare-contrast essays, was being compared or why. Words were randomly assembled and weirdly spelled, and does no elementary or high school teach the capitalization of the first person singular pronoun anymore? Some essays seemed, in their obscure reasoning, to make connections that would be apparent only to a lunatic. Was it the best work my students could do? That's a slippery question. The fact that they handed it in seems to indicate that, yes, on some level, it was the best they could do. But scattered liberally through the poor writing was much evidence of lack of care: crazy misspellings of grammar-school words, misspellings that the spell checker would catch but for which it could offer no alternative; words repeated, like the pounding of a sledgehammer, nine or ten times in a paragraph; crucial words omitted; batches of words pressed together in the hopes of forming a sentence, like old slivers of soap jammed together for one last shower. There were times I suspected an easy explanation to the whole mess: that the writers had not had their fingers placed on the home keys while they typed.

Here was my first hard lesson in life as an adjunct professor in the basement of the ivory tower. The students are poignantly desperate for success. Many of those I teach have done poorly in high school; college is not a goal for which they prepared single-mindedly for eighteen years. College is a place they landed in. I teach those whose names don't come up in the debates about advanced placement courses, adolescent over-achievers, and cutthroat college admissions. Mine are the students whose high school transcripts show poor attendance, indifferent grades, and blank spaces where the extracurricular activities would go. But now, shanghaied into college classes because of the demands of the workplace, they have seen the light—in a panicky sort of way. They want to do well. I want them to do well, and I teach subjects about which I am crazily passionate.

Many nights for the past decade, I have taught in a classroom crackling with positive energy. No matter where I lead, the students follow. If in my literature class I choose to spend an hour on the splendidly written opinion by the Hon. John M. Woolsey in the case of *United States of America v. One Book Called Ulysses* (". . . whilst in many places the effect of 'Ulysses' on the reader is somewhat emetic, nowhere does it tend to be an aphrodisiac" [the students don't get it at first; "emetic" throws them for a loop until I prod the memories of the young and not-so-young moms: "Ipecac!" they cry]), or if in my college composition class we detour off into such an arcane point of grammar as restrictive vs. nonrestrictive relative clauses, the students stay with me. On those nights when I am in the teaching zone, the class will follow where I lead.

For a while, I thought I was all the legendary charismatic teachers rolled into one: Mr. Chips and Conrack and Jaime Escalante and Robin Williams in *Dead Poets Society*. I assumed my results would match theirs. But now I better understand the immense hazard-strewn distance between teaching and learning. On any given night, I may very well be entertaining, informative, illuminating, and even inspirational on the subject of essay writing, but ultimately my gyrations are those of a semaphore signalman on the horizon, and it's every man for himself on a dark battlefield navigating past indolence, despair, fear of failure, fear of success, lack of foundational skills, lack of time, lack of aptitude, the allure of Internet surfing, lack of sustained interest. It's hard to teach writing for the same reasons it's hard to change any human behavior at any time. The students' essays are poor for the same reason my sporadic efforts to learn French have invariably stalled. Though she owns books and floor mats and has taken lessons at the YMCA, my wife can do no yoga.

When the essay that prompted this book was published in the *Atlantic Monthly,* education-minded bloggers were bent out of shape by my characterization of the students' writing as being so profoundly poor. Alex Reid, an associate professor of English and professional writing at the State University of New York at Cortland, wrote that he supposed "what makes such students the 'worst' is that they are distant from a certain ideological notion of students. They are perhaps unlikely to share in conventional notions of literacy and academic discourse."[4]

My notion of college-level discourse is indeed conventional, and no, the students don't share in it at all. Professor Reid's language is academic and polite, and the very essence of *euphemism,* which I try to get the students to stop indulging in. Mike Rose, who has written several books on education and literacy, clucked his tongue at me for being disrespectful to the students and spoke of the methods he used when teaching remedial college classes:

> And because many of our students . . . did display in their writing all the grammatical, stylistic, and organizational problems that give rise to remedial writing courses in the first place, we did spend a good deal of time on error—in class, in conference, on comments on their papers—*but in the context of their academic writing.* This is a huge point and one that is tied to our core assumptions about cognition and language: that writing filled with grammatical error does not preclude engagement with sophisticated intellectual material, and that error can be addressed effectively as one is engaging such material.[5]

Rose goes on at great length about the lots of other ways I could have achieved my educational goals. Remediation is what he wants me to do, but he seems to forget that I do not teach remedial or developmental classes, and cannot transform my bona fide honest-to-God fully accredited college class into one. The truth, of course, without any sugarcoating, is that the work submitted by my students is often so garbled that it is impossible to understand what they are thinking.

. . .

I read the compare-contrast essays that the students had written. I knew that we would have to start at the beginning. *A sentence is a group of words expressing a complete thought.* I wanted to go back there. I felt the tug of the past. I wanted to start at the very beginning and replicate the nineteen years of language arts study. I couldn't, of course, so I compromised. We would start not at the roots of language or usage but the roots of thought.

I read one essay aloud.

"Here we have a piece delineating the differences between cats and dogs," I said. "'Dogs are friendly, cats are not. Dogs greet their owners at the end of the day; cats do not. Dogs appear grateful for everything they get in life; cats do not.' Now, what's the problem with this essay?"

"It's not true?" said one student uncertainly.

"Why isn't it true?"

"You can't just say all cats are a certain way. You may have had a friendly cat."

I smiled to myself. She was young, not too long out of high school. *You can't just say.* Are there any words more chilling to a writer? The high school teachers had schooled her in a curriculum of political correctness. She knew that she shouldn't demean cats by stereotyping them. She was a nice young woman, I'm sure, and she'd never say a mean or unfair word about any living thing, particularly in a classroom setting.

"I actually think what the essay says is true," I said. "I've never known a friendly cat. No, the ideas behind the piece are, in some senses, valid. But in my mind the essay is not completely satisfying. Why is that?"

I got several halfhearted and confused answers.

I was starting to get a little ticked at the students, I must admit. It seemed I was working a lot harder than they were.

"Think of it this way," I said. "You're at a party. And there's a beautiful person on the other side of the room—a person that you really, really want to get to know before the night is out. You sidle up to him or her. You introduce yourself. The person reciprocates. There is electricity. You feel a bit of magic. Your heart flutters. You really need something great to tell this person. You need the start of a conversation. You desperately require some witty repartee. And so you lean over to the person and, with all the suavity you can muster, you say, 'You know, dogs and cats are really different. Dogs are friendly. Cats are not.'"

The class laughed. The writer of the essay, whom I had not identified, laughed as well. He reddened rather dramatically.

"So what's the problem?" I asked.

The laughter cut off. Confusion and uncertainty.

"What's the problem?" I cried. "You're all laughing. What's so funny?"

My nice young friend who was on the side of cats answered again. I think she wanted to redeem herself. "You would never say that at a party."

"Why not?"

"It's kind of . . . obvious."

Hallelujah. Now we were getting somewhere.

"So why would it be good enough for this assignment?" I asked. "The writer must seduce the reader, just like you want to seduce someone at a party. I, as a reader, have a lot of other stuff I could be doing. Why should I read anything? I could be watching a movie or eating a good dinner or surfing the Internet. Why the hell would I want to read about dogs and cats?"

They understood, the class. They got it. They knew that what had been written was absurd, but it was just an assignment, with no relevance to the real world. For the indifferent student, all work is busy work, empty effort to occupy time and, hopefully, garner some credit in the end.

"I think you all just may have to think harder and work better," I said.

By semester's end, I believe the class had made some small progress, but in truth it's hard to say. They were a challenge, and I was brand new. Certain assignments they made a complete hash of, and I, because of my inexperience, couldn't help them even a lick. Their research papers, for example, were utter disasters, because I didn't realize at how low a level they were operating; to dip into educational-speak, I didn't know how fragmented and disjointed their schematas were. When I explained to them how to develop a thesis and how to use passages from scholarly articles in journals to buttress that thesis, I didn't realize that I was speaking a completely foreign language: they had never seen, had never touched, had never even heard alluded to, this mysterious entity called a scholarly journal.

As a new instructor, I regretted my incompetence. That semester, I failed only the hardest cases, those students who stopped handing in assignments or even coming to class. Some of the nursing students and the middle-aged moms, who tended to hand in papers twice the required length, finished with low B's, which was already a compromise, as in my heart none of them did true B work. I gave one A. Everyone else swam in the polluted waters of C and C-minus and D.

My administrative systems were not yet locked in place. I had given some students the benefit of the doubt. Some students claimed to have handed in assignments of which I had no record; I had to assume the mistakes were my fault. I was still a naïf. I did not yet realize that some students, behind their earnest masks of good effort, were coldly, ruthlessly—like any high school punk, like smarmy Eddie Haskell—playing me for a sucker. I looked at that marvelous college-Gothic architecture, the arches, the trefoil windows, the spires pointing to heaven, and I was still thinking of college as a place of elevated virtue—of nobility.

My eye for grades was not yet sure. Some of those C's and C-minuses should have been D's; some high C's could have crept up to very, very, very low B's. But none of the students seemed to notice. I submitted the grades and never heard another word about any of it. *I can do this*, I thought rather merrily. *Not too bad*. I was happy to have gotten through it unscathed. We were in a college classroom, though we were often not doing college work. A visitor coming upon my class, in that stone fortress of an arts and humanities building, might think that we were enacting some sort of college idyll. We could, if the visitor squinted a bit, be at Harvard. But make no mistake: beneath the surface of that serene and scholarly mise-en-scène roiled waters of frustration and bad feeling. I was teaching students who were in over their heads.

5

The Four Stages of a Plot

It was always a great affair, the Misses Morkan's annual dance.
Everybody who knew them came to it, members of the family, old friends of the family, the members of Julia's choir, any
of Kate's pupils that were grown up enough, and even some
of Mary Jane's pupils too. Never once had it fallen flat. For
years and years it had gone off in splendid style as long as anyone could remember; ever since Kate and Julia, after the death
of their brother Pat, had left the house in Stoney Batter and
taken Mary Jane, their only niece, to live with them in the
dark gaunt house on Usher's Island, the upper part of which
they had rented from Mr Fulham, the corn-factor on the
ground floor. . . . Though their life was modest they believed
in eating well; the best of everything: diamond-bone sirloins,
three-shilling tea and the best bottled stout.

—James Joyce, "The Dead"

EVERY SEMESTER, in English 102, Introduction to College
Literature, we read "The Dead." I think about the genteel
poverty of the Morkan sisters and their niece. I think of their
real estate choices. Yes, they were only renting the dark gaunt
house, but there were many small luxuries in their lives. They
were happy. They lived on a small scale.

How on Earth did I get where I am?

Here is my story in real estate. It adheres to the classic four-phase form of the short story, the form I teach the students: exposition, rising action, climax, denouement.

Exposition. I grew up in a placid residential neighborhood on the edge of the city, a place of great spreading shade trees and above-ground pools and ice cream trucks with bells that tinkled gently. My upbringing could be called suburban in some ways, even though I lived in the city and the bite of the city was always faintly present: in the candy stores with wooden telephone booths in the back, where all manner of shady business was conducted; in the teenaged gangs who prowled the streets and hung out in the parks; in the boxes of untaxed cigarettes stored in the garages of neighbors working for organized crime. The itinerant scissors grinder—he worked off a horse-drawn cart, of all things, and this in 1965!—was known to be a numbers runner, even by us children, who had only the dimmest notion of what numbers running was. When the sun shone brightly, the quartz and mica in the sidewalks glittered, the ladies who ran the fêtes at the Lutheran church poured glasses of blue Kool-Aid, and the sound I remember most was the buzzing and clicking of bicycle gears.

My friends' parents owned their houses. Mostly, the houses were little attached boxes of brick, here and there a small ranch. My most affluent friend lived in a Queen Anne with a wrap-around porch and forest-green shutters and a flagpole in front. His father, with great ceremony, raised and lowered the flag every evening at dusk. My family rented. We lived on the second floor of a two-family house above our landlords, a middle-aged Italian-American couple, John and Angie Vigilante, and Angie's mother, Mrs. LoGerfo. Toothy Mrs. LoGerfo was bedridden. She was dying, I was told as a child, though she seemed cheerful enough, in her toothy old-lady way, when I caught glimpses of her. She was dying, as it turned out, but only in the way we all are dying, as she lived for another dozen years.

My life inside that apartment was proscribed. There were lots of things I couldn't do. The Vigilantes took great pains that Mrs. LoGerfo be comfortable, and while that was a pain in the neck for me, I had to respect how protective they were of her. I couldn't play in the alley because that would disturb Mrs. LoGerfo. I couldn't throw a rubber ball against the garage door because it wasn't our garage door. And it would disturb Mrs. LoGerfo. So there would also be no basketball hoop on the garage. I couldn't blare the TV. I couldn't jump in the living room because that might dislodge their ornate chandelier. I couldn't use the side door because I might disturb the Vigilantes' nephew, Jimmy, a weedy young man who looked, in his dark suits and rimless eyeglasses, like a seminarian. Jimmy was getting his Ph.D., it was said. He lived in the basement, but I never figured out where. His existence seemed Anne Frank–like. I was afraid of the basement, and avoided it, but sometimes when I took out the garbage, I risked a peek down there, and I saw no place habitable. This wasn't a basement but a cellar: stacks of boxes, a pyramid of loose pipes, mops and brooms, an old free-standing bird cage, peach baskets, cinderblock walls, and a slop sink. Sometimes I thought he slept in the coal bin; I always expected to see him sitting on the pipes, hunched over his dissertation. But I never did. In truth I forgot for years at a time that he lived down there, but then he would reappear, coming out the side door with his grad student satchel, and I'd feel weird and jumpy, as though I was being watched, all the rest of the day.

That my family was one of the few in the neighborhood who didn't own a home didn't really bother me. I seldom thought about it. My friends mentioned it only once. A kid named Tommy asked me about it one day, and we settled the matter rather quickly. I had just come outside. He looked up at the apartment windows and, with a cross expression, placed his hands on his hips.

"Why don't you get your own house?" he asked.

"I don't know," I said. "I think we might soon."

Tommy never brought it up again.

Why my parents were not homeowners was not discussed. There were only hints. We seemed no worse off than anyone else in the neighborhood. After my father died, my mother would say only that she had always wanted a house but that my father had a fear of mortgages, and a sense that he would never be able to do the necessary repairs. He was a city boy, a union official most comfortable in a topcoat and fedora, tucking into a plate of chops at a local steakhouse. He also, she told me, had a chance after the Depression to buy the grocery store that he had managed, but had shied away from making the deal.

Then one day I realized something important. I had come home from school and, while fumbling for my keys on the steps, I looked closely, perhaps for the first time, at the screen door, which was ornately designed with a busy pattern of scrolls, swags, and intertwining vines and branches. There, in the center of the door, encircled in a ring of decorative leaf-work, was a great script "L," looking for all the world like the symbol for the British pound. I knew in that moment that Mrs. LoGerfo's name was the one on the house's title, and my perception of the family dynamics downstairs was turned on its head. I had thought it was nice of the Vigilantes to take such good care of Mrs. LoGerfo, but in that instant I realized how little choice they had. They weren't young people, the Vigilantes, and that house was the key to their economic well-being. When I walked the dog in the evening, and I saw fat

John Vigilante, a man plagued by multiple hernias, leaning against the gate, pensively smoking a cigarette—he was ordered outside to smoke decades before such a thing was commonly done—I saw that he was practically as much a tenant as I was, his movements just as proscribed.

Mrs. LoGerfo's toothy grin, all of a sudden, made sense to me.

I never forgot my lesson about the power conferred by real estate, but as I got older I never particularly burned to be a homeowner. Some people positively ache to do it; for some, piloting a ride-on mower across their holdings is the summit of existence. But I felt I was called to the life of art. I wanted to write, and living in an apartment gave me the time to do that. Except for the ever-looming possibility of cockroach infestation, I enjoyed apartment life. I liked having neighbors. I had been blessed with unobtrusive ones. I have always taken comfort in the faint stirrings of life going on outside my apartment walls. The sound of a stereo a couple of doors down adds a nice rhythm to my movements. I love the sound of a husband and wife arguing across the hall. *Better them than me*, I think, and feel very cozy. I like the vague sociability of a laundry room. I like the smell of food in a hallway, garlic or meatballs or the sharp sweetness of crumbled bay leaves. I like the sound of a dog's toenails click-click-clicking on a hardwood floor.

After marrying in the mid-1980s my wife and I bought a two-bedroom apartment with a river view. The neighborhood was not so hot. There was vague, empty talk of gentrification, some of it quite strident, with some in the neighborhood for it and some against. Nothing came of it while we lived there. The problems of the neighborhood ran both deep and wide, and no one seriously believed it would ever improve. We didn't really care. There was a funky charm to our building, even to the drunken doormen in their threadbare uniforms. We rented out our second bedroom to a friend, and lived more like college students than people nearing thirty. We installed a nice butcher block in the kitchen. We lived there happily for several years. I waited tables in the afternoon and pursued my calling. I wrote essays and a couple of half-novels. Periodically, I would grow discouraged, but then I would sell a short piece or two, just enough to stoke my ambition and make me at once hopeful and miserable.

I continued to wait tables, working lunches at a place favored by local executives. I wheeled around trolleys full of food, transferring meals from sizzling platters to plates of white china: slabs of scrod and T-bone steaks and ladies' portion filet mignons the size of a Rubik's Cube. I struggled with my writing. I had nothing to write about. My life seemed too restrained. I thought that part of the problem was that I was seeing the same meal played out day after day; I couldn't shake the feeling that I was privy to only a fraction of life. I tried working a few dinners, but it didn't help.

On Black Monday in 1987, the stock market crashed. That day, I was serving the tables in the bar. There was a TV on. The stock prices crawled by at the bottom of the screen. My customers weren't eating. They weren't drinking, either. Their faces were ashen. I looked at the TV screen in great puzzlement. I couldn't make head or tail of the numbers and symbols. The silence in the bar was eerie. The only sound was that of my trolley wheels clattering on the tile floor. I brought lots of uneaten food back to the kitchen that day. The owner of the restaurant sat at the bar. He looked up to the TV screen then down to his cup of coffee, up then down, up then down, like a child playing peek-a-boo.

I felt so much on the outside of things. I knew nothing of stocks and finance, the real world. What gall I had trying to set myself up as a novelist. Who was I to think I could illuminate anything for anyone else? There seemed no one quite as ill equipped as I to take on such a task. I felt very stupid. I leaned against the wall in the restaurant's kitchen and thought about my life, and tucked into someone's virtually untouched plate of coho salmon.

Rising Action. Meanwhile, my wife had gotten pregnant. Clearly it was time to grow up. I started to feel that trying to be a novelist had actually stunted my experience. I didn't quite abandon my literary dreams, but I knew I would have to do more living before I had anything to write. We sold the apartment to a dancer who loved the butcher block. Maybe, I decided, I should be a teacher. Maybe that's how people like me wound up. I walked out the front entrance of the apartment building, past the red-eyed doorman, resumé and temporary teaching license in hand, to the nearest school, which happened to be a middle school. You could do that in those days. There was an acute shortage of teachers, and the job didn't pay much at all. Anyone who could spell, and some who couldn't, could be licensed to stand before groups of poor readers. Everyone with half a brain worked in private industry; nobody, and I mean nobody, wanted to stand in front of little kids and work on vocabulary lessons. I walked into the school without an appointment, as though I were a deliveryman. The principal hired me on the spot. He couldn't believe his good fortune. He led me over to the secretary so I could fill out my W-4. "He's going to make a fine, fine addition to the faculty," he said. She seemed unimpressed.

As far as teaching gigs go, middle school is generally considered the bottom of the barrel. I liked it. Seventh graders were the worst, but I never tired of how they tortured you for a year, vanished for the summer, and reappeared in the much more reasonable guise of eighth graders. They would greet me warmly by name, shake my hand and ask about my family, as though we were all corporate executives. I thought I would teach forever, but I left the classroom after a few years to take a job that paid more in a tatty corner of the government. We moved to the rural exurbs, to an affluent little village in a crease between the mountains and farms. The daily commute was a challenge for such an urban creature as myself: I spent my mornings stuck behind school buses and afternoons pinned behind tractors and hay wagons. In this new environment, my wife and I were conscious of our status as greenhorns, but we puzzled it all out: the penny socials and the church suppers, the gun shops, the silos, the gangs of chickens walking on the roadside, signs saying TOPSOIL WANTED and ads for such mysterious processes as rototilling.

We bought a very small home. It was a cheesecake-yellow 1950s dormered Cape Cod of about nine hundred square feet. Tiny. The house always reminded me of a Bavarian cottage. A storybook home. It sat in a little development of several streets among other Cape Cods. On the inside, the place didn't seem quite so small. The rooms were cunningly fitted together like puzzle pieces. No wasted space. There were two largish bedrooms upstairs, one down; living room, bathroom, dining room, and kitchen. The house had lots of wood trim and oak flooring and a back porch. This was what we could afford, and we bought it. So what if the distance from the farthest corner of the living room to the end of the kitchen was about ten steps? This was not just a starter house but a baby house—perfect for people who weren't handy, who really knew nothing about houses. My wife and I mused about the repairs I would have to learn to do. "Really, I don't think you'll even need a ladder," she said, which was true. Standing on tiptoe, I could practically reach the gutters.

I have fond memories of life in that house. The children were in a golden age. We had lovely neighbors with children of their own, and my kids forged strong friendships. I taught my own little gang to play baseball in the front yard. It looked like the move was a successful one. No more did I think that I hadn't experienced enough to be a writer. Kids will do that to you. I paid my mortgage and raked my leaves and stained my little deck. I rebuilt my front steps. I took a writing class, and the novelist-of-repute who taught it loved the book I had managed to finish. He had a big-time New York agent he would show it to. Off the thing went. I felt the greased gears of a wonderful narrative moving forward rather marvelously. No doubt, it was only a matter of time before a life in literature was mine.

No doubt. *No doubt.* It's a phrase I have come to associate with the 1990s, when the world was on the rise. How fitting that Gwen Stefani and No Doubt, the band, sold 27 million records in that decade. I remember when I signed up for the 401(k) plan at my government job (oh yes, we all knew about stocks and share prices now; how far I had come from my days cracking lobster claws at the restaurant!) and the Human Resource guy advised me to park my money in the riskier stock funds. He said he was averaging a return of about 10 percent a year. What happens, I asked him, when they go down? He looked at me pityingly. Clearly I was going to be a difficult employee. "They don't go down," he said.

But then my narrative, the one whose contours I could see so closely, derailed. The agent didn't like the book. Rather loathed it, was the feeling I got. What! This, clearly, was not supposed to happen. The great story of my literary discovery had been aborted. The lesson, which I didn't quite grasp, was that stories don't always move forward as we think they will in an orderly and logical fashion. Sometimes the machinery of a tale lurches and shudders and stops altogether. Sometimes the crankshaft starts spinning in the opposite direction.

"Well, that will have to be your *second* book," said the novelist-of-repute. He said it and I agreed and neither of us believed it. He was sad for me. I vowed hollowly to keep trying. I knew that I wouldn't be able to start another book. I was on the road to forty years old. I read reviews of first-time novelists and felt a growing bitterness. I was sure they were friendly with the people reviewing them.

Periodically, our real estate agent would send us a postcard, reminding us that she was available for all of our needs. Maybe it was time to trade up. Our lack of tax deductions, specifically a larger mortgage deduction, was bothersome to our accountant. He wanted us to spend more. To spend more was to make more to spend more to make more. And the children were getting bigger—older, yes, but physically bigger; the house now seemed unable to contain the lot of us. Daily life took on the flavor of an episode from *Alice's Adventures in Wonderland*; I started to feel that I might scrape my head on the ceiling if I wasn't careful and that, with any sudden movement, some family member might poke an arm through the sheetrock. There was enormous pressure on our single windowless bathroom. The light and fan and flushing mechanism seemed to run twenty-four hours a day. Why couldn't we have a real house? A house with some scope, some gravitas? I longed for a substantial house, a house with hallways and a foyer and a bit of extra space. My great love affair with literature had come to a shocking end, and I was on the rebound. To have nice floors and large closets and a great big living room seemed to me the pinnacle of existence.

The millennium turned. Everyone we knew was trading up, flipping their houses, moving forward. The nice families with whom we had lived in the little development atop the network of streams had all moved out, which made our decision seem somehow inevitable. This was a madness that fed on itself. There was a computer in a corner of our sons' bedroom; while the boys slept, my wife and I would huddle around the screen, whispering with excitement as we surfed the Web sites of real estate agents and mortgage companies.

Climax. We went for a week at the end of the summer to Miami Beach. We stayed at the Deauville, on Collins Avenue. The place was crawling with European tourists. It was slightly seedy in a good, comfortable, relaxed way. The Beatles had famously stayed here in 1964, and I took a few pensive strolls through the disused ballroom in the basement, where the band played on a live remote hookup for Ed Sullivan. The air was chockablock with ghosts, girls in beehives and bikinis and women in toreador slacks, older leathery women playing canasta at kidney-shaped tables in between inert dips in the kidney-shaped pool. I swore I smelled suntan oil and Brylcreem. I watched a scuba diving class moving as one in one quadrant of the pool. We came into the lobby from the pool and our wet footprints disappeared into the carpet—oh, the glories of 3M and Monsanto! I was happy to be able to afford this look at the lost glory of America in the Sun and Fun Capital of the World. We meandered through the art deco district, stepping gingerly into an additional level of nostalgia; took in a show of local art at the Jackie Gleason Theater; zoomed up and down the causeways in our rental car, rock and roll blasting, Pepsi tickling our throats.

At night in the hotel room, we watched the Little League World Series. The Danny Almonte controversy raged. How old, really, was the pitcher for the Rolando Paulino All-Stars, the pride of the Bronx? Fourteen or twelve? All sides of the controversy launched their own investigations. Little League dads who happened to be lawyers issued sharply worded statements. Gumshoes were hired to track down the birth certificate. We watched Danny strike out 16 batters in his victory over Oceanside, California, who couldn't get anywhere near the ball. We were transfixed. He did look big and overpowering on the mound. It was all so compelling, and so charmingly, dizzyingly, unbelievably irrelevant. Danny Almonte was the last news story that caught my attention before the planes hit the towers. It was on September 1, 2001, that the *New York Times* reported Danny's actual age as fourteen; the country reeled at the news. Expressions "of disappointment, anger and frustration came from President Bush, Mayor Rudolph W. Giuliani, Little League officials, and others who spoke of the team's pain and of lessons about honesty in sports," wrote the paper. An editorial on September 2 reminded us that "the opportunity offered by sports must never be allowed to void all the other opportunities children should be eligible to encounter as they grow up. In a literal sense, Danny Almonte has been defrauded by his father, Felipe de Jesús Almonte. That is the real crime, not the attempt to pass his son off as a 12-year-old."

What an affluent and carefree country that we could spend time agonizing about such things. No wonder we were the envy of the world. Who wouldn't want to be an American, in our Levis and our Ralph Lauren flannel shirts, the sparkling taste of Pepsi dancing on our tongues?

I wonder if any generation is lucky enough to be spared the trauma of the epochal, life-changing event? My mother talked about two: Pearl Harbor and the assassination of JFK. She remembered both moments in detail, and often noted that she was doing the same thing when she heard about both events: ironing. I couldn't appreciate the lightning-bolt devastation wrought by both events. They seemed part of the general churning of recorded history. Most news seemed to me distant and small, like scenes viewed through a telescope held the wrong way around. A few events stood out a little to me:

Nixon's resignation, the Oklahoma City bombing, the first World Trade Center attack in 1993—but even that was a byword for incompetence: six people dead and thousands helped out of the towers with nothing more than dirty faces. The newspapers were always full of stuff, but really nothing much ever changed.

Who can write about September 11? Is there anything more heartrending, nearly a decade later, than the image of those doomed souls at the top of the North Tower, clinging to the broken windows, waving towels? The memory is haunting, pitiable, sick-making. I drove home that day through the cornfields, which I imagined as stretching from sea to shining sea, and marveled at the empty blue sky: not a single plane was flying. I don't know why I found this so hard to comprehend, but I did. Two days later, an already wild-eyed friend made even crazier-seeming by the attack folded a $20 bill into the shape of an airplane and bid me behold—there were the smoking towers, there was the broken Pentagon. He was very upset, but I found his little origami stunt heartening. The American distraction factory was still operating on three shifts. Our compulsion to focus on the silliest aspect of any news story was intact. America would survive. I watched the news, and grieved, but never quite realized how quickly life, and the world, can change. I experienced the terror of the moment, but it didn't frighten me to my essence—it didn't scare me enough to keep me in my little safe house, biding my time. The planes could hit the tower—unthinkable!—just the way markets could drop, General Motors could go bankrupt, Bear Stearns could fail.

For someone so involved with literature, I missed one of the great themes of September 11: that life does not just churn and pulsate but sometimes tears and cannot be repaired; life can change irrevocably in the blink of an eye. Actions can have consequences. A man was capable of making a mistake that lasted a lifetime.

In the summer of 2002, our real estate agent, aware that we were ready to leave the Bavarian cottage, told us that she had a house that we really needed to see. It was beautiful. We would appreciate it. It wasn't even on the market yet. Would we care for a peek before the signs were hammered into the lawn?

I was flattered by the attention. I felt truly a part of the community. After September 11 I had the feeling shared by virtually every red-blooded male in America: that because I had not been in New York City on that day, that because I had not been called to trudge into the towers on a doomed rescue mission, that because I was not a fireman, that because I was alive and unscathed, I was not truly a man. I had not participated directly in September 11 or its aftermath, and no one was asking my opinion of its implications, either. I was a failed artist, a mute inglorious pundit, the author of one unpublished and several abandoned novels. I had by that time given up on a life in the world of literature. Playing in the field of real estate signaled an alternate form of legitimacy for me. Finally, I was entering the middle class. I found myself thinking a lot about hardwood floors and updated wiring and what went into the selection of a general contractor. General contractor. I liked saying those words. I liked knowing what they meant. I immersed myself in *The Field Guide to American Houses.* I may not have been able to publish my writing, but it seemed within my grasp to house my family in a half-timbered Arts and Crafts or a spindled Queen Anne. Suddenly, a finished attic seemed the key to personal happiness. I grew rather obsessed with Internet mortgage calculators, which told me always we could afford the houses we were looking at and now seem as rigged as a fairground game: "Swing the Hammer, Ring the Bell, Buy the House!" Our attention focused on a romantic just-stately-enough three-bedroom home a block or so from the center of our village, a symbol of an earlier era of American prosperity. We muted the television so as not to be distracted by the new violent world order and asked our real estate agent, who seemed to be with us all the time, like an unmarried aunt who had come to stay for good, if we should go ahead with the deal. She said yes. We understood her economic interest in the purchase, of course, but in those heady times, everyone's economic interests seemed miraculously intertwined, and all for the good. Yes, the price was steep, but didn't we stand to make a nice profit on the Bavarian cottage? This new house seemed to be increasing in value as the three of us stood on the porch jawing about it. Our plan was the same as everyone else's: buy the wonderful house, be very happy and prosperous, live a life out of Norman Rockwell, and then, once the children went off to college, sell it at a dizzying profit.

We loved the house. We loved its solidity, its large bedrooms, the fresh-looking apple-green tiles in the kitchen, the set of bowed windows in the dining room. We loved the tidy garage and the family room and the fourth bedroom, which would serve as an office. We loved the ornate scrollwork on the radiators, and the comforting way they hissed. We picked up one corner of the rug and gasped with pleasure at the grandiloquence of the hardwood floors. How happy could we be here? I was happy as things stood; the thought of an additional layer of happiness, like a sprinkling of sugar atop an already delicious pie, was intoxicating.

The house was expensive. Two years earlier I would have laughed at the price. How could I possibly afford that? But the parameters of real estate are an ever-shifting business, with no place of solid footing—like a pit of quicksand, if you'll forgive a too-handy simile. I sometimes regretted having sold my river-view apartment; apartments in the building were now fetching close to a million dollars. Why couldn't I just have paid that little mortgage every month? I could have paid it with the change I lost in the sofa. But it somehow doesn't work that way.

This house cost a lot more than the Bavarian cottage. But everything, in those heady days, still seemed possible.

"That's a big nut every month," said my wife warily.

A few wispy cirrus clouds of doubt streamed across our sunny blue sky. Was it really a good idea to start a new 30-year mortgage in our midforties? We'd have to meet that big monthly nut until we were in our seventies . . . No. We would sell the house at a nice profit before that. No doubt. No doubt. What would we get? That all depended, I said with great self-importance and a distinct lack of foresight, on what the market was doing when we opted to sell. The world of real estate was expanding, like the aftermath of an economic Big Bang, and I could not imagine the inevitable contraction. Real estate saws trilled faintly in my ears, like a Beach Boys song sounding distantly from a radio at the seashore. "Location, location, location!" Oh yes, my village was lovely. Twin church spires! Quaint firehouses! A beautiful little jewel of a library! (I loved to look through the cupola atop its roof and imagine the bit of blue sky was a little slice of the infinite.) "Real estate never decreases in value." No sir. It never did, it never had, it never would. And I didn't think of myself as greedy. If my house merely retained its value, that would be fine. "Better to have the worst house in a great neighborhood than vice versa." Yes. And my new house wouldn't even be the worst. It was solidly in the middle. "If you're choosing between taking vacations and having a nice house, buy the house, because having a great house is like being on perpetual vacation."

Who thinks up this stuff?

We had the house inspected. We knew an inspector whom

we trusted and respected, but owing to a series of misunder-
standings, we didn't get him but another inspector who worked
for the same franchise. She was tall, immaculately groomed.
Her shirt with her name in script on the pocket and her work
pants were crisp and creased. She had never owned a house.
She was thinking about buying a place. My wife and I must
have started a little. She showed us her credentials, her residence
inspector postsecondary certification plus her residence inspection protocol, a score or more checklists in green binders,
which we would receive a copy of. "I've done hundreds of these
things," she told us in blasé fashion.

Perhaps I am too ruled by prejudice, but I know what I want
in a residence inspector. I want a man who's been living in
houses and fooling around with them all his life. If he's short
and squat and smokes, all to the good. I want someone who
can stand in an entrance hallway, pressing his hands mystically
to both walls, and *feel* in an instant the vital signs of the house,
checklists be hanged. I want someone who doesn't tick off individual areas of inspection but sees the holistic connection
between the loose drain grate in the basement and the faulty
exhaust vent on the roof and the relationship of function to the
secondary and tertiary issues: indecisive thermostats, weak-
willed toilets, overeager circuit breakers.

We thought of waiting for our own inspector but there was
no time. The project had taken on a life and momentum of its
own, which is always dangerous. It did seem to us, and to the
realtor, the sellers, and all the attorneys involved that if we
didn't have *that* inspection on *that* day, the deal would fall
through. We were terrified that someone would jump in and
snatch the house away from us. Isn't that absurd? We imagined
all manner of people carrying attaché cases full of cash, waiting
to muscle us out. Of course, that was not the case. In all the
time we have lived here, no one has knocked on our door with

an attaché case, begging to be allowed to buy the house—not even before the housing market collapsed in 2008.

My wife had the first inkling that this was all a mistake. It came to her in the night, as though she had been ravished by an incubus of insight. When I awoke, she was pale, drawn, wide-eyed with terror. She said she hadn't slept. This was all, she said, a horrible mistake. What were we thinking?

I dismissed her fears. I thought she was just being alarmist. But my wife is a woman of blinding intelligence; I should have listened to her. But oh, the tangles of a marriage! I judged our very ability to vault ahead in the real estate world as prima facie evidence that we should; I dismissed my wife's impulses toward caution as mere, well, caution. It may not have been a sophisticated analysis, but I thought she was being a chicken. Our dynamic was of the fairly standard male/female variety, but of course we put our own spin on it.

I made us press onward. Everything, I was sure, would turn out for the best. My wife disagreed strongly. She was ready to cut our losses and run. But my mix of Candide-like optimism and bullheadedness eventually prevailed. I called for calm and rationality. I was determined that we adhere to our plan. I refused to be pushed around by circumstance. Looking back today at all the trouble we had with this relatively straightforward decision, I sometimes wonder: how would we have coped together during times of historical crisis? Imagine us in our Pompeiian villa in AD 79. "Tremors? We're always having tremors," I can picture myself superciliously telling my wife. "I hardly think a few flakes of ash are going to hurt us. Let's see how the new fresco is coming along." Or on the *Titanic*. She'd have done fine in Lifeboat #1; me, I would have been happy to stay behind.

This is the male psyche. We won't be bullied. Our backs go up. We dig in our heels. We can be obstinate to the point of willful blindness. We are not prone to introspection. This cluster of traits, though sometimes productive, leading to things like the invention of the steam turbine, can also invite poor decision making. And in the wake of disaster, when the scaffoldings have collapsed around our ears, still we will not admit error. Instead, we palliate our womenfolk, who saw it all coming, and put the best face on things. I imagine Adam and Eve leaving the garden in their new animal skins. "All right, let's just move on," Adam buzzes in Eve's ear. "So your childbearing pangs will be great. So the ground is cursed, and we can look forward now only to thorn and thistle? Get used to it . . . Or rather, think of the possibilities!"

As the day of the closing drew near, the karma turned more and more sour. My wife was normally the paperwork person, but she abandoned it all in despair, and I now faced increased dealings with people like our lawyer, who I didn't think was filing our forms in a timely fashion. I found myself in the odd position of pressuring him to move forward with a deal for which even I was losing enthusiasm. My daily existence had taken on the skewed logic of a too-vivid dream. I seemed to be moving through molasses. I felt, too, a blossoming sense of paranoia: my beautiful little village seemed populated by predators who would ensnare me in bad deals, swindle me, take from me what meager fortune I had amassed.

Never before had I felt more an outsider. The real estate agent, my attorney, the seller's attorney, the building inspector, and county clerks and the tax assessor—how could I have gotten mixed up with the lot of them? They all went to school together. Christ, they were probably all related, by blood and by marriage. Their faces, peering at me at the closing, all seemed to look alike. I was sure that none were in debt, that none had ever gotten himself in a hole for such a big mortgage. Their money, I imagined feverishly, came from the hard work of their serious rural forebears, who sold bushels of corn and baskets of eggs and cans of milk and then were shrewd enough to sell the farms to developers, who marketed overpriced McMansions to citified suckers who could scarcely afford them.

I've seen plenty of movies and TV shows in which young marrieds take possession of new houses. They always seem happy: filled with hope, brimming with plans, nervous in a good way, giggly. My own vision of things is darker. I think of Lucy and Ricky Ricardo finally buying that house in Connecticut after all those years renting—she, livid and thick of frame, and he, puffy with drink—and I think: it's a good thing the series is in its last season, for surely now these two weary middle-aged mortgagees will kill each other. John Payne and Maureen O'Hara in *Miracle on 34th Street* find Santa's cane in the new house, and I think that soon the misery will commence. Little Natalie Wood, up in her dormered bedroom, just might hear, at night, the sound of grown-ups arguing.

We took possession of our new house on a gray midwinter's afternoon. Our team of moving men trooped in and out of the front door with boxes and furniture, and if I squinted and looked at them a certain way it seemed they were actually moving us *out* of the house, not in, like one of those optical illusions where the spinning statue changes direction, and I found myself sort of relieved for a moment. But then, of course, reality would intrude, harsher than ever.

The house had seemed rather stately when we looked at it; now it just seemed dark. Gloomy. All the furniture from the Bavarian cottage didn't come close to filling the rooms. We would buy more, I thought, and then the parade of expenses began. I had budgeted for a new roof—even our tyro home inspector could see that we needed one of those—but in her inexperience she had missed an underlying problem, and I thus learned more than I ever wanted to, at an enormous cost, about the need to have one's soffits rebuilt, and the always-intriguing interplay between soffit and fascia.

When we owned the Bavarian cottage, I never gave a thought to the national economy. But now, I died a little death with each plunge in the stock market.

I pined hopelessly for the past.

The world seemed to be sinking into anarchy. I couldn't watch the World Trade Center stuff anymore. I felt deafened by the din of terror and misery.

I lay in bed at night and pondered what to do. There was so much to be done I didn't know where to begin. I lay with the lights on and studied the beautiful old wallpaper in the bedroom. It was a lovely pattern, bunches of pink and green and yellow stems on a somber ocher background. It was beautiful but it was very old, peeling and cracked in places. It would really have to be removed, and yet I had bought the house partly because of the beautiful old wallpaper, which I think sums up rather neatly the unfocused and contradictory quality of the decision.

In buying the house, we did find Norman Rockwell. But we had been overambitious. I had wanted hardwood floors and a foyer and an attic, and I got them, and all the expense that went along with them. I had needed life to fill my books; now I was in the grip of more life than I could possibly handle. For the first time in my life I worried about money. When I heard a strange gurgling in a pipe, I worried. When the refrigerator appeared to stop working, I opened the door fifteen times in an hour and felt the food, and I worried. I sat down and tried to write my way out of my worry and the pen hung poised above the page. I couldn't focus on anything. The milk in my coffee tasted a little sour. I worried, and I denied my worry to my wife because I didn't want her to worry. She tried to persuade me to be as worried as I actually was, and then we fought and both worried even more.

"If you're choosing between taking vacations and having a nice house, buy the house, because having a great house is like being on perpetual vacation." I was in yet a third situation, a place the adage failed to mention: I certainly wouldn't be taking any vacations, and neither would I be in the house very much, because it was soon obvious that I would have to crank up my second income. Whatever the state of the wallpaper, it would stay up. The time had come to kick my second career as an adjunct professor of English into high gear.

Denouement. I define it for my literature classes as the untying of the knot. Conflicts are resolved, the various plot strands untangle, the characters resume something akin to normal life, and the reader experiences catharsis, a release of tension and anxiety. I have a little trouble teaching this one because I'm not at all sure denouement actually exists.

6

Community College

A NY RESENTMENT I MIGHT HAVE HAD about having to
work a second job melted away. I couldn't worry about
the toll it might take on my happiness or my closeness with my
family or my aging body. I couldn't worry about not seeing
the children. I needed to adjunct up a storm. Pembrook College had been after me for a while to take on more classes; I
called them up and told them airily that my schedule had
"cleared up." They took care of me. But I needed more. My
new goal was to teach classes fifty-two weeks a year.

Late that summer, I approached Huron State, a community
college within reasonable commuting distance. They were interested. My experience at Pembrook made me an appealing
candidate. I was interviewed by the chairman of the English
department and a second teacher, two women who reminded
me, in both round shape and apparel, of a pair of nuns who had
just gotten the directive not to wear the habit anymore. The
interview went well, except for a moment right near the end.
It sounded like I had a pretty full schedule at Pembrook; why,
they asked with just a trace of suspicion, did I want to teach
even more?

You know how it is in job interviews: you can't admit to
needing the salary, much less to having made a cataclysmic
financial decision threatening to push you over the edge. I

thought fast. Adjuncts, I had come to understand, lived on the fringes. These two gals would assume I was a nut; the idea was to present as the right sort of nut.

"I'm trying to save for the kids' college," I said evenly, madly simplifying. "Trying to avoid loans."

I had conveyed what I wanted. I was concerned with education. I was a hard worker, a beast of burden. I had perhaps a bit of the right-wing survivalist in me, a man who would prefer to pay college tuition, if not in gold coins, at least in cash. Strictly speaking, what I told them wasn't entirely untrue. I did have college tuition looming, and I did have an aversion to debt. There was no need to tell them how I got that aversion.

They hired me on the spot. And, since they always needed good English adjuncts, they'd appreciate, if I knew anybody. . . .

I walked out of the interview feeling not exactly buoyed but somewhat relieved. I strolled pensively around the lovely, peaceful campus. Several of the buildings were quite old, but most, according to their cornerstones, were built in the 1950s, of a dusty yellow brick that conveyed a businesslike feeling of solidity. Several wiry and hawklike old women, who I later learned belonged to a local garden club, tended the impressive flower beds. The sun shone beautifully off the ladies' white hair. They seemed so happy, their lives so well lived. The campus bookstore was open, and several clerks unpacked textbooks from cartons. I had a real sense of new beginnings. Of course, I remained a man in his forties, and this was no time for a new beginning. Our buying of the house coincided almost to the moment, unfortunately, with our first glimpses of retirement. I had never thought about retiring from my day job; my work life stretched before me, I thought, infinitely. But all of a sudden I was getting service pins and being treated as an elder statesman. Conversations with colleagues started to move down the same detour: "So when can you pack it in?" they would ask. Did I really look that old? I didn't tell them what I was feeling: that I had made quite sure that I would never be able to retire, thank you very much. I would not be living in a condo on a golf course. I would not be joining a garden club and tending the black-eyed Susans at the local college. No, I wasn't going to take the usual path. My current plan was to drop dead at my desk.

Huron State put me in an English 101 class. The class was larger than any I'd had at Pembrook, and the students were younger. Of my twenty-five enrollees, no more than two or three were classic middle-aged returning students. They, of course, sat in the front seats. Their books were stacked neatly before them; they hung on my every utterance. Everyone else was young, but as the class progressed I realized they weren't as young as I had initially thought. They were in their twenties, and already beaten down. They had not gone directly from high school to college. Their essays revealed that they had spent some time in the world, time enough for unexpected pregnancies and broken marriages and parental estrangement and substance abuse difficulties and, always, thrumming along in the background, the relentless pulse of the stifling dead-end job. One girl mentioned in her first essay that she worked in a local café and had sold me the cup of aged Sumatran I had bought before that first night's class.

I hadn't thought at all about the philosophy behind community colleges. I knew their tuition was low; I knew they would take anybody. I could rattle off the press release: that the mission of the community college was to make college available to those who might otherwise be shut out, and I supposed that to be a noble goal. I did not know that their advocates possessed the zeal of missionaries.

. . .

In 1998, the American Association of Community Colleges noted the following about its constituent schools:

> The network of community, technical, and junior colleges in America is unique and extraordinarily successful. It is, perhaps, the only sector of higher education that truly can be called a "movement," one in which the members are bound together and inspired by common goals. From the very first, these institutions, often called "the people's colleges," have stirred an egalitarian zeal among their members. The open door policy has been pursued with an intensity and dedication comparable to the populist, civil rights, and feminist crusades. While more elitist institutions may define excellence as exclusion, community colleges have sought excellence in service to the many.[1]

It is all, in theory, wonderful: American egalitarianism at its best. We are happy believing that we can and should send everyone under the sun to college. This seems a noble initiative. Academia is all for it, naturally. Industry is all for it, and some companies even assist with tuition costs. Government is all for it; there are lots of opportunities, for the truly needy, for financial aid. The media cheerleads for it: Oprah, *The View,* National Public Radio—try to imagine someone coming out against the idea of everyone in America going to college. To be opposed to such a scheme of inclusion would be positively churlish. And now that we find ourselves stumbling through the worst economic downturn since the 1930s, the thinking is that community colleges are even more vital to the survival of our nation. "Community colleges are going to be an absolute catalyst to help people get back on their feet," says United States

Secretary of Education Arne Duncan at a roundtable organized by Senator Mike Enzi of Wyoming.[2] Bill Cosby tapes public-service announcements in Detroit in support of the Wayne County Community College District.[3] And Barack Obama pledges to spend $12 billion over the next decade on the American Graduation Initiative, which would, as the president said in a speech delivered at Macomb Community College in Michigan,

> reform and strengthen community colleges like this one from coast to coast so they get the resources that students and schools need—and the results workers and businesses demand. Through this plan, we seek to help an additional 5 million Americans earn degrees and certificates in the next decade—5 million.[4]

The American Graduation Initiative was removed from the 2009 Obama health care bill at the last moment, so for the moment it is a dead issue, but defeated or not, the language of the bill, the ringing optimism coupled with blind faith in the power of education, is striking. The American zeitgeist of limitless possibility is a beautiful thing to behold. I, too, want desperately to believe in it. But some of the students I encounter in the community college world test my belief in the ultimate workability, the sustainability (to use the fashionable term) of what we have set up.

> Recent changes in American higher education, which represent a substantial departure from previous practice, have extended college access to unprecedented numbers of minority, disadvantaged, and nontraditional (age 25 and over) students who are often less academically prepared than their peers. . . .[5]

The general preparation of my Huron State students turned out to be quite poor. I would have to figure out a way, and I wasn't at all sure I could, of reconciling the remedial work we were doing with a standard college curriculum. If you do ninth-grade work in a college classroom, does it automatically become college work? This is, I suppose, the ultimate question.

. . .

The writing of my new students was even worse than what I had encountered at Pembrook. Almost none were at college level. I did not attend anything resembling an Ivy League school, and Pembrook had tempered my expectations. But some of my community college students were not even at high school level. Remember "I" spent some time in the dreaded junior high classroom, and some of those students were miles ahead of my new college class.

I've taught in community college for nearly ten years now, and the writing hasn't gotten any better. How often is the first person singular, the letter "I," uncapitalized? Too frequently to count. I know, I know—I'm a grouch with a stick up his ass. Language is all casual, e-mail and texting have altered styles dramatically. Everybody's e.e. cummings. Who am I to deny the transformative vibrancy of language? What's the big god-damn deal anyway? Unfortunately, for me and I think for many others, fair or not, the lowercase "i" is a marker of shoddy thinking. I tell the students in no uncertain terms: do this, and the arguments in your paper, whatever the merit, will not even be considered, because no one will want to read what you say. I know this is true, because when I see "i" for "I," it is only the contract I sign as an adjunct instructor that keeps me reading.

Misspellings, of course, abound. "Tight nit" for *tight-knit*; a hero as a "knight in shinny armor"; "ludacris" for *ludicrous* (shame on you, rapper, for what you have wrought!); *theirs, there's,* and *they'res* chasing one another around in a fugal counterpoint of inaccuracy—what's the big deal here, Ms. Grundy? English spelling is difficult, and that's why the spell checker was invented.

Like it or not, college is not merely an extension of high school, another four years of bells, study halls, lunch, gym, and extracurriculars. Without heaping too much solemnity upon it, college is something that one must ascend to. No one would expect to pass a calculus class if he had not yet mastered basic arithmetic. Why, then, are most attempts to adhere to basic standards in the use of the English language in college courses heaped with scorn?

John Rouse, a rhetoric and composition theoretician, writes of a student struggling to begin an essay. In his abortive attempts, the student takes opposite sides of an issue, struggling to see which one he is able to write about. Now, I admire this student's practicality—I tell my classes that an important, if overlooked, factor when selecting a topic is that it must give you sufficient material to write about—and, as a writer, I sympathize. Often I have jumped full-tilt into a piece only to discover, as the prose came slowly and crankily, that I didn't quite believe in the position I had taken, and I would be better served approaching the writing from a different angle. But Rouse doesn't cotton to that sort of thing:

> Notice how in his desperation this student is willing to take any position, to agree or disagree or both at once—any position that will supply the needed words and satisfy the demand of authority. Here with this first writing assignment begins a training in that amorality so useful to authority everywhere.[6]

Rouse objects vehemently to the teaching of grammatical structures as just one more way to keep the beleaguered student in his place. He sees grammar as inherently sinister:

> Of course the inadequacy of traditional grammar as a description of the language is well-known in the profession, but no matter—it still retains a useful disciplinary value. It helps train young people to be concerned with the rules laid down by authority, even when those rules do not fit the situation. Language training is always behavior training.

The problem with Rouse and his ilk is that they presuppose a level of student difficulty with the structures of English that still allows instructors to understand their papers. I do not care if my students get "who" and "whom" wrong; the distinctions between "shall" and "will," or "which" and "that" are stumpers to me, and I wouldn't expect the students to be able or willing to negotiate them. But I do believe in teaching basic grammar and usage, even if the lessons are invariably rushed and ad hoc. College writing, the manipulating of ideas in a sophisticated fashion, requires a sturdy latticework of form; doing the thinking about sentences, which should have happened in high school, trains the mind to approach ideas with rigor. The birth of subtext, like the nurturing of a fragile Asiatic lily, requires proper fertilization: nouns and verbs, sentences that parse, that we can understand. Writing teachers don't go off in search of error. We don't shudder with a surreptitious thrill when we find it; we don't read as "policemen" or "examiners," in the words of David Bartholomae, who seems to think that an inability to understand poor student writing is the teacher's fault anyway.

The teacher who is unable to make sense out of a seemingly bizarre piece of student writing is often the same teacher who can give an elaborate explanation of the "meaning" of a story by Donald Barthelme or a poem by e.e. cummings.[7]

It goes without saying that we're not teaching creative writing here. We don't approach the spatterings of a first-grade art student in the same way we do a Jackson Pollock. What I encounter regularly in my students' writing are yawning canyons of illogic and error. Certainly the students don't read back to themselves what they write, but also, while they are writing, they appear to work with but the thinnest sliver of their consciousness engaged. They don't seem to remember that sentences need verbs; they deal freely in a currency of disconnected phrases and sentence fragments. It is difficult to know how to proceed with college instruction when this is the place at which we begin.

A woman writes in her research paper about America in the late 1940s and gets many details about World War II, details which are common knowledge, wrong. Her storehouse of knowledge about the world is inadequate to the task. In a paper on government wiretapping, a student seems to think that the American Civil Liberties Union is indeed a union. In an essay on acid rain, a student writes that water molecules in the sky absorb toxins and send them back to earth—because they have nothing else to do. A literature student, analyzing Flannery O'Connor's story "Everything That Rises Must Converge"—in which a mother and son ride a city bus to her exercise class at the YMCA—writes with confidence that it is set during the Civil War.

In no other age but our own—idealistic, inclusive, unwilling to limit anyone's possibilities for self-determination— would some of my students be considered ready for college. They have been abducted into college, sold a bill of goods. Despite having performed indifferently in high school, t were told that they have no choice but to attend college. Barack Obama speaks at Hudson Valley Community College, and says:

> We're here because this is a place where anyone with the desire to take their career to a new level or start a new career altogether has the opportunity to pursue that dream. This is a place where people of all ages and backgrounds—even in the face of obstacles, even in the face of very difficult personal challenges—can take a chance on a brighter future for themselves and for their family.[8]

The president is a cheerleader for community colleges. Were I looking at it from the outside, I might be right there with him. His words might make me experience the tug and swelling of inspiration in my chest. I might feel the endless possibilities of America. But I am in the classroom, struggling to teach unprepared students, and I can't stop thinking about the very real obstacles and difficult personal challenges his oratory glides quickly over—obstacles and challenges that sometimes cannot be overcome. President Obama goes on in the speech to detail his outline for the since-abandoned American Graduation Initiative, much of which was to be paid for by the American taxpayer. Increased funding for Pell Grants. New tax credits for college tuition. Funding to the states to close budget shortfalls for public universities and community colleges. President Obama talks about helping five million Americans earn degrees from community colleges in the next decade. How many new enrollments will that mean? A great many of my community college students are already on the path to crushing defeat. I'm not sure we know what to do with the students we already have.

7

Remediation

I F I HAD BEEN VERSED in the world of community college before my first night teaching at Huron State, I might have been less surprised at the low level of work. Thomas Bailey, the George and Abby O'Neill Professor of Economics and Education at Columbia University, puts the matter bluntly when he writes that "a majority of community college students arrive with academic skills in at least one subject area that are judged to be too weak to allow them to engage successfully in college-level work. Thus, a majority of community college students arrive unprepared to engage effectively in the core function of the college." The usual solution when confronted by students with such poor academic skills is to enroll them in "developmental" or "remedial" courses. The numbers of students enrolled in such courses is revealing. One study, using data from the National Educational Longitudinal Study sponsored by the United States Department of Education's National Center on Educational Statistics, says that 58 percent of students enrolled in two-year colleges had to enroll in at least one developmental course. A national database set up by Achieving the Dream: Community Colleges Count, using information from 83 community colleges, sets the figure at 59 percent.[1]

The numbers are daunting. The University of Colorado at Boulder mandates a writing exam, and 85 percent of students turn out to require developmental writing.[2] Exacerbating the problem, and putting both community college administrators and instructors in a difficult if not untenable position, is the fact that both placement in and testing out of developmental programs is a quirky business. Rules and regulations vary by school and by state and with each individual remediation teacher. Dolores Perin, in "Can Community Colleges Protect Both Access and Standards? The Problem of Remediation," studied 15 community colleges in six states and reports that a "wide variety of practices were used to determine student readiness to advance in or exit from remediation." Students don't want to enroll in remedial courses—it is embarrassing for them, and because no college credit is awarded for completion, students feel that they are wasting time and money. So what happens is what one would expect to happen: "assessment and placement mandates appeared to be softened either at the state or institutional level, with the effect of reducing the number of students who were required to enroll in remedial courses."[3]

When looking at regulations regarding remedial education, the term "crazy quilt" comes to mind. The Perin study reveals that the skills assessment is, in the overwhelming majority of schools, mandatory, but what exactly is done with those assessments varies wildly, the end result being that fewer students are placed in remediation than should be. A number of colleges studied did not test all skills areas. Others allowed instructors to sidestep the tests by signing students into their programs who hadn't been tested. Still others did not test students enrolled in vocationally based programs. The selection of tests and assessment instruments varied from state to state and college to college; some states mandated which tests to use, others did not, leaving the colleges free to choose. Assessment strategies also vary from year to year for reasons that have more to do with politics than educational theory. Perin reports a conversation with an administrator from a suburban community college in the Southwest:

> English was using up until [a few years ago] a holistic writing sample, where the English faculty would grade this writing sample by students and make a holistic decision whether they could go into college English or needed to be remediated. That got very controversial with the high schools, and so [the college decided that] anybody who finishes high school English can go right into college English and that was fine, the high schools are happy but the students aren't successful. They're not passing. So we have had just a radical drop in the number of students in developmental English and a rise in the number of students in credit English and a huge drop in success rate in credit English.[4]

Virtually all community colleges mandate placement in developmental courses for students who do poorly on the entrance examination, but very often feel great pressure to maintain the intellectual status of their institutions. As Perin puts it succinctly, given "the extent of the need for basic reading, writing and math skills, if all students who needed remediation were actually required to enroll in developmental education classes, the community college could acquire the reputation of a remedial institution." At one school, students who tested poorly in math and reading were mandated to attend remedial classes in only one of those areas; testing poorly in three areas meant remediation in two.[5] It's all like some vastly complex game show, where choosing Kathy Griffin in the corner square entitles the contestant to a free pass. The nadir of this sort of illogic is reached in New York, in a suburban community college which required students who scored poorly on the placement examination to attend remediation—no fooling around, now—but released them from the mandate if they signed a waiver.[6] And as for those who actually enroll in developmental education, Bailey tells us that, overall, "fewer than half of students who are referred to developmental education complete the recommended sequence."[7]

When I encounter a student who seems hopelessly unprepared at Huron State, I check the transcript and, almost every time, they have been through the wringer of remedial classes: developmental English 1, sometimes taken twice, developmental English 2. But developmental classes are by no means a foolproof solution, and getting through them doesn't necessarily mean that the students have mastered the material. The consensus seems to be that even the most hopeless student can eventually find an instructor willing to pass them along. Perin quotes a developmental faculty member: "I think if the student ended up taking a summer session with an easy teacher they'd pass them on with a C. And that's usually how they end up . . . they know how to work the system."

I can picture the student on his second go-round, the student who is perhaps not quite fully ready to leave the remedial class but, through dint of hard work, may be one of the best in that class. Would the remedial teacher really have the stomach to fail him again? I'm not sure that I would.

Some have ventured to say that there is no evidence at all that remediation at the college level works. Bettinger and Long, in their study of remediation, which tracked nearly 13,000 students in Ohio community colleges from 1998 to 2003, can come only to the rather disheartening conclusion that "students in remediation do not perform worse than similar individuals who do not enroll in remedial courses. . . . When we compare students with similar characteristics, we find that remediation does not appear to have a negative effect." The most they will say is that "math remediation appears to improve some student outcomes." They conclude with the rather weary observation about remedial programs in general that "one might have expected to find a greater number of positive effects."[8]

Hardly a ringing endorsement. Preparation for higher education takes twelve years, and it is all but impossible to make up for inadequate preparation in a semester or two of remedial work.

Semester after semester, I deal so often with students who are not yet ready for college that my sense of things gets a bit skewed. The student who is still using invented spellings at age eighteen or nineteen starts to seem the norm. I start to wonder: perhaps I am too harsh, too demanding; perhaps the idea of what a college student should be that I hold in my mind is just my own warped idealization. But then a student will turn up in my class who sets me right again.

I have had only a few of these students. Several semesters back, there was a girl at Huron State who read *Catch-22* on the breaks. Was it for a class? I asked her. No, just for pleasure. She got an A in the class. She couldn't have helped getting an A in the class; even in her more pedestrian moments of writing, her familiarity with the sheer existence of the printed word shone through. Her diction was appropriate, her sentences and her ideas complex enough. She was a perfectly serviceable college student. She was perfectly average, perfectly good, she should have been instantly forgettable. If I could have given her an A+ I would have.

Sometimes when a good student appears in one of my classes, it turns out they have been blown in from God-knows-what sort of complicated circumstances from halfway across the globe. Recently, in my English 101 class, I taught a woman in her early thirties. She had bright eyes, rather startling in their attentive shine. She wore long dresses, and necklaces that seemed to be made out of seashells. She read her first assignment aloud and stunned the rest of the class into silence. The paper was gorgeous. It talked about society's reluctance to allow teenagers, who have as children learned by emulating such adult behavior as speaking and writing, to safely imitate the more frightening adult behaviors, to explore sexuality and drink under safe, controlled circumstances. Nice job, good thesis. Her writing was sophisticated. Her language was awkward in places; I noted a just-discernible accent. Her first language turned out to be Tagalog, not English.

I asked the class what their first reaction was. They froze with uncertainty. I wondered if they could even tell whether the writing was good or bad. Finally, one astute young man, bless his heart, ventured a response. He said, with some incredulity in his voice, "It sounded like an adult paper written for adults."

The class agreed with him. "Adult papers written for adults" became my new definition for what we aspire to in our writing classes.

I am actually surprised that a larger sprinkling of good students doesn't turn up in my Huron State classes. I have come to think of two-year colleges as a great bargain. If you are a particular type of good student—someone who is in it only for grades and low cost, someone who can sit through rudimentary lectures without falling asleep, who can listen to the rambling and disconnected answers of your fellow students without wanting to bludgeon them, who can listen to your teacher's repeated attempts to pull answers out of a class without wanting to scream out the bleedingly obvious response—if you are someone who can avoid falling into despair when college classes have high-school-type discipline problems, and the library is so lightly used, and no one really ever reads a word of anything, then a place like Huron State is a great buy. An in-state full-time student pays less than $2,000 per semester. Students who are on the ball can sail through two years at low cost with minimal effort, earning a 4.0 GPA, spiritually regenerating their professors and earning their eternal gratitude in the process.

. . .

The students at Pembrook and Huron State leave me with two choices: teach at a true college level and fail everybody, or dumb things down enough so that more students can pass. For a long time, I didn't know what to do, and so I did both, or neither, depending on the class, depending on my philosophy, which was constantly in flux. I would teach at a college level, but then someone would ask me if the *New York Times* was a newspaper or a magazine. I was suspended in a great workplace inconsistency. I'd been there before, treading the air (like a cartoon character who has wandered off a cliff) between the steep walls of policy and reality. "Because of generally weak skills found among community college students," says Thomas Bailey, "professors in many college-level classes must teach in such a way as to address the needs of students with weak skills." He goes on to discuss the phenomenon of "hidden remediation," the surreptitious introduction of basic skill instruction. Well, I was secretly remediating like crazy, speaking in the same class period of deconstructionism and subject-verb agreement. I could teach my students how to write a sentence, but I couldn't really give them college credit for it. Or could I?

My classes and I flailed in the drink, and kicked, and swallowed water, and came perilously close to drowning, and at the end of 15 weeks a decision had to be made: nudge the terrible grades upward, give them lots of credit for making progress and pass some people along, or adhere to a set of standards and fail most of them. Could a student not yet ready for college learn the skills in 15 weeks to become so? Could he, at the conclusion of my class, write a fully formed, fully realized college essay, even a D or a C one? We weren't, after all, asking for miracles, but the answer was no. The students at Huron State were worse than those at Pembrook. I'd failed my share at Pembrook, but here I hit new heights, or new lows.

My eventual single-semester record would be nine out of fifteen students failed.

David Mazella, an associate professor of eighteenth-century British literature at the University of Houston, would have it that the fault lies completely with me. He writes that I am an "unhappy soul," a modern version of Dostoyevsky's Underground Man, and really, their poor work, or at least my reaction to it, is all my fault:

> In my mind, the notion of grading-as-ranking almost always flips over and becomes a way in which we as teachers are reminded of how we have been ranked and sorted ourselves, into institutions and departments with reputations good, bad, or indifferent.

He believes that my apprehension of the students' work as being alarmingly substandard really has nothing to do with them. It is a manifestation of my own sense of powerlessness, and my own need to bully:

> The temptation, at institutions like mine and Professor X's, is to impersonate the kind of punitive, absolute authority that renders grades to its helpless students as if they really were blessings and curses. The temptation to act out in this way, I think, actually gets stronger the further one is from any real or effective authority in one's institution or profession.[9]

I went to the Huron State campus to turn in my grades after that first semester. This was before the days of online grade submission; the deadline was 9 A.M. In the registrar's office, little knots of instructors, adjuncts and full-timers, drank coffee and did last-minute averaging. The air was thick with weary sighs, sarcastic commentary, and the click of calculator keys. Huron State required instructors to turn in an additional form when a student received an F. The office floor was littered with these things, discarded forms with mistaken entries and blank extra copies. The scene looked like the aftermath of a modest academic ticker-tape parade. The helpful secretary had a big stack of the things on either end of her counter. "Anybody need more?" she asked. "Anybody need more F forms?" Several instructors wondered aloud: when were they getting rid of these things? It really was too much of a burden to have to fill out so many.

I braced myself for the howls of outrage. I thought surely I'd be fired; I waited for the torrent of irate e-mails from the students. But no such response came. The students were silent. They were used to failure. They'd been failing for years. This was just another bad report card, although now there was no requirement that they have a parent sign it. Not a single student complained. Some weeks later I got an official looking letter from the college. I worried until I tore it open to find my contract for the following semester. A helpful adhesive arrow at the bottom showed me where to sign.

8

The Good Stuff

I T TURNS OUT THAT despite everything, I really enjoy spending my evenings with 15 or 20 pupils both apt and inapt, our eyes glued to the blackboard, as together we try to hammer into shape the most malformed and misshapen escarpments of prose imaginable. We take paragraphs straight from the nightmares of E. B. White and turn them, after much work, into beautiful things. This is a laborious business. Crafting good writing is dead slow even for the best writer working without encumbrance; for me and for my 20 apprentices, thinking and writing and editing together, time accelerates in rather an Einsteinian fashion: an hour disappears in a flash as we focus and tighten and buff the writing to a shine. With every improvement, every strengthening of diction, every mistake removed, I read or a student reads the paragraph aloud again, and in time we are all marveling at the sensual pleasure good prose can give. Good writing in the mouth is like sweet vanilla ice cream. But it takes forever to get anywhere, which is okay, because I want the students to appreciate what kind of effort it takes to unravel and improve what the writing pedagogues would call "inexplicit texts." Good writing takes hours and hours, but is there any intellectual endeavor more satisfyingly enveloping? Even the students who profess to be uninterested in writing fall under the spell of the transformative process. What we do is true classroom alchemy, starting with little lumps of lead and emerging with, if not gold, something a lot shinier.

Few things I do are anywhere near as engaging. If I am ill with the flu or my lower back is bothering me, I have forgotten about it by the time I finish unpacking my little instructor's satchel at the front of the room. Teaching is a restorative tonic. If some disaster is befalling the house, if a mysterious stain on the ceiling of a room beneath the bathroom is increasing in circumference, I forget about it while teaching. If my wife and I are fighting, teaching clears my head and soothes my soul. Thinking of her unhappy tears me to pieces; the teaching of writing can distract me.

There are many things to love about teaching writing and literature. It happens that I enjoy nothing more than trying to convey to a class something of my passion for a great short story, or the satisfaction a writer can feel upon nailing a point with a phrase that tells.

Through a most circuitous route, one lined with heartache, I am back in the game of literature, the game I had abandoned to chase my notion of a middle-class life. My day job is nothing to be ashamed of, but it is, in the immortal usage of the late graphic novelist Harvey Pekar, quotidian. My job does not transcend. It is cut from the very heart of job-ness. I make schedules and approve purchases and improvise madly when the staff calls in sick—really, exactly the same stuff I did in high school when I was the de facto manager of an ice cream stand. I haven't come very far, have I? My English degrees haven't been relevant to my work life for years. I had given up thinking about the power of writing and literature. Becoming an adjunct brought me back to a world I had nearly forgotten and, of necessity, submerged me completely in its vast waters.

It's one thing to have the typical English major's glancing

acquaintance with *Hamlet*. But that won't be enough if you are suddenly required to *teach* the thing. In the full flower of middle age, I have been forced by circumstances to cultivate new expertise; I now have the satisfaction of being intimately acquainted with the wonders of *Hamlet,* having read and taught it more than a dozen times. I know it far better than I ever did as a student. I still can't get over the sheer largeness of the thing, the way it's drenched in Shakespeare's obsessions and passions, from his preoccupation with his career to his impatience with bad verse and his wonderment at those who would laugh at catchphrases, like the audience at *Saturday Night Live*. He has no patience with comics who break themselves up onstage ("And let those that play your clowns speak no more than is set down for them: for there be of them that will themselves laugh, to set on some quantity of barren spectators to laugh too. . . ."); he doesn't fathom the groundling ancestors of those who dug Tim Conway breaking up Harvey Korman on the old *Carol Burnett Show*. When I think of Polonius reading Hamlet's love letter to Ophelia, and coming across the word "beautified" and dismissing it ("That's an ill phrase, a vile phrase—*beautified* is a vile phrase. . . ."), I think of Robert Greene's *Groatsworth of Wit,* published a decade earlier, and its dismissal of Shakespeare as an "upstart crow, beautified with our feathers." The years melt away, and I shiver at the immediacy of Shakespeare's long-festering resentment. Would anyone in his audience have understood the reference? It doesn't matter; he couldn't help himself.

Hamlet is nothing less than the William Shakespeare Reality Show.

Here is another fringe benefit of my job: teaching composition has improved my own. I live writing every day, and think about it constantly. I move in a Zen state of focus, transforming life events obsessively into stacks of paragraphs. My students' minds take a straightforward event and mangle it in the telling like peppers and onions in a food processor. I understand now how that happens. I know what destroys their prose. I know their vocabulary limitations, and their biases. I recognize the residual colon paste of half-digested high school instruction. I am familiar with their inability or unwillingness to see clearly, to stretch, to think, to dig deep. Their pen nibs slip automatically into the groove of the ready-made and the cliché. They seem to apprehend the world as a collection of vague processes that defy description. They find it difficult to write using concrete detail. And they are afraid of writing. Who isn't? I was afraid when I sat down this morning. I walk into libraries now and look at the shelves of books and think of the authors: they were all terrified, but they overcame their fear. I have come to understand the enormous detrimental effect that fear has on prose. It saps writing of thrust and cogency. Fear is the enemy. I dive into a stack of essays and smell my students' terror. Writing requires *cojones,* the *cojones* to, as Adrienne Rich put it, dive into the wreck: to don "the body-armor of black rubber" and "the absurd flippers," to see "the damage that was done / and the treasures that prevail," and to emerge knowing, as all writers must know:

> *the wreck and not the story of the wreck*
> *the thing itself and not the myth. . . .*

I have grown, I think, if not less fearful in my own writing, at least aware of the place fear occupies in it.

How many other wonderful fringe benefits are there to an unexpected life in the college classroom?

Teaching literature has made me think, really think, about the inscrutable authors peering at me from those oh-so-familiar photographs in the textbooks. What else was Shirley Jackson about besides "The Lottery"? And I don't mean the gothic stuff, *The Haunting of Hill House* or *We Have Always Lived in the Castle*. I went to the college library and checked out a collection of her short stories. The book hadn't been borrowed in decades; there was the quaint checkout card in the back pocket, with the names of a few students from the 1960s and their Social Security numbers. The librarian's eyes widened in horror when she saw the numbers; she shredded the card and eyed me with great suspicion, as though I was running some kind of scam. The stories, I found, were utterly conventional, little well-made slices of romantic life, tales of young single oddballs in shabby little Manhattan apartments; they were the farthest thing from avant-garde, little bits of foreshadowing and irony, photographic descriptions and eccentric characters, like a tableau of knickknacks on a shelf, pleasing, perhaps, but hardly consequential. Nothing in the book could have prepared anyone for the volcanic eruption that was "The Lottery," but of course "The Lottery" does follow, it works the same way, uses the exact same devices and gimmicks with the simple insertion of ineffable genius.

My courses have led me to new authors, authors I would never have heard of. If you're not in the game of literature, or a retiree with lots of time on your hands, there is much that falls beneath the radar. Literature seems a vital and healthy place to me, now that I've read Charles Baxter and T. C. Boyle (I know! I know! They are well known to you, perhaps, but I was just a regular guy!), Sharon Olds, Alberto Ríos, Martín Espada, Mark Jarman. I used to argue that no one was writing anything good, but I was just talking. I didn't know a fucking thing. While I was reading the new guys—new to me—I spent some time with old hands, poets I hadn't thought about since college: Donne and Sexton and Hughes and Creeley. There are days I can't get the drunken lurchings of "I Know a Man" out of my head, can't stop thinking about the darkness that makes us whole and trying to make sense of the thing. It's so manically fraught with the possibility of incipient change, which no doubt appeals to me since my own life is so constrained. It's so America on the cusp of the 1960s, so *Mad Men*: " . . . shall we & / why not, buy a goddamn big car, / drive, he sd, for / christ's sake, look / out where yr going." Isn't that "shall" marvelous? What word could be more emblematic of a world on the brink of obsolescence than "shall"? Some days the passage beats in my head 50 or 60 times, which isn't an entirely pleasant sensation; the poem has, in Anne Sexton's phrase, grown "like a bone inside of my heart."

I teach the students about the changing literary canon. I talk about the rising and falling reputations of writers. Why do we teach the writers that we teach? One student, exasperated by my idiotic question, answered charmingly: "Because those are the ones in the textbook." Yes, yes, I said. But how did they get there? Who picked them? She had never considered that there was a political/intellectual/social process to textbook creation; she thought of textbooks as fully formed things, like pretty pebbles on the beach. I try to convey all that goes into a writer's reputation: the academic chops of his supporters, fashion, affirmative action, snobbery and reverse snobbery, book sales and the lack thereof, and academic connection. Sometimes a notable death helps; it certainly hurt John Gardner, he of *Grendel* and *The Sunlight Dialogues,* that his dramatic death on a motorcycle on September 14, 1982, was the same day Princess Grace of Monaco fatally cracked up her car. Gardner got no play. The older students understand what I'm saying—they've seen in their lives the mysterious ways fashion can change. The younger ones are vaguely upset by the notion. They feel, perhaps, stirrings of paranoia as they realize their place in the cosmos. The same girl as before: "Who actually decides? Is it a committee?" She can't get her mind around it. The young students are perhaps just learning that forces beyond their control exist in the world, telling them what to think; who knew that something so boring and irrelevant as a literature textbook could be just one more tool to tell them what to believe?

These discussions of the literary canon have brought me around to an appreciation of some of the poor bastards who've been thrown out of it on their ears. Henry Wadsworth Longfellow, for one. His very name is a joke, three bywords for all that is hokey and American in a tricornered-hat sort of way. I used to dismiss him. "Listen, my children, and you shall hear / Of the midnight ride of Paul Revere"—it's doggerel and bad history to boot; Paul Revere was probably off in a whorehouse on the eighteenth of April in seventy-five. What a glorification of the dead white male!

By the shores of Gitche Gumee,
By the shining Big-Sea-Water,
Stood the wigwam of Nokomis
Daughter of the Moon, Nokomis.

Feathers and headdresses, wampum, smokum peace pipe—it's too painful to think about. In the library before class one night, I grabbed a book of Longfellow's verse and actually read him, and all I can say is that his dismissal from the texts is our loss. He is a fine, fine poet, and his greatest hits are not entirely representative of his work. As a thinker and a poet, he reminds me in his approach of Wordsworth, and like the latter he walks a fine line between the profound and the campy. "The Arrow and the Song," so endlessly parodied ("I shot an arrow into the air, / It fell to earth, I knew not where"), works as a piece of romantic verse in much the same way as "I Wandered Lonely as a Cloud"—and, like that more respected poem, is simultaneously brilliant and a little silly. "The Village Blacksmith," under his spreading chestnut tree, is an American incarnation of "The Solitary Reaper." "Evangeline" has moments that are simply gorgeous. I will never go on a camping trip again without thinking of its haunting, atmospheric opening ("This is the forest primeval. The murmuring pines and the hemlocks, / Bearded with moss, and in garments green, indistinct in the twilight, / Stand like Druids of eld, with voices sad and prophetic"). "The Children's Hour," another slice of Romanticism, uses shadings and insinuation to catch the feel of an essentially uncatchable moment. Longfellow's language is stirring and memorable—"Thou, too, sail on, O Ship of State! Sail on, O UNION, strong and great!" He must have known he had a winner there—and I wouldn't have known about any of it had I not been abducted into the college classroom.

My time in the classroom keeps me marvelously connected to the larger culture. The students keep me young—it's an awful cliché, the sort of thing I try to banish from their writing, but it's true. I watch how the young ones dress, catch snatches of conversation, observe the dance of the sexes, and modern life seems vital and worthwhile to me, not just a debased version of what I have already experienced. I note my own interactions with the older students and understand, for the first time, the profoundly important role that age plays in relationships. The middle-aged teacher's aide, the middle-aged Toyota mechanic, the middle-aged English adjunct—we all understand each other because of all that we have seen, our common touchstones, our little shared segment of the unspooling ribbon of existence. We have watched Nixon resign. We've been to parties and heard side one of the Pretenders' first album played, over and over. We understand the concept of side one. We have all been beaten down by our children. Retirement worries thrum constantly in a fevered, anxious corner of our consciousness. As a basis for mutual understanding, age trumps sex, age trumps race, age trumps education and social class.

I can hear you now: more news at six, smart guy. These are my own epiphanies. This is as profound as I get. At the end of "The Dead," Gabriel Conroy realizes that everybody dies. It's at least as good as that, isn't it?

9

The Pain

THERE ARE MANY wonderful aspects to teaching English in college. I wouldn't trade the experience for anything, no matter how tortuous the route that got me there in the first place. But sometimes I feel so frustrated.

I do love what I do, but there is something missing. The students and I seldom complete the transaction, seemingly so fundamental, of my teaching and their learning. We do not experience the consummation devoutly to be wished. The students are never able to re-create the compositional points that I demonstrate. They can never incorporate what I say into their own work because they are not at that place yet. I am denied the teacher's orgasm—I've been dry-humping for a decade—because of a fundamental falseness in the system.

Robertson Davies wrote, in *The Rebel Angels,* that "Energy and curiosity are the lifeblood of universities; the desire to find out, to uncover, to dig deeper, to puzzle out obscurities, is the spirit of the university, and it is a channeling of that unresting curiosity that holds mankind together." Where did you teach, Davies? Someplace good, I am sure.

I ask my students to write about the books they have read. Several write about Harry Potter. Some tell me they have read *She Said Yes,* a young-adult novel about the Columbine killings. Also, *Scar Tissue,* by Anthony Kiedis, lead singer of the

Red Hot Chili Peppers. *Crank* by Ellen Hopkins, a young-adult novel in verse that Amazon calls "a *Go Ask Alice* for the 21st century." The collected works of Mitch Albom. *The Giver* by Lois Lowry, a high school novel but a *freshman* high school novel.

One of the things I try to do in English 102 is relate the literary techniques we will study to novels the students have already read. I try to find books familiar to everyone. This has thus far proven impossible to do. Many of my students don't read much, and though I tend to think of them monolithically, they don't really share a culture. *To Kill a Mockingbird*? Nope. (And I thought everyone had read that!) *Animal Farm*? No. If they have read it, they don't remember it. *The Outsiders*? *The Chocolate War*? No and no. *Charlotte's Web*? You'd think so, but no. So then I expand the exercise to general works of narrative art, meaning movies, but that doesn't work much better. That really surprised me—that there are no movies they have all seen, except one: they've all seen *The Wizard of Oz*. Some have caught it multiple times. So, when the time comes to talk about quest narratives, we're in business. The farmhands' early conversation illustrates foreshadowing. The witch melts at the climax. Theme? Hands fly up. (The students can rattle off that one without thinking. Dorothy learns that she can do anything she puts her mind to and that all the tools she needs to succeed are already within her.) Protagonist and antagonist? Whose point of view is the movie told from? Can anyone tell me the cowardly lion's epiphany? Are the ruby slippers a mere deus ex machina? What would you say is the symbolic purpose of the winged monkeys?

The movie comes in handy. Discussions are pretty lively.

My students are sometimes suspicious of ideas, those admittedly thorny and vexing things. The college classroom certainly seems an odd place for such sentiments to be on display, but I often encounter wide swaths of what can only be described as resentful anti-intellectualism.

Let me say at the outset that I am in no way opposed to anti-intellectualism. A philosophical stance is a philosophical stance; reading books and thinking about stuff are not pastimes for everybody. I do not worship at the altar of books. I have known people whose reading, meaty as it was, provided as much desperate escapism as obsessive ESPN viewing. I am not here to say that reading *The Alexandria Quartet* is inherently more worthwhile an activity than making flourless chocolate cake or collecting "Guinness Is Good for You" posters. Whatever floats your boat. I'm not willing to say that my intellectual pursuits have done me the smallest bit of good; in truth, they may have done little more than fill me with unrealistic ambition, impoverish me, and needlessly clutter my thinking.

However, remember: we're talking about college, where ideas are supposed to be the coin of the realm.

Our literature anthology spends some of its bulk early on fretting over a definition for literature. To that end, it juxtaposes a contemporary "literary" short story with an excerpt from a Harlequin Romance. The approach is snarky and could be effective, but the joke is lost on my students, who get the intent of the whole thing backwards. They can't make head or tail of the literature; the protagonist strikes them as too crazy. "People don't really act that way," says a middle-aged woman in nursing scrubs, shyly (wait till we read Carver's "Popular Mechanics," with the baby perhaps torn in half by the feuding couple), but the class is quite impressed by the realism of the Harlequin excerpt; it excites them, and gets them talking about literature in a way that no other writing will that semester.

I am no snob. I love Anthony Powell's *A Dance to the Music of Time* cycle of novels, but I love the 179-episode cycle of *I Love Lucy* reruns even more. Reading, however, is a prerequisite for doing college work. Lack of familiarity with the written word makes it impossible to write essays with any degree of sophistication. Michael Holden, assistant professor of English at Delaware State University, says of his students:

> They know almost nothing about their own country, its history, or the planet they live on. Worse, most of these students do not read. In the last 4 years, I have read 25,000 pages of student journals, which are an integral part of my writing courses. Writing this paper, I reflected on the contents of those thousands of pages and was struck by an astounding realization. Not one journal in four years and all those pages has dealt with a book that the student was reading outside of a required class assignment![1]

I am encouraged in my endeavors, but only a little, by the words of Thomas Bailey:

> [Some students may] make significant progress in developmental education, but their skills do not reach the college-level standard. Getting a student from a sixth- to a tenth-grade . . . level is a valuable social undertaking, even if it is not enough to provide a solid foundation for a college education.[2]

I suppose that helps. I am happy to do my bit for the larger society. I toil, unseen and forgotten, in the basement of the ivory tower after dark. Sometimes, ours is the only class in session. What must our building look like from the highway, one window lit by pulsing blue fluorescent light? I wonder how it all end. What will become of my students? What grade does one give a college student who progresses from a sixth- to a tenth-grade level of achievement?

Sometimes, when I have to give bad grades, I feel like a beacon of morality, an unyielding standard, an ever-fixed mark, like the silver meter stick stored in the French vault from which all other meter sticks once derived. Sometimes, on the other hand, I feel like nothing more than a hardass.

I just came inside from a session of raking leaves. What a handy metaphor! Just as I am never sure what system to use to grade my classes each semester, so I waver each fall on how to go about doing the leaves. Do I rake them into piles and *then* onto the blanket, or do I skip the piles and rake them directly onto the blanket? Each method seems sometimes like less work, sometimes like more, depending on the time of day, my mood, whether I am feeling precise or slapdash, and the ache in my back. Do I grade on improvement and/or effort and/or sincerity? Raking is invigorating, but it gets tiresome, and I grow weary of theorizing about it. Have I mentioned that my property consists of a lot-and-a-half: not enough to subdivide or sell, just enough to rake. And mow. And weed. And rake again. As I rake and sweep up the leaves I come upon sheets like papier-mâché of leaves from last year, or several years ago, that I missed. I have the feeling that I'm just getting behind with everything in my life. I would flatter myself and say the metaphor is reminiscent of one by Robert Frost, but I know that he was much better in the yard than I am, always picking apples and patching his wall and such.

· · ·

Rarely do I venture onto my college campuses during the day. One afternoon I come in to pick up a new teacher's edition of my writing textbook. I wander the corridors. Classes are in session; doors are shut. A few students meander through the halls. The place looks, in the bright light of day, like a real college. There are ads and notices on the bulletin boards lining the corridors: ads for screenings of *Halloween,* information about the tutoring program, stuff for sale: cut-rate textbooks, a DJ setup with a pair of turntables. One item catches my eye: an ad for a Web site, Simplified Nursing, "where you can learn about and purchase easy-to-read books written to help nurses and nursing students. . . .":

How many times have you struggled to learn something? It can happen in a classroom, with a textbook, on the job, in a seminar, or even in your home when you want to reset the clock on the VCR. Then, suddenly you get it! You slap yourself on the forehead and then think, "Well why didn't they just tell me that in the first place? Why do they always make this stuff so complicated!"

The ad interests me. I read further. The books use illustrations to convey their points. The book *Drug Calculations for Nurses Who Hate Numbers,* for example, shows a drawing of a 150-milligram pill broken into thirds—each segment drawn as a little character, with a smiling face—to explain how much to give if the dose is 50 milligrams or 100 milligrams.

I don't immediately realize that classes have ended. Classroom doors open and students pour forth. I am in an awkward spot, blocking traffic. Professors pack their satchels and chat at their desks with stragglers. These professors don't look like the adjuncts I am used to seeing. These are regular-looking professors, prosperous-seeming chaps, tall and weedy fellows in long oxford shirts, women with hair cut in tidy wedges. One guy is fat, bearded, benign—the spirit of Robertson Davies himself! The place smells of tenure and, emanating from a faculty office near the stairs, freshly brewed Starbucks coffee. In the office, two professors in lab coats hold their mugs in anticipation as the brewing cycle finishes; one affectionately strokes the pate of a skeleton mounted on a stand.

These are the full-timers. They leave their classrooms, satchels in hand, and eye me with apparent suspicion. What am I doing there? They know all the daytime faculty, at least by sight. Who the hell am I? What's a fifty-year-old man in a necktie doing skulking about?

Daytime at the campus has a carefree quality I never see. The sun is shining. Moods seem brighter. The students, not having arrived from an eight-hour job, shuffle languidly in flip-flops and T-shirts. Department secretaries lace up their sneakers and pair off for midday walks and lunch. The professors are relaxed. They have paid sabbaticals and great parking spaces and guaranteed employment. For them, the recession is a rumor. Cheerfully haughty, they remind me of the professors I had so many years ago. Their students will head off in many different directions, toward many different types of employment, but each class day's unspoken lesson is that being a tenured college professor just may be the sweetest gig there is.

My students and I are of a piece. I could not be haughty, even if I wanted to be. Our presence in these evening classes is evidence that something in our lives has gone awry. In one way or another, we have all screwed up. I'm working a second job; they're trying desperately to get to a place where they don't have to work a second job. All any of us want is a free evening. We are all saddled with children or mortgages or sputtering careers, sometimes all three. I often think, at the beginning of the class, that a five-minute snooze, a sanctioned nap period, would do us all good. We carry knapsacks and briefcases spilling over with the contents of our hectic lives. We reek of coffee and tuna oil. The daytime students are fed by the college food service, which understands its mandate to be at least marginally nutritious. My people eat cakes and chips out of machines—when there's anything left in the machines.

The poignancy of my students can be overwhelming. I see them trying to keep all the balls in the air: job, school, family, marriage. Of course it isn't easy. On our class breaks, they scatter like frightened mice to various corners and niches of the building, whip out their cell phones, and try to maintain a home life at a distance. Burdened with their own homework assignments, they gamely try to stay on top of their children's. *(Which problems do you have to do? . . . All right, then, just the odd numbers. That's good, right? One, three, five, seven, nine and you're done. Don't think of it as five problems. Just do them one at a time. Finish that and then do the spelling. Now put Daddy on.)* I hear husbands and wives trying to conduct a whole domestic life within the boundaries of a ten-minute phone call, talk of parent-teacher conferences and appointments with plumbers that often disintegrates into argument. "What do you want me to do?" I have heard it said many times by trapped people standing in empty classrooms. "What do you want me to do?" I think sometimes that we'd all be better off without cell phones. After the breaks, it's difficult to reconnect with some of the students. I can tell they are replaying the last phone call in their minds, frustrated and helpless as they sit trapped in the classroom while the world outside, they imagine, goes to hell.

As a writing instructor, I have a unique perspective. A botched calculus or biology exam reveals only the student's ignorance of the material being tested, but a piece of bad writing lays bare all intellectual deficits. And because essay topics are often rooted in the personal, as they have to be to get any decent writing out of the students, I am far more likely than a math or biology instructor to hear my students' tangled backstories.

Now, some of my students are merely young and silly and disinclined to do the required work for the class. They know they're goofing off, and they sort of care, but pretty early on they throw up their hands. All of life stretches out before them, all possibility, and it is impossible to take people like me seriously. Consider Jason. Jason is a cheery sort, with a fringe of dark curly hair visible under his omnipresent baseball cap. He has a pert sort of nose and little bow lips; I can see the cute child he once was. He comes to class faithfully, mostly I think to ogle the girls. Jason has thus far, this semester, handed nothing in, not a single assignment.

I meet with him after class to discuss the situation. "I love having you in the class," I say, "and I wouldn't for the world suggest that you stop coming. But you've got to know that there are issues we need to talk about. Where are the assignments?"

This is the approach I have cultivated over the years. I chide him gently because the situation is so absurd: why would someone come so dutifully to class yet not hand in a single assignment? I am careful not to suggest, even faintly, that his time would be better spent elsewhere. I don't tell him that he's going to fail and there's really no point in his continuing. To suggest that he shouldn't come anymore, to be discouraging, or mean, or uncaring—it's simply not done, even though in college our goal is to get the students to evaluate data, to make good inferences, to think, above all else, critically. I cannot state, and I cannot elucidate from him, the obvious conclusion that the mathematics are working against him: he would have to do brilliant work at the Harold Bloom level to overcome all the lateness penalties.

"I've got a lot going on," he says, vaguely abstracted, as though I was taking time from his other important work. He opens a binder full of fresh, blank paper. "Could you tell me which ones I've missed?"

The implication is that his personal assistant merely forgot to ensure that I received them. "Well, all of them."

"Could you just tell me what they are again?"

I make a great show of opening my grade book, even though I know that every box next to his name is blank. He writes down what I say. "The Hawthorne essay, the Flannery O'Connor essay, the first poetry comparison, the second poetry comparison. Everything we've done."

"Got it," he says. "I appreciate it."

The young are stone deaf to good advice, I know, but I can't resist trying. "The best advice I can give you is just do something," I say. "You've got to do something. Anything. Don't think of the assignments as a group. Do one at a time. You're enrolled in this course. It's only sensible to do the work."

Our interview over, he flees.

What I have said will make little impression. He will attend class faithfully; he will not hand in any assignments. On the evening of the final exam, he will be the first one finished and out of the room. And when the grades are posted, he will log on to the Web site and, in the moments of suspense after he has typed in his college ID and password and hit SUBMIT—the system is primitive and slow—he may think that perhaps he has achieved a C. *I hope it's a C it's probably a C I think I did good enough for a C.* And then the F will unfurl before him. *Ah shit. Oh well.* What a world of emotion lives in the moment between those two brief sentences! He will try again next semester. He bears no one ill will. His optimism is really rather extraordinary; I hope he never loses it. We meet on campus in a few weeks and he is as friendly as can be, as though he still feels a hangover glow of fulfillment from our wonderful time together.

"What are you taking?" I ask.

"102. You know. I think this time I'll do okay."

"Are you up to date with assignments?"

He flashes an evil smile. "Pretty much."

That's the story of many of my students: they are young, they are a little lazy, the future is opaque to them. Other students have had a harder time of it. I read essays about divorce and substance abuse, unexpected pregnancy, emotional cruelty both delivered and received, and past brushes with suicide. I read about exhaustion and desperation and, more often than you might think, about how impossibly difficult they find college work. The sheer shock of college is a recurring theme in my students' papers, and inspires some of their most heartfelt writing. Even with their limited academic gifts, many have managed to cruise their way through high school. American public education has not served these students very well, and now, as they enter college so vastly unprepared, there is a real poignancy to their growing recognition of this astringent truth.

How can I stay angry at them? They want me to show them what literature is all about; they know, dimly, that those who matter in the world are versed in its mysteries. They call me "professor." It stabs me when they do. I used to tell them not to; I told them I was an instructor, and not entitled to the honorific. They called me "professor" anyway. They did it without thinking. I stopped making a fuss about it. Why should I rain on their parade? In my mind, I was a government worker masquerading as an academic. Why should I let my feelings of fraudulence interfere with their college experience?

I drive home that night in my old car. Is the radiator leaking? I seem to be leaving small green puddles whenever I park. I have one headlamp out, but if I keep my brights on, both work. I pull up to a quiet traffic light near the college. A car waits across the intersection from me. My brights are shining right in his eyes. He flashes his own lights a few times to get my attention, but I ignore him. I don't feel I can click mine down. He just thinks I'm an inconsiderate asshole. I burn to tell him: That's not me! There's more to me than that!

10

College as Eden

THE COLLEGE CAMPUS is a marvelous place. The sun glints off the buildings, bathing the sidewalks in light and warmth; you can't help but feel nourished and optimistic. Knots of students grab books and buzz off toward class. Most times that I'm not sitting grading assignments, I feel the pleasure of the place. Nowhere are employees friendlier. The staffers could not be more accommodating to students who have lost their way in the forests of financial aid or class schedules; they will stop whatever they are doing to go with a student to find a lost calculator or binder.

One night before class I sat in the office with one of the secretaries. She had just returned from a vacation in Florida, visiting her son and her grandchildren. We were looking at pictures when a frazzled, sleepy-looking student approached the desk.

"What can I do for you, sweetheart?" said the secretary.

The girl had on a green sweatshirt. She wore what looked like a religious medal, and ran the short chain between her teeth nervously. "I need to leave a message for my teacher. I won't be in class tonight."

The secretary reached for her memo pad. "What's the name?"

"Roslyn."

The secretary noted it down. "And what's the name of your teacher?"

The student froze in mid-chain-suck. There was an awkward pause.

"I don't know," she said.

We were about midway through the 15-week semester. I expected the secretary to glance in my direction, but she didn't. Pointedly, she did not look at me. Instead, she picked up her iced coffee and took a sip. "Can't think of it?"

"No."

"I hate when that happens. Subject?"

"Math."

"Male or female?"

Again, a moment of uncertainty. But Roslyn conquered it. "Female."

"Great. We have a bunch teaching tonight. Is she tall or short?"

Roslyn shook her head. "Regular."

"Blond or brunette? Light hair, dark hair?"

"She has dreads."

The secretary nodded. She looked up the name of the course on the schedule. Roslyn nodded with joy. The secretary finished writing out the note.

"I'll put this in her box," she said, "and you're good to go."

Roslyn grinned and thanked her and departed. My secretary friend watched her as she left. Never took her eyes off her. She sighed and picked up her iced coffee. She did a bit of housekeeping with it, adjusting the two little straws, nestling them together, and took a long thoughtful sip. She would not compromise Roslyn's dignity, even in her absence.

"Florida's beautiful," she announced to me. "But the weather takes some strategy. You've got to be smart about it."

It seems to me that those who work for the colleges walk around with half-suppressed smiles, as though they were privy to a delightful secret. The administrators, the lunch ladies, the cooks, the security guards, the little birdlike post-mistress who runs the campus mail room—they seem almost giddy with satisfaction. (Okay, maybe one or two of the lunch ladies have an occasional dark moment.) Yes, there are irritations: the copiers jam and the salaries aren't enough and some of the students will break your heart. But who else earns their bread in a place of such opportunity? Truly they can say, problems notwithstanding, that in their work they do no harm.

Colleges are nice places. It's hardly a surprise that every day, stories in the news demonstrate the way we worship at the foot of the ivory tower. The stories are so ubiquitous we don't even notice them.

In Martinsville, Virginia, Major Ray Ferguson returns to his home county to bring "his message about the importance of college and making the right choices to eighth-graders at Fieldale-Collinsville and Laurel Park middle schools, as well as JROTC cadets at Bassett and Magna Vista high schools." Because of work and family responsibilities, Ferguson took thirteen years to complete his four-year degree in logistics from Georgia Southern University. He tells his audience how "it opened up a tremendous amount of doors. . . . [College] took me down a whole different path." Now he's deploying to Afghanistan, but he will continue studying; he hopes to earn a doctorate in homeland security.[1]

Major Ferguson's story is one of triumph, and I can't think of a reason he shouldn't delight in passing on how well things have turned out for him. The problem is that we in America forget that stories of triumph are by definition the exception rather than the rule. If everyone could triumph, it wouldn't be any kind of triumph at all.

For a student to succeed in college, he requires, at times, superhuman drive and energy and resourcefulness. A thirst for knowledge is good, too; familiarity with a daily newspaper, a magazine or two, and a book here and there is helpful; toss in a sprinkling of God-given smarts and, please, some writing skills. Never would I want to cheapen the accomplishments of those who really have conquered college, who were perhaps able to get past the shortcomings of their previous schooling and climb onto the honor roll. That is truly something.

But why should college be for everyone? The recruitment drive is relentless. In Chappaqua, New York, home of Bill and Hillary Clinton, 20 Bronx high school students live for a month with local host families. The Chappaqua Summer Scholarship Program, which has been around since the late 1960s, gives the teens "the chance to live in the burbs while getting a hit of Shakespeare, computer science, writing, filmmaking, tennis and swimming. . . . Worked into the mix is a strong message of the importance of college, and the kids are taken to local college campuses and tutored for the SATs."[2]

In Detroit, Tigers slugger Magglio Ordóñez founded the Ordóñez Family Scholarship, "which will provide $2,500 a year for full-time study at any college or university in the United States." At the formal announcement ceremony, Ordóñez "encouraged the young people in their love of baseball, and spoke to them about the importance of college."[3]

For Americans, college looms as a great metaphor. Michelle Obama tells *Time* magazine:

mean, I grew up in Chicago on the South Side, and liter-
y a 10-minute drive away was the University of Chicago
ll of its grandeur. And I never knew anything about that

institution that was a few minutes away from me, and that was so telling, even to the point that my mother worked there. She worked there for four years as a secretary to the legal office. But I never set foot on campus. We came through, we picked her up, we left. It was sort of like another world that didn't belong to me. I didn't think about college in that sense when I was younger. So it was a very foreign place, even though it was a stone's throw.[4]

It's never too early to get started. In Phoenix, 50 kindergartners from the Acclaim Academy spend a day at Estrella Mountain Community College. They had originally just wanted a campus tour, but the director of early outreach at the college sees a great opportunity, and plans "a morning's worth of activities to introduce the students to college life."[5]

The State of Washington Higher Education Coordinating Board reports that a record number of parents with newborns have already enrolled in the state's prepaid college tuition plan. House Higher Education Committee chair Deb Wallace (D-Vancouver) says that parents "should feel good knowing that this is the best investment they can make in their child's future." Senate Higher Education Committee chair Paul Shin (D-Edmonds) agrees. "When parents and grandparents set aside money for college when children are little, they send a powerful message about the importance of a college education," he says.[6]

· · ·

Not surprisingly, the colleges themselves are in favor of more college enrollment. It would be a bit weird, I suppose, to see highly placed representatives of any other industry stumping so shamelessly for their products and services. But when the subject is education, we don't even notice, for we as a nation are, above all, woefully insecure about our own learning. When we see such a headline as "Texas State University President Talks about Importance of College to Memorial High Students," the incongruity barely registers.[7] Americans venerate education, perhaps unduly. It is, I think, one of our more charming national traits. We think of educators as something close to saints, and schools as impervious to bottom-line concerns. Yet with every increase in enrollments comes a positive tick on someone's performance evaluation, another measurable achievement for someone's curriculum vitae. And with every increase in tuition revenue comes more incentive to grow. New stadiums and state-of-the-art student centers and green dormitories have appeared on campuses across the country, often accompanied by oversize tuition hikes. As most Americans' salaries have remained flat or vanished altogether, the cost of attending college has been rising exponentially year after year. The tuition increases have vastly outpaced inflation. From one corner of the country to another, at community colleges and state schools and the Ivies, the story is the same. Check the headlines: "Suffolk County College is Raising Tuition," says the *New York Times*—that's Suffolk County Community College, and its price is going up by 7.7 percent.[8] "MCC Eyes 11.7% Hike in Tuition"—that's Mott Community College, in Flint, Michigan.[9] "Why Is College Tuition So High?" asks the *Charleston Post and Courier.* "In South Carolina, Costs Have Nearly Tripled in a Decade," the headline continues. The College of Charleston has increased tuition this year, recession be damned, to in-state residents by 14.8 percent.[10] An article in the *Chronicle of Higher Education* trumpets the arrival of "The $50K Club: 58 Private Colleges Pass a Pricing Milestone." The writer notes that for "the nation's private elite colleges, $50,000 is fast becoming the new normal."[11]

But I can't accuse the schools of villainy.

Oh, it is sometimes tempting. Sometimes one looks askance. The colleges at which I teach sometimes seem like busy factories, mounting second and third shifts of learning when the daytime students are busy with such regular extracurricular pursuits as tapping kegs. Why leave a blackboard unused?

> Winston Chin hustles on Tuesdays from his eight-hour shift as a lab technician to his writing class at Bunker Hill Community College, a requirement for the associate's degree he is seeking in hopes of a better job.
>
> He is a typical part-time student, with one exception. His class runs from 11:45 P.M. to 2:30 A.M., the consequence of an unprecedented enrollment spike that has Bunker Hill scrambling to accommodate hundreds of newcomers. In the dead of night, he and his classmates dissect Walt Whitman poems and learn the finer points of essay writing. . . .[12]

This story actually got me thinking about my own schedule. A 4:00-to-6:15-A.M. Fundamentals of Poetry would suit me to a tee.

Colleges are blessed with a magical business model. They market a product that American consumers do not need to be sold on, and I don't suppose we can blame the colleges for that. From top to bottom, from coast to coast, our society views college not as a consumer product at all, but as both a surefire, can't-lose financial investment and, even more crucial than that, a moral imperative.

USA Today ran a story in 2009 that wondered if, in a recession, the cost of college was really worth the economic benefits.[13] The story led with an account of a young woman who came out of college with a double major in journalism and anthropology and $80,000 in debt; her difficulties began when she got laid off from her job as an information technology recruiter—a profession, I note, not even in her major field of study, leading me to wonder exactly how crucial her degree was. The thrust of the story was that although college is necessary to maximize income, the amount of the college "earnings premium" has been greatly inflated, encouraging students to take out loans that are imprudent. College graduates will not earn an additional $1 million over the course of their work life, as has been reported. (That's an old saw, like others I have heard: remember "If you're choosing between taking vacations and having a nice house, buy the house, because having a great house is like being on perpetual vacation"?) The figure is closer to $450,000, and that must be reduced by the amount of college debt incurred.

After the story appeared, readers who wrote letters to the editors found themselves displeased by the reductivist argument. "The educated person is more likely to contribute ideas and values necessary to sustaining a democratic society," said one correspondent. "To look at education in economic terms alone is cynical and shortsighted; it does a disservice to your readers." Another wrote that "in our increasingly global, knowledge-based economy, no one can expect to thrive—or even maintain a middle-class lifestyle—without some form of high-quality postsecondary degree or credential."[14] But is this really true?

Colleges benefit from many Americans' refusal to worry about who is going to pick up the tab. But that may be changing. In the professional literature and the popular media, there is a growing urgency to the warnings about the economic quicksand of higher education. Our recent recession has transformed the rather routine warnings of years past about how expensive college is into clarion calls about how really, truly, crazily expensive college is. Tamara Draut, vice president of policy and programs at Demos, a national public policy and research organization, posits that since federal student aid has shifted from grants to loans, we have moved to what she calls a "debt-for-diploma system." She characterizes growing student debt as a "drag" preventing an entire generation of young people from getting ahead.[15]

In the *New York Times,* the chairman of the Religion Department at Columbia University laments the way university admissions officers have for years marketed their product using the lifetime-income-earnings saw. "But with the cost of an undergraduate degree well into the hundreds of thousands of dollars, this argument is no longer persuasive," he says. "The collapse of our public education system and the skyrocketing cost of private education threaten to make college unaffordable for millions of young people. If recent trends continue, four years at a top-tier school will cost $330,000 in 2020, $525,000 in 2028 and $785,000 in 2035."[16]

It is currently all but impossible to wipe away federal or private student loans. Congress, fearing that newly minted graduates would immediately file for bankruptcy, saw to that. According to the three-pronged "undue hardship" test established by the Second Circuit Court of Appeals in *Brunner v. New York State Higher Education Services Corporation* back in 1987, a debtor wishing to discharge student loans must show

> (1) that the debtor cannot maintain, based on current income and expenses, a "minimal" standard of living for herself and her dependents if forced to repay the loans; (2) that additional circumstances exist indicating that this state

of affairs is likely to persist for a significant portion of the repayment period of the student loans; and (3) that the debtor has made good faith efforts to repay the loans.[17]

That second prong of the test, the one concerned with "additional circumstances," is the tricky one. As Charles Booker writes in the *Journal of Law & Education,* debtors "have to prove not only that they are currently overwhelmed and unable to pay, but that they have honestly tried and that such conditions will last long into the future. In particular, there must be unique or exceptional conditions that can sufficiently be shown to last for a significant portion of the loan. This presents a tremendous roadblock, as student loans can last upwards of 30 years." Debtors must "substantiate the position that their financial struggles will continue over any possibility of obtaining future resources."[18]

High-profile bankruptcy expert Elizabeth Warren has been warning of the dangers of student debt for years. "We tend to talk about student loans in the abstract, 'ten or twenty thousand dollars—it's not that much,'" she told the *New York Times* in 2006. "But I think it's really about what it means to be 28 and try to make loan payments and health insurance premiums and still put something aside for a down payment for a house. Think about how much extra room you have to have in your budget to cover those three things. Most can't do it."[19]

The mortgage meltdown has served as a grim reminder that, even in carefree America, the good times don't necessarily just keep rolling on. Narratives all have endings, and those endings can be cataclysmic. I don't advocate bankruptcy as a simple solution to excessive debt, but at least it is a solution. Notwithstanding the recent Supreme Court decision in the Espinosa case—which could conceivably crack the door to the discharging of academic debt through bankruptcy—there is at the moment no solution to student loan debt. It doesn't go away. It is a catarrh that will not dissipate, a strangulating blockage that cannot be cleared. It can squeeze the very life out of a debtor, and we seem rather cavalierly to be encouraging more and more students to take it on for fewer and fewer rewards.

. . .

Americans believe in college. A poll conducted several years ago by the *Chronicle of Higher Education* found that "the public's trust in colleges ranks near the top among all kinds of institutions, right along with its faith in the U.S. military and in churches and religious organizations. . . . Nearly 93 percent of respondents agreed that higher-education institutions are one of the most valuable resources to the United States."[20]

That was back in 2004, but, if anything, the American public is more college-crazed than ever. Nearly 70 percent of all those who graduated from high school from October 2007 to October 2008 went on to enroll in some manner of college program.[21] All this pushing for college has worked. College enrollment increased from 17.5 million students in the year 2000 to 20.5 million in 2006, an increase of about 17 percent.[22]

The American college juggernaut is in full swing, and unless someone finds himself imbued with the entrepreneurial spirit, there are few other options. "The evidence for the individual economic benefits of college is overwhelming," says Sandy Baum, professor emerita of economics at Skidmore College and senior analyst for the College Board. "While the wage premium for a college education is not at its highest level ever, it is larger than it was five years ago, and typical four-year-college graduates earn more than 50 percent above typical high-school graduates."[23]

My students believe this; that is why they are there. But

some of them, I think—particularly when they are asked, as prospective medical technologists, to turn in a paper comparing Nathaniel Hawthorne's "Young Goodman Brown" and "The Minister's Black Veil"—may have an inkling that we all have been caught in a trap of our own making. They may think of all the second-tier colleges of the United States, after sitting through three classes of *Hamlet* with me, as "springes to catch woodcocks," as Shakespeare would say.

The requirements for higher education in many occupations are self-imposed, and probably not really necessary. As Stephen J. McNamee and Robert K. Miller Jr. point out in *The Meritocracy Myth*:

> With so many Americans receiving college degrees . . . the overall return on the investment has declined. To put it simply, the labor force is being flooded with new college graduates. There are fewer "college level" jobs being produced by the economy than there are new college graduates. The result has been an increase in both underemployment (e.g., college graduates waiting tables) and credential inflation (employers requiring higher levels of education for positions without a corresponding increase in the demands of the positions themselves). Under these conditions, many students perceive that getting a college education would not help them so much as the lack of a college education would hurt them.[24]

And why wouldn't employers want their workers to have at least a couple of years of college under their belts? What's the harm? Doesn't college broaden the mind, expand the spirit, make for a measured and reasoning workforce? Isn't an expansion of college enrollment a societal good? I think that most Americans sincerely believe this is so, though the aspirations of their prospective employers may be more pedestrian. Here are McNamee and Miller again:

> In the process of credentials inflation, higher education degrees come to be required even for some jobs that may not be very intellectually demanding or for which an advanced degree would hardly seem necessary. For example, a college degree may not actually be needed to manage a video store. But if the pool of applicants for such a position comes to include holders of college degrees, they will tend to be selected over those without degrees, and soon a college degree will become a requirement. . . .

Of course the biggest winners in the game of credential inflation are the colleges themselves. We think of colleges as entities that wouldn't dirty their hands even thinking about money. We forget that each individual employee—from the janitors and security force, through the adjuncts and the full-time professors, up to the directors, vice presidents, and even the college president—has an economic interest in growing enrollments. In an industrial society, according to McNamee and Miller, not only do the educational requirements of jobs increase with technological change, but jobs not necessarily touched by technology are "continuously upgraded" in their skill requirements. The end result, as they tell us, is "educational expansion: educational requirements for employment continually rise and more and more people are required to spend longer and longer periods in school."

But Americans, in their naïveté, do not think much about college expansion. Higher education is an unalloyed good. Treasury secretary Timothy Geithner, speaking about college access at a meeting of the White House Task Force on Middle-Class Families, is right on point there talking about the college premium. He and Sandy Baum are singing off the same page of the hymnal. Geithner notes that a "college education is one of the best investments a family can make. Beyond the many intangible rewards, economists estimate that college graduates earn 50 percent more than otherwise similar high school graduates over the course of their lifetimes." [25]

How pleasing that must be to his boss, for Barack Obama is the number-one college booster in America today. He has a special place in his heart for community colleges. What better news in a recession, I thought, when I first heard the rumors, still dim and indistinct, that community colleges would have a large role to play in America's continuing economic recovery. Here I was worried that class enrollments would shrink, and I as an adjunct, low man on the totem pole, would be taking cuts in pay and hours.

Not so.

Obama's shelved American Graduation Initiative called for America to "once again" lead the world in college graduations by the year 2020. The Community College Challenge Fund would provide grants and funding for all sorts of things, including the improvement of remedial and adult education programs, the acceleration of students' progress, and counseling and career-planning services. [26]

It all seems pretty pie-in-the-sky to me. Remember the figure: 50 percent of community college students drop out before the second year, a fact that the American Graduation Initiative readily acknowledged. [27] According to the fact sheet,

> Nearly half of students who enter community college intending to earn a degree or transfer to a four-year college fail to reach their goal within six years. The College Access and Completion Fund will finance the innovation, evalu-

ation, and expansion of efforts to increase college graduation rates and close achievement gaps, including those at
community colleges.

Even President Obama, in dark moments, has alluded to
the underside of expanded enrollment: the fact that so many
students are not able to complete the program.

At the colleges where I labor, particularly the community
college, student attrition is an enormous problem. I see the
statistics borne out in my own classes, where rosters of 25 regularly shrink to less than half that. Open admissions policies have
thrown open the doors to all comers, but graduating from college does not happen automatically the way high school graduation can. Some of the students who wind up in my classroom
report how they were mediocre or poor students and yet found
themselves carried along year after year in the general high
school wave, promoted without having mastered sufficient academic skills.

A study released in 2008 by the Center for Labor Market
Studies at Northeastern University looked at all graduates of
the class of 2000 in Boston public schools. Of the 2,964 graduates, 1,904 of them—64.2 percent—went on to college. Most
attended locally: Bunker Hill Community College, University
of Massachusetts at Boston, Roxbury Community College,
Massachusetts Bay Community College, Northeastern University, Quincy College, and UMass Amherst.

Seven years later, only 675 students—35.5 percent—had
earned a bachelor's degree, an associate's degree, or even a one-
year certificate. The students who attended community college
could muster only a 12 percent graduation rate.

On its editorial page, the *Boston Globe* decreed that action
needed to be taken, that "the colleges, and especially the com-

munity colleges, need to step up with some big ideas on how to turn entering students into graduates." Ideas were already being floated, some with a tinge of desperation. The Boston public schools were already "ramping up academic rigor by offering more college-level courses." It isn't clear, of course, how students who wouldn't pass college-level classes in college would do it in high school. The superintendent of the Boston schools proposed the creation of a "newcomers academy" for immigrant students, and floated the idea of single-gender classes.[28]

None of this is news to the adjunct instructor at the college of last resort.

11

Grade Inflation Temptation

COLLEGES EMPLOY INSTRUCTORS not just for their expertise but for their willingness to administer grades, which is by far the most gut-wrenching and distasteful aspect of the job. Grading student work, like writing parking tickets or leveling property tax assessments, is not employment for the tenderhearted. No one enjoys grading assignments. The classroom itself is often a joyous place, with instructors and students striding together toward some enlightenment, but the evaluating of tests and essays and research papers turns those same instructors and students into adversaries, often leaving bitterness and hard feelings on both sides. What makes things sticky for the instructor is not just the subjectivity of the whole process but also the dazzling multiplicity of factors that clamor to be weighed before each grade is assigned. Semester after semester, I find myself buffeted and sometimes unmoored by my own shifting assumptions and expectations regarding the students and their relationship to the curriculum.

I fail plenty of people, but it's a struggle.

There is something in the human psyche that shrinks at sitting in judgment of another's efforts. I suspect that grading has been a sore point for teachers since Ichabod Crane hit the tenure track. To hand out grades with complete objectivity, to adhere to however well considered a rubric, to give the students exactly what their assignments deserve is a daunting task. Without constant vigilance on the part of the instructor, grades will tend to rise.

Certainly there seems to be grade inflation at the Ivies. In 2007 more than half of the grades received at Harvard were in the A range.[1] Maybe this is to be expected. Harvard is a clubby place, with a "we're-all-A-students-here" mind-set. And maybe their mind-set is correct. Harvard's acceptance rate now hovers around 7 percent; it takes only the best of the best, proudly turning away hundreds of valedictorians, National Merit Scholars, and students with perfect SAT scores.[2] It's quite possible Harvard's professors can't make quizzes or tests tough enough to stump those who make the cut.

At the colleges where I teach, the issues are different. Many of my students have landed in the world of academia with only the scantest scholastic preparation. Their efforts are meager and unsatisfying. Do they fail? Do whole classes fail? And for those few students who are at college level, who have perhaps overcome adversity to get themselves to a B or B+ level, doesn't it seem churlish to award them the grades they actually deserve and not give them a little rewarding boost?

Sometimes it is said that adjunct instructors are the worst offenders when it comes to grade inflation. In her cleverly named study "A Is for Adjunct: Examining Grade Inflation in Higher Education," Brenda S. Sonner spends two years studying a small, unidentified public university that relies heavily on adjunct instructors. She concludes that "adjunct faculty give higher grades for comparable work than do full-time faculty."[3] Ronald C. McArthur studies full- and part-time humanities faculty for three semesters at a small two-year college in New Jersey and concludes that students are "substantially more likely to get a grade of A from an adjunct professor than from a full-time professor."[4]

The studies are somewhat vague about the source of this adjunct grade inflation. McArthur says that the reasons "are not clear," though he suspects that adjuncts "are being held hostage to the student evaluations. Wanting to receive a good evaluation could influence a grading decision." Sonner is more decisive, and she agrees. "It seems reasonable to conclude that adjunct faculty, who are employed on a term-by-term basis, are hesitant to give lower grades as it could create student complaints that would result in the adjunct not receiving an offer to teach in subsequent quarters."

Though my experience may be singular, I have never felt the smallest bit of pressure to be a "popular" instructor. The colleges have never suggested any uptick in my grades. I am under no pressure to assuage disgruntled customers. My colleges' official stance is one of vehement opposition to grade inflation, and I believe they are sincere. They don't need to worry about enrollments; students, cognizant of the requirements of their jobs, are beating down the door to get in. Both Pembrook and Huron State caution against grade inflation in their adjunct workshops; Pembrook goes to the trouble of generating a little spreadsheet comparing the grades given by full-timers and adjuncts.

A tenured professor at Huron State says that she hasn't given an A on an English 101 assignment in twenty years. The English chair at Pembrook told me that nothing pleased her more, on a course evaluation, to see that a student wrote that a professor seemed too tough. "The world is a tough place," she said, "and they've just got to get used to it."

I'm not sure, however, that college administrations are always aware of the intellectual depths to which some of the students have sunk. Let me now use the sort of modern-speak cliché I so decry in my students' writing: there is a disco
At my last yearly adjunct meeting at Pembrook, my old

Dean Truehaft, he of the boxy wool three-button suit who oriented me to the whole adjunct game so long ago, still athlete-trim, spoke about academic rigor. With great Weltschmerz, he chastised the adjuncts: "People, we can't just give out A's and A-minuses." His comment floored me. I nearly choked on my wedge of student dining services carrot cake. The imperially slim dean seemed, at that moment, pathetically out of touch with the realities of one large swath of his student body. I have discussed grades with other adjuncts, and, believe me, we're not giving out A's and A-minuses with jolly abandon. If the issue were merely A's that should be B's and B's that should be C's, my professional existence would be a more straightforward one. The real question is a lot thornier, and one that doesn't seem to come up at adjunct meet-and-greets: what exactly constitutes base-level college work? Who are we serving by admitting so many students who couldn't do it without years and years of remediation?

. . .

Most English departments adhere to a standard rubric for grading freshman compositions. The guidelines issued by Modesto Junior College in California, for example, delineate an A paper as a "markedly exceptional, superior essay." The paper "addresses the assignment thoroughly and analytically," with "fresh insight that challenges readers' thinking." It provides "adequate context for readers (i.e., necessary background information, brief summaries, or definitions of key terms, etc.)." It uses a "clearly focused and sufficiently narrowed controlling idea (thesis)." It presents a "logical progression of ideas." It "analyzes ideas and issues skillfully using sound reasoning." In terms of mechanics, the nuts and bolts of expression, it "displays superior, consistent control of syntax . . . sentence variety . . . diction . . . punctuation, grammar, spelling, and conventions of Standard English." Other rubrics I have seen stress the importance of a clear authorial voice.[5]

Let's be brutally frank. I've never been handed such a paper.

The guidelines for the A paper could really apply to an essay by David Foster Wallace. His approach was analytical, and his insights fresh. His work always challenges the reader. It is chock full of context, the control of syntax is superior, and there is a polished authorial voice working.

The B paper is a "clearly above average essay." The Modesto rubric actually doesn't make much of a distinction between an A and a B paper. The B paper deals with the assignment "clearly and analytically, setting a meaningful task." I love that phrase, "meaningful task." It is difficult to get my students to believe that their writing must have a purpose. They don't believe that there is a job to be done, an idea to be gotten across, that writing is not just a string of words conveying a shopworn or self-evident idea. The B paper presents a "clearly focused" thesis and "clear and coherent organization"; it "evaluates and analyzes ideas and issues carefully (but not with the skill or sophistication of an A essay)." The mechanics of the B essay, the diction and punctuation and syntax and all that, are exactly the same as that of the A essay, except that the control is only "consistent," not both "superior" and "consistent."

I'd put a Chuck Palahniuk novel such as *Choke* at about a B, being organized but sometimes not sophisticated. I'd put Anna Quindlen at about B level, too: her theses are focused but somehow a bit lacking. B-minus.

The C paper displays only "some analysis"; it has a thesis but not necessarily a good one. The organization is "adequate," but "the focus may not be as clearly maintained as in the A and B essay." Examples and details are "less developed and less persuasive" than those in the A and B essay. The control of mechanics is "adequate"; mistakes do not "slow the reader, impede understanding, or seriously undermine the authority of the writer."

According to this rubric, most of the best papers I have ever gotten are C's.

The D paper is "seriously flawed." The thesis is "unclear." the paper "lacks focus and a clear pattern of organization." The paragraph structure is "flawed." The syntax "lacks sufficient control," and the errors do tend to "slow down reading and impede understanding."

Ah, yes. The flash of recognition.

These are the waters in which I swim regularly.

An F paper? That's "fundamentally deficient." It "fails to address [the] assignment or does so minimally." It lacks a thesis. The organization is illogical. The paragraphing is "inadequate or nonexistent." The mechanical errors "greatly impede understanding."

Writing is a peculiarly unforgiving endeavor. Good writing is good writing, whether done by grade-schoolers, college freshmen, syndicated columnists, or Booker Prize short-listers. Though the grading criteria seem overambitious, an A college paper really should jump off the page. It should surprise. It should even jolt. Its language should, if not crackle with subtext and implication, at least please.

Based on strict adherence to such grading criteria, my students would forever be doomed to dwell in the place of F's and D's. Occasionally, very occasionally, a student may stand on tiptoes and crane her neck and breathe the sweeter air of a C.

. . .

I fail lots of students, more at Huron State than at Pembrook. But it's not easy to maintain my resolve. Failing all those in a class who deserve to is like trying to keep 23 helium balloons at ground level with your hands. They tend to rise.

First of all, twenty-first-century American culture makes it more difficult to fail people. Our society, for all its blathering about embracing diversity and difference, really has no stomach for diversity and difference when it constitutes disparity. We don't like to admit that one student may be smarter, sharper, harder working, better prepared, more energetic, more painstaking—simply a better student—than another. So we level the playing field. Slow readers get extra time on tests. Safe harbor laws protect substance abusers. Students who miss class for religious reasons, as it says in the boilerplate language Huron State suggests that I place in my course syllabus, may be absent without incurring a penalty. While fairness and inclusion are desirable, and while I have no argument with the impulse behind any single policy that strives to mitigate the capricious nature of life, the effect in the aggregate has been to render distasteful the whole idea of one human being passing judgment on the efforts of another. It is a reflex: to be understanding and compassionate about the curveballs life has thrown our fellow human beings. A noble reflex, but at odds with the very nature of grading. How can an instructor even enforce the simple concept of deadlines for assignments? Cars break down, don't they? Computers crash. Infants get sick. Our quest to provide universally level playing fields has made us reluctant to keep score.

And professors have become demystified. Surely that's not bad, right? Isn't it good that students do not quail in their professor's presence, that they feel at ease enough to send friendly, jaunty e-mails? A young man kept up a steady correspondence with me during the course of our semester together. He had questions about missed classes, he wanted to substitute a different paper topic for the one assigned, and so on. The e-mails invariably began with "Hey there"; his trademark sign-off was "Later, peace." We seemed to be something like pen pals, two bros collaborating on the worthy goal of his passing the course, which he didn't. He didn't do the reading and failed a bunch of quizzes and the final exam. His final missive to me, no less breezy than his others, suggested that our friendship had suffered a breach. He was dissatisfied with his final grade of F. There was, however, a remedy. He asked me to change one of his paper grades from a C to an A-minus or B, which would raise his overall grade enough so that he passed the course.

When I attended college, grading was a fairly straightforward matter. Professors assumed that their students had successfully completed work at the more difficult end of the high school curriculum, and grades were in part based on whether those students had successfully progressed to postsecondary levels of thought and expression. There was a universal baseline of skill. I would no more have questioned an instructor about a grade than I would have questioned God. I understood that my Shakespeare professor knew in his very marrow that my paper on Sonnet 50 was a B. How could I even dream of changing his mind? (And he didn't use written grading criteria, either. The need for a set of formal written guidelines only arose when the papers the students were submitting no longer aligned with the instructors' internal scale. Written guidelines manifest desperation; they almost always appear in times of noncompliance. As the pool of college students expanded, skill levels declined, and instructors found themselves grading more and more papers that left them frankly puzzled.)

The professor was the expert; he sat on high, like a photographer perched on a stepladder to get the best view. I don't want deference. That's the last thing I'm looking for or deserve. But the fact that there really is no deference, that there is very little social distance between instructor and student, impairs the instructor's ability to dispense grades. Students view instructors not as oracles but as college employees bound by rules of fairness and disclosure. This is a good thing, but grades then become highly negotiable.

The whole system of grades may be too nineteenth century for our modern taste. Nevertheless, the system remains in place. I have to give grades, and I frequently have to give bad ones, but the system rankles and depresses me in a way it did not rankle and depress previous generations of college instructors. My resolve to give grades blindly, based solely on the work and without regard for the consequences to the student, is compromised; my stance as an arbiter of academic success is debilitated. Passing a failing student starts to seem like one more "accommodation," like extra time given for an exam, to make college life fair.

I am keenly aware of how important these courses are to their livelihoods. Colleges have insinuated themselves everywhere, and the need for college credits is an important part of contemporary work life. The attainment of degrees and certificates is now routinely linked to promotions and higher salary scales. The licensed practical nurse may need 65 more college credits to get her R.N. The aspiring laboratory technician takes core courses in medical technology but also three years of prerequisite courses in the liberal arts and sciences—including English 101 and English 102. B.A. candidates in sociology with a specialty in criminology will be prepared, in the words of the catalogue, for "scholarly careers" in sociology, criminology, and social deviance, as well as jobs in victim counseling, corrections, and law enforcement. Virtually none of my students are headed for scholarly careers in social deviance or anything else. They will work—or are working—as bailiffs or federal marshals; in sheriff's departments; as nurses of all kinds; in the billing or human resource divisions of large institutions; in county, state, or federal prisons; as court or correctional officers; or as caseworkers in the caverns of whatever social service agency will have them. Whether much of their college coursework will actually be of any use to them, other than qualifying them for the job, is questionable.

It must be said that colleges make no exception for their own: every semester, I teach a fair number of college employees in search of their own certificates, credits, degrees, and accreditations. Spending their days in the college culture, most of them do okay, thank God.

How intense it all is! I came from a rather different world. I was an English major in the 1970s, and the idea of making a living from my degree was a hazy one, which is one of the major reasons I now work a second job. I spent four leisurely years imbibing, along with my major's requirements, the classic mixed assortment of liberal arts bon-bons: a bit of sociology here, a dip of the toe into ancient history, a painless science requirement, calculus (which was truly difficult; I took it my first semester, before I had learned to choose courses more wisely), cultural anthropology, an Old Testament seminar, Introduction to Theater. I cared not a whit about any individual grade. I saw no endgame. College was for me a four-year equivalent of the Grand Tour, and I spent that time very much outside society, wandering intellectual pastures, exploring my interests and aptitude, having fun and delaying the start of adulthood.

My students, in contrast, are up against it. The clock is ticking. The pressure is on. They need, desperately, to get through their programs. They work during the day and attend school at night in the hope of at least moving into nicer cells in their daytime prisons. Their college life has an urgency mine never did. My students, some of whom have never written anything actually cogent, have to pass College Writing to be a firefighter or court officer or prison guard. Others need to get through College Literature, to make sense of "The Waste Land," in order to have any hope of saying good-bye to shift work and maintaining a normal relationship with their children.

When I give a failing grade to a student, I am not just passing judgment on some abstract intellectual exercise. I am impeding that student's progress, thwarting his ambition, keeping him down, committing the universal crime of messing with his livelihood—not to mention forcing him to pay the tuition charge all over again. The stereotypical ivory tower is a realm far removed from workaday concerns; in the tower's basement, where I labor, any poor grade I issue may mean disastrous economic consequences. So I think long and hard before giving poor grades. I agonize. I get that sick feeling in the pit of my stomach. When I fail someone, I suffer Dickensian visions of starving children, missed mortgage payments, dunning creditors.

I know that part of what the college pays me to do is maintain academic standards. As I tell my students: teachers don't fail students, students fail themselves. I know that by passing the incompetent I will cast a shadow of defilement upon the degrees of those more talented souls who have managed to navigate college successfully. But there are times when issuing a failing grade seems inhumane. I am forced to fail plenty of students, and I am well able to do it; that said, I have certainly given C's that should have been D's and D's that should have been F's.

. . .

I often require students to write comparisons of poems. Normally, I assign works that live in college textbooks yoked together in thematic pairs: the meditations on fatherhood ("Those Winter Sundays" by Robert Hayden and "Digging" by Seamus Heaney), or John Ciardi's "Suburban" and Margaret Atwood's "The City Planners." Last semester I used "A Pink Wool Knitted Dress" by Ted Hughes and "Wreath for a Bridal" by Sylvia Plath. The poems are standard college fodder for comparison. They are a thematically matched duo: both deal with weddings, and they are often paired in literature texts because of the circumstances of Plath and Hughes's own marriage. Plath's poem is rather obscure, and typically overdone: a dreamlike evocation of a marriage and consummation with nature imagery that is lush and overripe. Hughes's poem is a dryly comic recounting of a threadbare ceremony that would seem to recall his and Plath's own nuptials. I give the class lots of biographical information about the two poets, and provide guidance questions. What, I want to know, is the stance each poem takes with regard to love?

One of my students, a woman in her midtwenties, obviously came to class each evening directly from work. She dressed in dark pantsuits and wore the tallest, pointiest high heels I have ever seen. Her paper set this year's benchmark for confused student prose. A hallucinogenic lit-crit puree of *Finnegans Wake* and *Bridezillas,* for long stretches it was indecipherable. As I was reading the thing, I started to grow angry, which is hardly the rational and correct approach—but sometimes I just can't help myself.

I tried to imagine the circumstances that would result in her submitting an assignment of such desperately poor quality. The thing read like the free association of a disordered mind. I pictured her writing it in a bar, or while driving to class or skydiving. Maybe she composed it as one long text message to herself. By any rational standards, this was failing work. Failing.

I calmed down and gave her a D.

I hear the cry: grade inflation!

Her writing was deficient in many areas. The problems with the assignment didn't stem from the fact that she knocked this one off in a hurry and it didn't come up to her usual crisp standards. This student could not write standard English, yet she had already successfully completed English 101, College Writing. Someone on the faculty (and for one panicky moment I feared that it might have been me) had determined that she could navigate expository prose at the college level. The evidence of my senses disputed this mightily. Nonetheless, I was haunted by a nagging sense of unfairness. Was it right for me to fail her based on her wretched prose when she had already been certified as at least marginally competent in this area? The college had signed off on her completion of the writing requirement, and now I wanted to renege on the deal. None of it seemed quite fair, but passing this woman along didn't seem quite the ticket either: sending her out into the world thinking she could write at least competently—with the transcript in her hand that says so—was like sending a toddler out of the house for the first time on her own after a five-minute lecture on traffic safety.

Other factors pushed me toward the D over the F grade. I looked at her work and detected faint, pinprick reflections of my own teaching. She repeatedly referred, for example, to the voice of the poem as "the speaker." Bingo! I grabbed at it like the last bit of meat on a picked-over turkey carcass. She did that one thing correctly. She didn't refer to the poet, or the narrator, or the author, or to Ted Hughes, or, as some of my students are inclined, to Ted. (Langston, Tennessee, and Ernest have also turned up in papers.) She wrote about "the speaker." Mentioned it repeatedly, in fact. I make a big deal of that in class: how we can't confuse the writer of the poem with the speaker of the poem, and how one way poets can be thought about is in the distance between their lives and verses. She had been listening. She had emerged from my class with an ever-so-slightly deeper understanding of poetic mechanics. Not much deeper, I admit; deeper by about the thickness of one coat of paint. We could say only, based on her paper, that she seemed to have understood one concept. I would never for a moment have considered giving her an A or a B or a C, but how proficient does one have to be to simply eke out a passing grade? If she was to come to understand more fully, over the duration of fifteen weeks, five concepts, would that be sufficient?

I receive worse work than that. I get papers that are out-and-out F's, things that are just as badly done but lack any value at all: poorly written summaries without even the smallest attempt to probe meaning. From this sort of work I get not even the briefest wink of reassurance that the students paid any attention in class.

Here's one student's anonymous evaluation of my college literature class, and I don't get the feeling he or she is pulling my leg:

> Course was better than I thought. Before this I would of never voluntarily read a book. But now I almost have a desire to pick one up and read.

My students almost think of my interest in reading and writing as eccentricities, as this evaluation makes clear:

> I really like [Professor X], this is why I took the course because I saw he was teaching it. He's kind of enthusiastic about things that probably aren't that exciting to most people, which helps make the three hours go by quicker.

. . .

Even for someone like me—someone whose pulse quickens a little at the thought of *Lolita* or *Catch-22,* someone who vows to read *Ulysses* all the way through in retirement and wonders (in passing, but certainly a few times a year) whether there can possibly be anything in all this adulation of Marilynne Robinson—writing about literature is not something I was born knowing how to do. It's a knack, and it takes lots of practice, like driving a stick shift; it seems impossible to master at first but can eventually be done without thinking. It took me years to be able to drift into the contradictory state of consciousness that combines close reading with a trancelike receptivity to themes and subtext and patterns of symbols. Now I can do it in my sleep. My student might be able to get good at this, or at least better than she was, but I doubted that she would ever have interest enough or time to, and I have started to wonder why she should bother trying.

Is it fair to penalize the students for being unable to grasp, in fifteen weeks, the passwords and coded language and shibboleths and secret handshakes of the world of Introduction to College Literature? The students I encounter in English 102 have spent a lifetime in English classes thoroughly in the dark; they stand outside the great Masonic hall of literature with their noses pressed up to the glass. I'm a good person to lead them inside, but it will take time.

I have always wondered about the ultimate disposition of my students. I have wondered, sometimes, at the conclusion of a course, when I have failed such a large percentage of my students, if the college will send me a note either (1) informing me of a serious bottleneck in the march toward commencement and demanding that I find a way to pass more students, or (2) commending me on my fiscal ingenuity, since my high failure rate forces students to pay for classes two and three times over.

What has happened is precisely nothing. I have never felt any pressure from the colleges in either direction. My department chairpersons, on those rare occasions when I see them, are friendly, even warm. They don't mention all those students who have failed my course and I don't bring them up.

Our American unwillingness to count even the most hopeless of us out in the educational marathon may be one of the
most debilitating ideas in contemporary culture, a jagged gash
through which vitality and truthfulness and quality slowly
drain away.

I find the ultimate institutional indifference to marginal
students something of a good sign. Yes, there are remedial
classes, and writing labs, and interventions by the academic
advising people, and meetings with at-risk students. But how
much can or should the colleges do? In the end the students'
fates are in their own hands, and if they aren't willing or able
to put in what could be a tremendous amount of work, they
will not pass. They must sink or swim.

Sink or swim. When was the last time you heard that in
contemporary America? When was the last time we heard of
a clearly defined, rigid, nonporous boundary?

My two colleges maintain their standards. Dean Truehaft said
it long ago on the night of my initial orientation: give them what
they deserve. I often joke that some of my students take English
101 and 102 twice or three times, and what a financial bonanza
for the college this must be. But the truth is quite otherwise. My
101 and 102 classes are taken early in a student's time, and failure
in those classes has a particularly discouraging effect. Students
who fail repeatedly simply give up after a while, and do not
graduate. In Boston, remember, 88 percent of local students did
not finish community college. Eighty-eight percent! An occasional bonus of double-tuition notwithstanding, community and
lower-echelon colleges would find themselves more solvent if
more students graduated. A nod, a nudge, a wink, a whisper to
the instructors, and everything would be hunky-dory.

But such is not the case. The colleges for which I work main-
n their integrity. A passing grade is a passing grade, and a
d grade means something; in my experience, grade inflation

is not pronounced. When the *Boston Globe* opines that colleges "need to step up with some big ideas on how to turn entering students into graduates," my blood runs cold. If the pressure mounts on colleges, and community colleges in particular, to get all their students through the program, grades will inflate tremendously and degrees and certificates will be worthless.

In educational circles, English 101, freshman English, is known as a gatekeeper course. Students who can't get through it can't move on. So I am a gatekeeper. I will teach my students. I will work with them as much as I can. (Remember, I don't get paid for office hours.) I will guide them to resources. But I will not pass them if they have not earned a passing grade.

We're not talking nuance here. My students who fail do so with an intensity that is operatic. They lack skills on a grand scale. To check if students are keeping up with the reading, I give unannounced quizzes. Sometimes I ask if characters are alive or dead at the end of the work. Hamlet—alive or dead? Polonius—alive or dead? Gabriel Conroy—alive or dead? Talk about not going into detail about a character's motivations or epiphanies. We're talking simple existence or lack of. And yet my students fail.

My colleagues are with me. A supervisor once asked for a bunch of midterm exams to see if she agreed with the grades I was giving. She said I was doing a good job, but she had one quibble. One of my D's should have been an F.

The students who attend class faithfully, who try, who actually go to the trouble of rewriting their papers, who put in the effort—they do improve as writers, but they just may not get far enough to pass.

. . .

When I assign compare-contrast essays, or cause-and-effect essays, or persuasion essays, I tell my students what every writer comes to understand: that for greatest effect and maximum clarity, they must write about what they know. And they do. They write freely and openly and without self-consciousness about their lives: about failed plans and disappointment, about dysfunctional homes and unwanted children (who always, at the end of the compositions, turn out to be the greatest gifts they have ever had), about addiction and poverty and just how wrenching and difficult life can be.

A harried-seeming young woman, Goth in the extreme, who always comes late and never says a word, writes that she has a couple of hundred bucks saved up from when she was in grammar school and she's probably going to be broke and exhausted for the rest of her life. A Chinese student writes of her childhood outside Beijing. She remembers delivering lunch to her father every day, and how his coworker always said, admiringly, that he had the smartest little girl in the world. Now, in America, she feels nothing but illiterate.

Another student, a child of divorce, buys a ticket for her father to take his girlfriend to see U2, but winds up going with him herself and mending some fences.

A woman in her late twenties named Kerri writes of her experiences as a mother. There are several young mothers in the class, and on the breaks Kerri and the others gravitate to one another. They talk shop: of nutrition and playdates and tantrums and sibling rivalry. Their conversation is lively. As the semester progresses, I note their growing addiction to one another's company; the breaks can't come fast enough for the group to assemble and compare notes. They seem pleased with life. They glow with satisfaction and take a vaguely superior stance toward the younger women in the class, who are not yet in the game of motherhood. Kerri makes the others laugh and has a large laugh herself.

From reading her writing, I know what her new friends

probably don't, that stay-at-home motherhood has been something of a disappointment.

Now when I look at Kerri, I see not just a student struggling under the weight of school and family responsibilities. I see a woman gripped by a quiet, middle-class despair, the same despair that spawned the work of Betty Friedan and some of the dark domestic poetry of Anne Sexton, whose "Cinderella" we read in class.

Kerri smiles and jokes with the other mothers, but now I'm in on her secret. I see her struggling with guilt about what she feels, carefully watching the other mothers and searching for clues to answer the big question: Are they really as fulfilled as they seem?

Sometimes students have to tell me directly about their lives when life intrudes on their work. A student writes on the final test of the semester:

> This may or not be my best work. I tried though. Although I was prepared, I got laid off this morning and had a brutal day because of it. Thank you. . . .

I sometimes feel, as I read my students' writing, that I know them better than anyone else. I sometimes feel as though I am the only one to whom they tell their deepest fears. This can't help but interfere with the process of grading.

. . .

Toward the end of my College Literature class, I introduce students to postmodernism, with its dismissal of the patriarchal master-narrative in favor of a multitude of small, local narratives, a "constant interplay of voices and worldviews," as critic Ian Marshall puts it, conceived " . . . to deliberately evade the possibility of unity and monolithic meaning."[6] I tell my class:

the postmodernists (and we cannot help being postmodernists all of us) believe in not just one story but many stories—or *texts,* as they would say—with none having primacy.

The students dutifully write down what I say, and at the outset this concept of postmodern fragmentation is just another vague literary idea with no particular relevance, a term on their vocabulary list along with *litotes* and *synecdoche* and *sonnet.* We read Margaret Atwood's "There Was Once" and Lorrie Moore's "How to Become a Writer" and various stories by Tim O'Brien and excerpts from *Persepolis.* I tell them that we are all living in the thick of postmodernism, and try to convince them of the significance of its orthodoxies. What I don't tell them is that postmodern modes of thought are largely responsible for their being in a college classroom in the first place.

Recently, at a developmental session for adjuncts, I was handed a thick packet, an explanation and endorsement of something called the Learner-Centered Paradigm. It was taken from the book *Learner-Centered Assessment on College Campuses: Shifting the Focus from Teaching to Learning* by Mary E. Huba and Jann E. Freed. The Learner-Centered Paradigm is meant to replace the Teacher-Centered Paradigm, which is now thought to be bad—very bad indeed.

In my packet, the two paradigms were compared point by point.

In the Teacher-Centered Paradigm, knowledge "is transmitted from professor to students." Doesn't that sound terrible? Who's the dunderhead who came up with that one? In the Learner-Centered Paradigm, students "construct knowledge through gathering and synthesizing information and integrating it with the general skills of inquiry, communication, critical theory, problem solving, and so on." The students, like squirrels, are expected to gather information as though foraging for nuts and berries, out of which material they are to construct knowledge while the instructor stands by idly. Learning is somehow whipped up out of some ether in the classroom.

In the bad Teacher-Centered Paradigm, the emphasis "is on the right answers." Who in God's name ever thought that would be any good? In the Learner-Centered Paradigm, the emphasis "is on generating better questions and learning from errors." The nice thing about this approach is that raw material is plentiful: errors of all kinds—errors in usage, errors in thinking, childish errors in spelling—flow in my classroom like oil in the Gulf of Mexico.

In the Teacher-Centered Paradigm, the professor's "role is to be primary information giver and primary evaluator. . . . Only students are viewed as learners." In the Learner-Centered Paradigm, the professor's "role is to coach and facilitate. Professor and students evaluate learning together. . . . Professor and students learn together."

Obviously, if professor and student are learning together, the professor's position as an authority figure is at risk. When I grade a student's work as acceptable or unacceptable, I am asserting my expert's narrative as having ultimate primacy, and that transaction, so unbalanced, so rooted in inequality, does not sit well in our contemporary minds. It is difficult for me to fail students because there is always an explanation for their bad performance, or for my perception of their performance as bad. Death to unity and monolithic meaning!

And what could be more monolithic in meaning than a poor grade?

Later on in the packet, instructors are given a hundred or so tips for the first three weeks of class. These are adapted from something inelegantly called the "Teaching Effectiveness Network" of Sinclair Community College, which has been adapted by Joyce Poulacs of the University of Nebraska at Lincoln's Teaching and Learning Center.

> Introduce yourself by PowerPoint, videotape or CD, short presentation or self-bio.
>
> Hand out an informative, attractive, professional and learner-centered syllabus.
>
> Tell students how much time they will need to study for your course.
>
> Explain how to prepare for the kind of assignments (essay, multiple choice tests, group work presentations) you assign.

I understand how we got to such a place. I understand the impulse to make college a welcoming and unthreatening environment. I can't even say that I think, in theory, it's a bad idea. Who would endorse the idea of anyone, under any circumstances, being frightened? And I understand the economic factors: that if we're admitting to colleges hordes of students who have no business being there, college really has to be welcoming. The effect, though, is to leech all authority from the instructors by having them dance attendance on the students, and to render them impotent.

> Ask the person who is reading the student newspaper or reading text messages on a cell phone what is in the news today.

Over and over, the idea is reinforced that the relationship between students and teachers is collegial. Rather than teach, instructors are asked to wait on the students, to understand them, to seek their approval, and to befriend them, if they will have it—all of which makes the issuing of grades a dicey proposition.

> Find out about the student's jobs; if they are working, how many hours a week, and what kinds of jobs they hold.
> Greet students at the door when they enter the classroom.
> Have students write out their expectations for the course and their own goals for learning.

Granted, I've never heard of any other professors, adjunct or tenured, who actually do any of this stuff. But nonetheless, the college zeitgeist is impossible to ignore. Night-school teachers are particularly vulnerable to a kind of academic Stockholm syndrome. I feel it acutely: that we are all in this together. On a hot summer night in July, I teach *Hamlet* to a class of nine in a stifling room without air-conditioning. The ventilation system is being overhauled; what better time to effect repairs than when no "real" students are around? I can't argue with that. Ours is the only class meeting on this floor. A great silence seems to envelop the room. The students must feel that they are the only ones in the world doing work on this steamy night. I feel the same way. We are one in our misery. How on Earth did we all wind up here? We break at eight o'clock and wander the halls aimlessly. There is nowhere to go. I peer absently into the locked computer lab, where 30 screen savers dance on monitors. I have spent the class break sitting on a toilet even though I don't have to go; I need a few minutes alone.

We are the Academy of the Night, a sobriquet worthy of

Anne Rice or Stephenie Meyer. We are of the college but not completely; ours is a ghostly reality. Little more than squatters, we inhabit the place but don't own it. At 8:15, when we return to our labors, I start to think of the classroom as a tiny becalmed lifeboat holding the ten of us. I can almost hear the creak of the old timbers, the water slapping at the side. I talk about the *Ur-Hamlet* and the First Folio and Shakespeare's opinion of actors who would ad lib. The students twirl their pens and shift in their seats as their hindquarters drift off to sleep. We are, all of us, in a small and quiet hell. I care deeply that the line in the First Quarto reads, "To be or not to be, ay there's the point," but the students most assuredly don't. They're just trying to get to a place where they can make a buck. I find myself viewing the study of literature as one more indignity visited upon the proletariat, like too-frequent traffic stops and shoes with plastic uppers and payday loans.

. . .

Not long ago, I had dinner with a tenured professor of journalism at a four-year college. She had her own take on grading. Her grades were based solely on student improvement. A C-student who makes what she amorphously defines as "progress" receives a B; any hardworking B-student can get an A, whether or not the work actually merits it. She seldom fails anyone. Most of her students, she admits, are really not prepared for higher education. She is lending a helping hand. And because I know that in every system devised by man, somebody's getting screwed, I asked her: what about the occasional good students, the ones who can assemble a parsed sentence, who may actually deserve an unsullied B or A?

"They don't need my help," she said, and I would swear that she sniffed.

She is the decider, in George W. Bush's notable coinage, of

who needs help and who doesn't, and suddenly, without notice, we have moved far afield of the job description for a college professor.

The Bureau of Labor Statistics reports that in 1975, 31 percent of college teachers were female; by 2009, the number had grown to 49.2 percent.[7] There are more women teaching in college than ever, and it is quite possible that their presence, coupled with our discovery of the postmodern narrative, has had a feminizing effect on the collective unconscious of faculty thought. Strong winds of compassion blow across campus quads. Women are more empathetic than men, more giving, simply more bothered by anyone's underdog status. Many of the female adjuncts I have spoken to seem blessed and cursed by feelings of maternity toward the students. Women think about their actions, and the consequences of their actions, in a deeper way than do men. Women may not be quite as inclined to sigh and, with a murmured "fuck it," half-angry and half-miserable, possessed by the fatalism of someone throwing the first punch in a bar fight, mark an F in the grade book.

I administer grades fairly, but how difficult it is. Everyone and everything is in ascendancy, and I must pull them back to Earth. Grading writing fairly is as hard as writing itself. For the writer, the blank page is like a window to the teeming world, and he or she must sidestep distraction to harness only what will support the thesis. The writer sees too much, as does the instructor. In every assignment submitted the instructor sees all that surrounds the writer: the past, the future, possibility, disappointment, local narratives, desperate circumstances, sinking hopes, even the ghostly rattling chains of previously failed English courses. The view for the grader is kaleidoscopic; all that authorial backstory makes for quite a din. Who could possibly concentrate? The challenge for the teacher is to dredge for the work: for the quality of thought and expression, and not the writer's circumstances. The work and only the work.

No good deed goes unpunished, by the way. My student who wrote the D paper was not at all happy with her D. She was, in fact, rather outraged. She e-mailed me, saying that a professor friend of hers had gone over the paper and pronounced it good to go.

A professor. Him, or her, I would really like to talk to.

The outcome of it all was that I graded more fiercely the next semester. The F's were F's, the D's were D's, some of the borderline D's were F's—though, I knew I would soften. . . .

I had an art teacher in high school who once said something I think very important. He was teaching us to sculpt clay, and he said as we began, "There are several important things you want your sculpture to do." I was young at the time, and enraptured with my newly acquired vocabulary of art. I thought he was going to talk about form and function, about depth and resonance. He went on: "Here's the first one. Your sculpture has to stand up solidly. It can't wobble." I was disappointed at the time, but have come to see his instruction as profound, and the words of not just an art teacher but an artist. Art can't wobble. Writing can't wobble. We expect our houses to be plumb, our tables solid—why not our paragraphs?

12

The Textbooks

FEW PEOPLE NOT INVOLVED with college English in some fashion have occasion to look at the textbooks we use. I've worked with a number of different books, and found them a rich vein of cultural information above and beyond what they purport to teach.

I take my hat off to those contemporary writers who manage again and again to crack the college anthology market. I had never heard of Suzanne Britt, but her name will be instantly recognizable to anyone who teaches English 101 as the author of "That Lean and Hungry Look," the comic comparison of fat people and skinny people that can be found in the compare-contrast section of whatever textbook one happens to be using; ditto for "Neat People vs. Sloppy People." The author's bio tells me that Britt teaches English part-time at Meredith College in North Carolina: an adjunct made good! The essays are mildly amusing and exactly the same, which I suppose doubles Britt's marketability for textbooks. It's a sweet deal for a writer, to have such ephemera reprinted year after year, thereby hardening into classic work. It's good economically, of course, but how nice to have one's writing remain a part of the consciousness of generation after generation of college students. Britt could easily have been forgotten completely, but her whimsy lives on, tucked away in a corner of thousands upon thousands of collegiate minds, not to mention a more prominent place in the minds of English instructors. I've been teaching both of Britt's pieces for a decade, and can more or less recite them by heart.

Britt is a marketing genius, in her small way, but there is another writer I can think of who makes her look like a piker. An extraterrestrial trying to get a handle on our literature using English texts as a guide might rank Shakespeare first and Judith Ortiz Cofer second. "The Love Song of J. Alfred Prufrock" comes and goes in new editions; "The General Prologue to the Canterbury Tales," once a staple of college texts in simplified language or not, seems to have disappeared for good; "The Secret Sharer" is wavering, wavering, blinking on and off like a distant lighthouse glimpsed through the fog. But the works of Cofer live on, poems and stories and essays in every college edition. I find her poetry pretty teachable. I have a soft spot for "My Father in the Navy: A Childhood Memory," which my students respond to with enthusiasm; in its use of connotative meaning, the meaning that swirls above and around the language, it is an absolutely perfect vehicle for showing them the way poetry works.

The collections of nonfiction writing that we read for English 101, supposedly models for the student's work, seem oddly and haphazardly assembled. There are nice pieces, of course. I've used "The Chase" by Annie Dillard in several classes. An excerpt from her full-length memoir *An American Childhood*, "The Chase" finds large thematic significance in a simple anecdote from childhood, and though the language is quite poetic in places, the essay serves as a model for something that could be done, on some basic level, by a student. Ditto the work of Sarah Vowell: as famous as she is, as much the darling of National Public Radio as she has become, and as amusing and moving as her writing can be, there is often much of the college composition about it, theses and topic sentences and supporting details and tidy conclusions that, even when they shock, comfort the reader on some level.

But often I don't have a clue why certain pieces of writing just keep on appearing.

Is any student in 2011 going to write anything that remotely resembles "I Want a Wife," Judy Brady's protofeminist screed that first appeared in *Ms.* in 1972? And yet there it is, reprinted year after year.

Are any of my students going to write anything nearly as complex, leisurely, and reflective as E. B. White's "Once More to the Lake," which first appeared in *Harper's* in 1941? It's never a bad thing to read White, of course. The prose both invigorates and relaxes. Reading White is like drinking a milk shake. When the speaker of "Once More to the Lake" watches his son put on the wet bathing suit and feels the chill of death in his own groin, I feel it too. But White, mastermind of *The Elements of Style,* one of the great prose rulebooks, ironically follows a whole different set of rules in "Once More to the Lake." We need our student writers to be direct: to paint the chair as an object, the seat and the back and legs. White works indirectly, as only a genius can, painting the space around the chair.

Is any student helped by reading "The Plot Against People," a cry against technology, which could have been written by no one other than Russell Baker and seems very much a forty-two-year-old piece of work? Can my young students even understand the concept of being ambivalent about technology? I think they embrace technology wholeheartedly.

I keep waiting for William F. Buckley Jr.'s "Why Don't We Complain?" to quietly disappear from nonfiction sections of our literature textbooks, but there it is, year after year, edition after edition, though the world Buckley portrays, the buttoned-down and repressed world of 1961, no longer exists; my students, who hail from a place where everyone complains, loudly, about the smallest injustice, can't make head or tail of what he's saying.

Examples of nonfiction writing work best when they are current. Nora Ephron's "A Few Words About Breasts" is a great essay, a seminal work, but the world has changed so much since she wrote it that its effect for students is blunted. Pamela Anderson, Madonna's conical brassiere, TV shows such as *Nip/Tuck,* Sharon Osbourne saying she's planning to have her implants removed so that she can give them to her husband, Ozzy, to use as paperweights—all have unfortunately drowned out Ephron's comedy.

On the other hand, I am partial to teaching fiction that is old, burnished, and disconnected from my students' experiences. Does that sound odd? Students learning the mechanisms of literature sometimes find reminders of their own lives a distraction. A student of architecture must study blueprints and diagrams of buildings he or she has never seen, buildings foreign to his or her own aesthetic. A research chemist studying the genetic markers of multiple sclerosis need not have the disease present in his or her own family. I like to assign short stories and poetry that, while revelatory of the human condition, need not say very much about *our particular* human condition. Why not study "The Lady with the Dog," or "Bartleby the Scrivener" or Alice Munro's "Boys and Girls" or Margaret Atwood's "Death by Landscape"? I enjoy teaching Cheever's "The Country Husband," that epic tale of alienation and loss and acting out and redemption, that great stew of roiling emotions—but, thankfully, other people's roiling emotions.

How reassuring that so many of the stories I read in college are still there, 30 years on. I don't know if the reason is inertia or inattention, or if these editors actually think that this stuff is worthwhile. I don't know who's shilling for Charlotte Gilman, but there she is, year after year, with her "The Yellow Wall Paper." Can't have a textbook without "A Rose for Emily." It's not a party without "Flowering Judas" and "The Jilting of Granny Weatherall." Pulitzer Prize and National Book Award winner, to be sure—but who among non–English majors even knows who Katherine Anne Porter is anymore? Yet her Granny endures, slipping off into death, cruelly disappointed again. The boy in "Araby" lusts after Mangan's sister, that girl with the rope of hair and erotic way of turning the bracelet on her wrist, and still his passion is unconsummated, still he stands in the darkening gallery and burns with the realization of his own foolishness. The fictions play on, wondrously. Nothing is settled. No one has learned a damn thing and we won't either.

I consider a short story such as John Steinbeck's "The Chrysanthemums" to be a perfect tool for teaching the ways in which literature works. Here we have a highly fraught setup: a marriage with a few holes in it, a couple with a great unfulfilled need hanging over them like a winter fog over the Salinas Valley, a woman's pastime sublimating her real desires, a stranger who enters the domestic scene and reveals the truth, the chrysanthemums symbolically abandoned in the road. Quaint? Perhaps. Stolid, old-fashioned, just a touch sexist? Perhaps. But photosynthesis as a subject of study is pretty quaint and stolid too. Understand how "The Chrysanthemums" works and you've got a leg up on understanding how much of literature works.

Back when I was young and green at the teaching game, when I first assigned this story to my students, I had some concerns about its old-fashioned quality. These concerns evaporated when, before the next class, I asked a pair of students who happened to be black what they thought of it. They smiled and nodded with enthusiasm; their eyes lit up with pleasure and relief. "Oh, it was really good," one said, and then the other added: "It didn't have the n-word or anything."

Oh yes. We had been using the word "nigger" a lot in the class.

In the minds of textbook editors, the tortured history of race relations in America is a subject ripe for replaying, again and again. Its presence in the texts is unrelenting. Flannery O'Connor is one of my favorite writers, and I have come to appreciate her more since becoming a college instructor because she is incredibly teachable—full of large ideas, packed with potent imagery, violent and twisted enough to keep everyone awake. But she loves nothing more than having characters talk, in the most offhand way, about "niggers." "A Good Man Is Hard to Find," endlessly anthologized, is indeed a great story, but what is the literature teacher to do with that discomfiting business in the middle concerning the grandmother's old beau, Edgar Atkins Teagarden, who once left a watermelon with his initials carved in it on her front porch? She never received the watermelon "because a nigger boy ate it when he saw the initials E.A.T.!" I know the grandmother is supposed to be an embodiment of evil, and we can consequently file away her racism, but O'Connor herself, as her letters and the big new biography reveal, was far from fully enlightened about racial matters. This comes through in the story. My black students can sense it; when I teach the story, I feel that I am betraying them. They look up at me, earnestly taking notes, and I feel terrible. Here we are having a pleasant enough time in a literature class; why must they have their noses rubbed in the old racial attitudes? And, come to think of it, why must *I* have my nose rubbed in them? "A Good Man Is Hard to Find," "Revelation," "The Artificial Nigger"—sometimes I don't have the steam to teach these things, and so I fall back on photocopies of "Temple of the Holy Ghost," in which O'Connor's mockery is of religion and sensuality and class, or "Good Country People," in which she turns her scalpel, at least in part, on herself.

Flannery O'Connor is only part of the difficulty. The textbooks with which I am presented to teach college literature are chockablock with tales of racism and oppression. "Battle Royal" seems to be in every anthology. Can't be avoided. It was written by a black man, of course, Ralph Ellison, but that does nothing to lessen the discomfort level of the piece, in which a black valedictorian, invited to give his speech at a smoker, a gathering of his town's "leading white citizens," discovers that for the crowd's entertainment he and nine other black men will first have to take part in a battle royal, a group boxing match during which all participants are blindfolded. "Bring up the little shines, gentlemen! Bring up the little shines!" says the school superintendent when they are ready to begin. The narrator, with killing understatement, comments that he "suspected that fighting a battle royal might detract from the dignity of my speech." "Battle Royal," essentially the first chapter of *Invisible Man,* is nothing short of a racial nightmare. All attempts to concentrate on the mechanics of the story, the way the thing operates, are doomed by the events of the narrative, which is so dark, so twisted, which posits a world in which cruelty is so pervasive and wounds so deep, whites so sadistic and blacks so humiliated, that race relations can never be anything approaching normal. Maybe it's all true, but is this what the class and I have signed up for? We read "Battle Royal" and the old pot of enmity is stirred up. Soon everyone is a little angry, or a little humiliated, or a little ashamed. The glories of foreshadowing and symbolism and subtext seem rather beside the point.

The catalogue of charged material in the textbooks goes on. "Barn Burning" by Faulkner is full of minstrel show dialect and casual talk of "niggers." Excerpts from Richard Wright's *Native Son* are just as painful. "What It's Like to Be a Black Girl (for Those of You Who Aren't)" by Patricia Smith may be a perfectly estimable bit of verse, but its insistence on keeping me, the instructor, on the poem's outside (for I can tell you this much about myself: I am not a black girl) makes it difficult for me to teach. Natasha Trethewey may have won a Pulitzer Prize, but I feel too much the oppressor teaching her "Domestic Work, 1937." ("All week she's cleaned / someone else's house, . . .")

In Wole Soyinka's "Telephone Conversation," the speaker tries to convey the exact hue of his skin to the skeptical potential landlady on the other end of the line. Okay, so it's not the United States. It's probably Nigeria. I still don't want to teach the poem; I want to apologize.

What of "The Ballad of Birmingham" by Dudley Randall, in which a little girl who wants to participate in a "Freedom March"—she must think it's some sort of patriotic pageant—is instead sent off to the safety of singing in the children's choir at church, which is reduced to rubble by a bomb? The poem is chilling, as is Toi Derricotte's "A Note on My Son's Face," in which a black mother wishes for her child to be born white; when she peeks in the infant's bassinet, however, all she sees is "the face of a black man." How can I teach such a poem? How can I stand in my little classroom, under the buzzing fluorescent lights, in the quiet and airless blue-white gloom, and present, with academic nonchalance, the vision of a sick nightmare? As Sekou Sundiata says in "Blink Your Eyes":

All depends, all depends on the skin,
All depends on the skin you're living in.

 ordsworth was right: The world is too much with us.
 he of the nonfiction we study in College Writing is just

as loaded. In Maya Angelou's "Champion of the World," Primo Carnera knocks down Joe Louis in their heavyweight bout, which prompts the narrator to observe, "It was another lynching, yet another Black man hanging on a tree." Then there is Gloria Naylor's "The Meaning of a Word" (that word is "nigger," by the way). I try to avoid "The Fourth of July" by Audre Lord, in which a northern black family, unused to Jim Crow laws, can't get served at a soda fountain in Washington, D.C.; what a "travesty," the author says, is the Independence Day celebration for black people.

I can't fault black people for writing about race in America. As Margaret Atwood says, "Tell what is yours to tell. Let others tell what is theirs." Race is America's biggest and saddest story. The life of the black writer stands—a loaded gun. The black faces, young and old, look up at me from their desks and I find it difficult to teach those stories, poems, and essays. They make me too sad and worried about humanity. I try retreating to a neutral ground, where it is high and safe and postracial, where no mortar shells will scar our meadow of learning.

Perhaps I am too timid. Perhaps I am too old-fashioned, like a member of the family in Elizabeth Bishop's poem "Manners," sitting in the early years of the century on my horse and wagon, speaking politely to everyone while the newfangled automobiles zoom by, covering me with dust. I don't want to talk about race and I don't want to talk about social class, either.

The compilers of our nonfiction anthologies include, in addition to the professionally written essays of people like E. B. White and William F. Buckley, examples of what is called "student writing." I don't know if these things are real or m͏ ͏ up. If they are real they seem heavily edited; there's a h geneity to them, like a page of letters to the editor. Th dent essays, in an effort to appeal or have relevance t such as my own, tend to have about them an unmistakable tinge of the struggling lower orders. A supposedly lighthearted essay concerning the writer's difficult encounters with corporate computer systems features collection agencies, funds in bank accounts that desperately need to clear, car insurance about to be canceled, and perilously empty food cupboards. One essay, particularly poignant, explores the reasons behind the writer's lengthy history of academic failure; in the end, he winds up in a community college, and though things appear to be looking up a little, he's having trouble with some of his courses, and trying to figure out why he even has to take such courses as College Literature.

In one essay, a clerk in a convenience store deals with poverty-stricken customers who come in to steal or ask for food. Another deals with the hazards of working as a telephone solicitor. Another piece talks about someone who records too many programs on his DVR, programs he never gets around to watching; I can't help but notice that the writer is not addicted to reading books. A love of books, or indeed any mention of the written word, never comes up in these essays.

Some of my students come from poverty, and the last thing I want to do is remind them that they are poor. I'm pretty sure they already know. I take a different approach from somebody like Ira Shor, a rhetoric and composition big shot who teaches at the College of Staten Island in New York. Shor seems to feel it is his duty to bludgeon his students with fresh insights about their lack of advantage. He thinks a lot about class and its implications: his biography on the College of Staten Island Web site says that he was born in the Bronx, attended "weak public schools for New York City's white working class," and "grew up in a rent-controlled apartment among all-white families. . . ." At the Graduate Center of the City University of New York, he offers seminars in "literacy and conquest" as well as "whiteness studies, domination and oppositional discourses . . . and the rhetorics of space, place, and resistance."[1]

Shor writes about the importance of teaching about "evolving knowledges of social class"[2] to his community college students. "Why is the theme of social class urgent for classroom study, particularly at two year colleges, but also more generally in higher education?" he asks rhetorically.

I do agree, speaking from a spot squarely in the recession, with his point that "the current economic and political climates threaten the fragile work-family-school nexus in which college students live . . . ," but I'm just not sure why English classes are the place to enlighten the downtrodden. We are in a "new class war," he says; community colleges are underfunded; education for the working class is suffering.

One damning piece of evidence he presents is that basic writing and first-year composition courses at the College of Staten Island are taught by the English department's "new army of seventy-two adjuncts." The gauntlet has been thrown; I take that as an insult, sir! "All in all, then, we teach about social class to empower students to know themselves in their times," writes Shor, "to dream large and act wisely as alert citizens, to evolve into capable workers who build lives that nurture life, in a democratic society at peace with itself and the world." Me, I think my role is to teach tense agreement and topic sentences, and to instill in my students a writer's sensitivity to language, so that words like "rhetorics" and "knowledges" will start to sound funny to them.

The fact is that anyone in America can attend college if he or she so desires. That battle is won. The time has come to start worrying about paragraph unity and dangling modifiers.

13

An Introduction to the Research Paper

THE CULMINATION of my college writing class is the assignment of a research paper. Students are expected to assemble books, journal articles, and Web sites and, using the words of experts, studies, and statistics, assemble a coherent argument about something. The research paper illustrates the difficult time my students have with college. I spend no fewer than five out of fifteen classes teaching various aspects of the thing, and still, many of the students make a complete hash of it.

The English department teaches the research paper so that the students will be able to write papers for all their other classes. The idea is for students to take English 101 early in their academic careers so that we can give them the tools to do research in whatever their disciplines turn out to be. Both English departments I work for take this responsibility seriously, and feel that they are performing a service to the rest of the school. I have heard teachers in the other disciplines remark that the English department shouldn't be so puffed up, as they are doing a really shitty job of it.

The research paper assignment is meant to teach the fundamental mechanics: how to find sources, paraphrase or quote them, and make a list of cited sources, all the while not plagiarizing. Students must develop a strong thesis for their papers, and not just write what is called a "passive report," the sort of thing one knocks out in fifth grade on Thomas Edison.

I always do an introductory class on research. We all trudge down to the library and sit at the computer terminals. I ask my students about their computer skills, and some of the older ones say they have none, 'fessing up to being computer illiterate and saying, timorously, how hopeless they are at that sort of thing. It often turns out, though, that they have sent and received e-mail and Googled their neighbors, and it doesn't take me long to demonstrate how to search for newspaper and journal articles on Lexis-Nexis, EbscoHost, and Academic Search Elite. For my younger students, computers are second nature, and I remember one young man, particularly on the ball, who held his index fingers together in the shape of a cross as though warding off a vampire when asking me what my take was on Wikipedia. Even my younger students, though, fall short of the sort of cybercompetence one associates with collegians. Many have spent lots of time goofing off in front of computer screens but have fallen short of developing any actual expertise.

I explain to the students that their job is to imagine they are hosting a party. They are to take my arm and introduce me as a stranger to scholars A, B, C, and D, who fall on one side of an issue, and scholars E and F, who stand firmly on the other.

"That's some dull party," snorted my Wikipedia fellow.

The first problem I encounter in teaching the research paper is explaining to my students, as they pull up peer-reviewed articles, just what these things are. They have no familiarity with academic journals. Now, neither did I when I first strolled into college, but I did see that there were whole bunkerlike depositories of the things in the library, and small armies of pale clerks darting about, assigned to the storage and retrieval of the bound volumes. Once I got into the swing of my major, I always had my nose in an old issue of *Shakespeare Quarterly* or the *Bulletin of the Rocky Mountain Modern Language Association*. The things had heft, and weight. You could hold them in your hand; you could imagine a postman popping them into a mailbox. Some of the older ones gave off a particular smell, a faint tang of dust and mildew and oil from a thousand fingertips. Certain of the hotter articles would on occasion be ripped out, and this sort of vandalism reinforced the worth and import of the writings.

My college had a whole floor devoted to periodicals. I loved it up there. I loved reading the old English journals; I loved distracting myself from work with the few consumer publications the library had, the shelves and shelves of bound *Life* and the *New Yorker* and *Commonweal*. But today, at least in the school libraries I frequent, all is virtual. Journal articles are nothing more than a particular arrangement of pixels, no different from a Facebook page. My students never see a whole issue of a journal. They see a smorgasbord of different articles, like unrelated songs on an iTunes playlist, served up by the search function of WilsonWeb or ProQuest or whatever database they are using.

With the advent of remote access from home computers, research has become a lot more private. Students don't see their professors doing research anymore. I used to see my own professors spread out on tables in the library, jotting notes on index cards and looking thoroughly miserable. This helped me in my own work.

A few of the more seasoned nursing students have heard of the *Journal of the American Medical Association*. But they are in the minority. I still have to explain to the class not just about the use of scholarly journals but about where the things come from in the first place. I try to give them some idea of how the professoriate works. "All those books in the library—they've got to come from somewhere, right?" I say, and the class smiles indulgently, as though I am a dotty old uncle making a joke they do not quite understand, for they have no truck at all with books or any sort of intellectual commerce. They don't go anywhere where there are books, not even the college library. I once had a student who handed in a paper late, and this was his explanation: he got a late start because he couldn't *find* the college library.

I try to devise good, paper-ready topics for the students to help them out, but it's not easy. I wind up assigning things from history or sociology or current events because these are areas in which every student should be able to conduct discourse. Maybe the topics are a little spongy, but they have to be. What are we going to write, a paper on chemistry? Mathematics? Social or cultural anthropology? Too technical. English itself, meaning literary analysis, is far too technical for nonmajors to attempt. It wouldn't be fair to many students to assign a paper about *The Plague*; however, I see nothing unreasonable in expecting any college student, after conducting the research, to be able to compare the Tehran and Yalta conferences, or analyze whether or not municipalities should fund sports stadiums, or figure out whether school vouchers would be a cheap alternative in the long run, or present evidence as to whether boxing should or should not be banned.

When I initially suggest topics, and I talk about one that has even the faintest odor of the historical, some of my students complain that they are not into history. When I suggest a topic from current events, they sometimes ask, "What if you're really not on top of the news?" Fair enough; when I was in college I was too busy to be on top of the news. So I prod and poke around with them, hoping to find something suitable.

One education major who was planning to be a high school teacher (but wasn't into history) realized, after some leading questions from me, that she actually did know something about the history of federal education legislation, and ultimately that was what her paper was about. She said to me, with relief,

"When you said history, I thought you meant just presidents." Other students have a harder time of it; they can't seem to place their chosen field of study in any intellectual context. We return to the old problem that my students do not read very much. They do not understand that most educated people read a fair amount. For my students, reading is just another thing that they happen not to be into, the way some people aren't into scrapbooking or Pilates or watching *Lost*.

The research paper is a mix of high- and low-level skills. The more complex skills, the synthesis of arguments and the development of a thesis, are simply beyond some of my students at this stage of their academic development. Some are poor readers. Some cannot read a journal article—or even a *People* article—and summarize the author's stance. An alarming number of my students have trouble Finding the Main Idea.

Authoring a paper is one thing. Making sure it adheres to the Modern Language Association rules is quite another. That's a low-level skill, and they don't do so hot at that either. My students seem to have a lot of trouble formatting the works-cited page at the end of the paper, giving information about the books and periodicals used in the paper. Each entry follows a slightly different format, depending on what it is: a book, a journal from a research database, an online journal, a newspaper, a selection from an anthology. It can be very annoying work, as I am reminded as I type the notes to this book. But it is doable. My students' research materials fall into no more than five categories. They're not citing anything tricky, like e-mails or unpublished dissertations or transcripts of interviews they have personally conducted. They're citing books and Web sites and articles from the databases and that's about it. I give the students a sample "works cited" page. I tell them: make sure yours looks *exactly* like this one. We spend one, sometimes two classes writing works-cited entries and putting them on the board.

After much drilling, they *seem* to get it, but when the papers are turned in, the works-cited pages are a disaster—even after I've looked at their first drafts and told them their format is incorrect. They don't make changes. They don't fix it. They do not make any goddamned changes. Why not, I ask you? Why not? I understand why my students don't do what they can't do. But why don't they do what they *can* do?

I am frankly puzzled. Deciding what model to use for a particular entry is no harder than deciding whether a can of coffee on the supermarket shelf is regular or decaffeinated.

This is the conclusion I have come to: my students are suffering from some manner of despair. Unsuccessful students grow up thinking not just that their work has no value, but that it *never can* have any value, and thus they cannot put in the wholehearted effort that college demands. They cannot surrender to the demands of the work because they think it's probably shitty anyway.

The library is an exotic place. Once, as we started to do research, one of my students found the name and the call number of a book she wanted to use. She dutifully wrote it all down on a slip. "So what do I do now?" she wondered. "Give it to a librarian?" She and I were standing in the library stacks. "Some things haven't changed," I told her. "It's still self-service. You can pull it off the shelf yourself."

Maybe she missed the orientation. Some colleges have multiple orientations to lure students into the library:

> What other actions can colleges and universities take to get first-year students into the library? . . .
> Include the library as a stop on the campus tour that prospective students take with admissions representatives. Along with the newest residence hall and the state-of-the-art recreation facility, students and their families should see the library. They should be welcomed by a librarian

who delivers the message that the library is critically important to each student's academic experience. That message bears repeating at every opportunity, especially during freshman orientation. . . .

Try the Barnes & Noble approach. A comfortable ambience, Wi-Fi, and coffee may bring into the library students who are seeking a cozy alternative to studying in a residence-hall room. . . . [T]he University of Texas at Austin has revamped its undergraduate library to include "computers, a coffee shop, comfortable chairs, and 24-hour technical help."[1]

Often I receive papers without a thesis, papers that lapse into incoherence, papers that have not been proofread, papers that simply beggar all description. Sometimes I think—they've got to be kidding! A woman once turned in a frightful paper, one of the worst I've ever seen, but she was older, she could have been someone's grandmother, and I felt sorry for her. I thought for a moment about slipping her a C-minus or a D, but then I had a sobering thought: what if she were a plant from the *New York Times* doing a story on the declining standards of the nation's colleges? In my mind's eye, the front page of a newspaper spun madly, like in the old movies, coming to rest to reveal a damning headline:

THIS IS A C?
Illiterate Mess Garners "Average" Grade
Adjunct Says Student "Needed" to Pass, "Tried Hard"

Gotta be strong. Gotta give the F.

. . .

Every time I teach the research paper I drive the class a little harder. Each group does a bit better with it than the last. We labor mightily, week after week: thesis statements, parenthetical citations, proper works-cited format for a preface, introduction, or foreword. We're all sweating. One night, I was going on about the ellipsis mark in a way that I thought was compelling when I looked down to the back row of seats and noted a startling V of student arms: across an aisle, a young boy and girl held hands. She took down what I was saying in her notebook. He couldn't, his writing hand being committed. Instead, he looked on admiringly as she worked. At break time, I had a little meeting with the couple. "You just can't do that," I said, and they seemed sincerely abashed. They promised they wouldn't do it again. "When you're holding hands back there, no one else can concentrate," I said. They walked away, hand in hand. They looked barely twenty. She was squat, splay-footed, wide of pelvis. Her shoulder-length hair bounced as she walked. He, a skinny boy, swam in his T-shirt, which hung long on him, nearly to his knees. A casual interlacing of fingers, and I no longer felt quite able to assure the class that all of this research paper stuff was so terribly important. Life had intruded on our classroom. Maybe they had the toughest part of life solved. Privately, I celebrated their union, and I wondered at their prospects, their children and careers and hopes for marital happiness. I hoped they would have enough resources; I hoped their lives would never be cramped; I hoped they would suffer no want. They returned to the classroom sharing a carton of orange juice. He was so in awe of her.

She got a B on the paper. The one he turned in was quite a bit worse. I don't think he did much work on it. She must have been clasping his hand really tightly.

14

Life Editing

I BELIEVE IN THE EDITING PROCESS. I try to convey to my classes that the hardest part of writing is battling the blank page and emerging with some sort of draft, no matter how lumpy, which can then almost always be whipped into acceptable shape. How much simpler it is, how much more directed the work, to repair something rather than build from scratch.

Once we have our draft, no matter how lopsided or jerry-built, then we can spit on our hands and get down to the business of making it better. Once I have the raw material I have no fear. In my classes, we've put junky, half-thought-out paragraphs onto the blackboard and—by dint of great sweat, by rewriting every sentence multiple times, by devoting as much as two and a half hours to a single paragraph—come up with something that is, if not brilliant, then decidedly okay.

I believe in the power of editing in life, as well, which isn't always well advised. My faith in life editing renders me unafraid of taking the craziest course of action. It can always be fixed later, I think. I always want to do something rather than nothing, no matter how ill advised or boneheaded the action seems. I leap into life without fear.

Some of the decisions I have leapt into have worked out wonderfully.

The children, of course. What's to say? What would life be without them? No life editing necessary.

Getting a master's degree—that was a good decision. So was moving to the exurbs. So, in these uncertain economic times, when the unemployment rate hovers around 10 percent, was working for the government. It hasn't ever been particularly glamorous, and I may have looked a bit foolish in the go-go stretches of the 1990s, but I do appreciate the steady work.

Marrying my wife—that was a good one too.

I was lucky to find her. Even today, after things have been so hard between us, after the sound of her approaching footsteps in the house can sometimes send my heart racing with anxiety and anger, after her voice sounds to me harsh and drained of all love (and she, no doubt, feels a whole set of corresponding things about me), so many times we still have the capacity to ring out together like notes of a pleasing piano chord. We are the same people, the same consciousness, in a thousand small ways.

We are *Miracle on 34th Street* people, not *It's a Wonderful Life* people. Jimmy Stewart is too corny. Give us both the pleasures of John Payne.

We rush to tell each other about the same stories in the newspaper.

We are both almost comically indifferent to the weather. We never carry umbrellas.

We think alike. We see a lottery winner on TV and my wife wonders: if someone buys a friend a lottery ticket for Christmas, and the friend wins $250,000, what would be an appropriate amount to bestow on the gift giver? We both have an answer, without hesitation, and it is the same answer: $50,000.

We stand together outside the house and watch one of the holiday parades our little village is so fond of mounting. Our eyes alight on the same things; our heads snap in the same direction. Look at how tall that kid has gotten, we think at the same time. We watch with great fascination the manager of the local deli, who speaks with an eastern European accent. He is thin and angular, and he's got an equally angular eastern European wife. They sip tea and watch the parade. My wife and I can't stop imagining them as sculptors, and the same sort of sculptors at that: we imagine them mounting large installations made from found objects, old junk cars and the like. For whatever reason, even our craziest fancies are the same. The high school band passes: we like that. The Veterans of Foreign Wars pass: we well up at that. Here comes the 4-H club, and the local chapter of the Odd Fellows, and the Catholic church, and the volunteer firemen. The year could be 1956; my wife and I are swimming deep in the syrup and grain of Americana. And then come the Civil War reenactors, their shoes authentically tattered, the brims of their hats broken. They walk in a shuffle, half in a daze. These are men who have clearly seen too much on the battlefield. Except they haven't, really; one is an insurance adjuster, one works in a toy store. The spectators fall silent as they pass. It's an uncomfortable silence. No one quite knows how to react.

I make a snide remark about their fraudulence.

"It seems a harmless enough hobby," says my wife.

The idea of fraudulence hangs in the air. The house we bought seems to have poisoned talk. There are fewer and fewer subjects on which we can alight comfortably. If there is to be peace, I dare not mention Civil War reenactors again. I'd better not mention the Civil War. There are scores of subjects off limits in this way. The vacation we took to Florida. Ivy League colleges. Even our shared indifference to the weather. If we cared about ourselves more, if we weren't so blockheadedly oblivious to such things as rain, we would have taken care to feather our nest more, and not bought the house.

A sense of estrangement descends on us, raining on our parade, but mercifully it soon lifts. She, too, wants us to be normal. The Knights of Columbus march by in their tricorner hats beplumed with white feathers, their dark jackets trimmed with braids of white. She takes my hand.

All of our troubles may ultimately have made me a better, less rancorous person. I have always been a wiseacre, ready to make fun of anything or anyone. My wife, who laughs easily, was a good audience. Neighbors, relatives, local merchants, children's teachers—all were fair game. Once I became less happy, the jokes turned caustic, and she stopped laughing. My weaknesses were showing; my desire to drag down everyone else, like the poor reenactors, was now evident. And so I developed a policy of measured silence. I assumed a virtue that I did not possess, but eventually, liberated from the obsessive search for a punch line, I started to see the world more clearly, and more charitably.

After the parade is over and the crowd has dispersed, it is time to mow the lawn, a task I do not relish. My lawn is large and my mower small. It has a 14-inch deck. It takes a long while. Somehow, my grass is always too long and too wet when I get around to mowing. I have to stop frequently and tilt the machine on its rear wheels in a sort of landscaping Heimlich maneuver so that it can disgorge, like knots of chewed gristle, plugs of grass. I must be rather a forlorn figure, tracing square paths, marching back and forth, back and forth, losing the battle with nature. I vow, tomorrow, to pull weeds. I look more and more like my father, the renter of an apartment in a quasi-suburban setting. I never saw him in anything but a suit and fedora; he stood out from the other fathers, who sometimes turned up in sport shirts and sneakers. Why didn't he have the right accoutrements? Why did he insist on the suit? Well, now I know: he was a bit of a dandy, true, but more than that, he didn't want to spend the money on leisurewear. Neither do I. I wear discards from my work wardrobe: shorts cut from old work trousers, a frayed pinpoint oxford, wingtips without socks. I feel like the neighborhood tatterdemalion.

The task takes about an hour.

"How was mowing?" asks my wife as I sit in the hot kitchen drinking seltzer. Sweat pours off me. My head swims with fatigue. I feel as though I might collapse.

"It's good exercise," I say.

"That's probably the best way to think of it," she says, perhaps darkly.

I try to catch my breath. I am an old, poor, bare, forked animal. The chemicals in my body are out of balance; my toenails now routinely split and fall off. I suffer dyspepsia. For my health, I try without much success to eat oatmeal with the consistency of library paste. Outside the kitchen window, a crow caws in an ugly fashion.

Our household is wildly fraught. Everything drips with meaning. I know she's thinking: *It's okay to think of it as exercise. But you're at the age where you should really be able to choose your own exercise. How sad.* Or something like that. Or maybe she's not. I don't know anymore. Even in the smallest, everyday actions, I am no longer on sure footing.

Before anyone else has gotten up in the morning, I struggle to read a book that won't stay open and eat breakfast at the same time. This is difficult because my genteel, poverty-stricken mother taught me to butter toast one bite at a time. At her knee I learned to appreciate a world that lay beyond my means. The struggle with breakfast wears me out. I feel all my motor skills diminishing terribly with age. The pages of the book get greasy. I don't even taste the toast. All my upbringing, everything silly I have brought to bear on life seems, at that capstone moment, to conspire against me, and I want to cry out: I seem trapped in the wrong universe, neither exactly left- nor right-handed, not able to maneuver.

I hear the creak of my wife's step upstairs. I don't go immediately up there, and she doesn't come down. Our life has altered what it was. I hope we can go back to how we were.

I am addicted to her presence, as sad as it makes me at times. I have never loved another adult the way I love her, and so—it has to be—I've threatened to leave, barked the word "divorce" at her (Did I really mean it? Or was I just angry, the way everybody in a couple gets angry sometimes?), shouted and screamed, hammered dresser tops with my fists, thrown things, jumped up and down in frustration like a little kid, as though I could break the bonds of Earth's gravity, and that would make me feel better.

It's not easy to argue with the children in the house. One tries very hard to be undetected. We argue in whispers. We argue in bursts no more than ten seconds long. We have gone out to the driveway and argued in the car, as though we were listening to the last minutes of a compelling report on the radio. But often, we can find a vacant room in which to fight. The house is big enough for that. How's that for an irony? In the Cape Cod, there was no room to fight—there was no room to swing a cat—but we had thankfully little to fight about. This house, vast and dark, can seem to possess a malevolent spirit. I think of *The Amityville Horror, The Haunting of Hill House*—thank you, Shirley Jackson.

"Why are we arguing?" I say. "It's not like we're fighting about doing anything. We're not going to sell the house. We won't uproot the kids. We're just fighting about how we got here. It's all just—literary analysis. I don't care how we got here."

"I want to make a better decision next time," she says.

With one wrong move, one misstep, life can change forever.

I tend toward the obsessive-compulsive. I'm always checking running toilets to make sure they don't overflow. I try not to do it around the children. My anxiety might be contagious. I don't want them to be nervous. I don't want them to live in constant fear. But maybe my approach is wrong. Maybe they *should* know what I didn't in my bones: that with one misstep, life can change forever.

We shouldn't have gone to the closing, my wife and I. We should have blown it off, left all the vultures sitting there in the bank office with their reams of unsigned documents. We should have gone out to lunch. That would have been more productive. We were wonderfully unencumbered, with a check for more than a hundred thousand dollars in our pocket. We could have packed everyone in the car and headed west. Lit out for the coast. Like Sal Paradise and Dean Moriarty—with the kids, of course.

Life can't be edited, really. My wife and I view each other now through veils of argument. Our collective landscape is littered with the rubble of past quarrels. You can't erase hurt. Can't just delete it or drag it to the trash. We've been through a lot, the two of us. We can say the rich experience has been good. We can say our love is deeper. I know that it's sadder.

15

Resonance

S OME OF MY STUDENTS have had a rough time of it. They have suffered fractured home lives and job losses, unwanted pregnancies and galloping diabetes, turns of life that could bring a person to tears. But many of them are still young, and haven't been beaten down completely. The literature we read in English 102 does not resonate for them. It bores them, and how I envy them their boredom. For them, the living of life still seems something separate from the sorrows and tragedies portrayed in literature.

And I understand, for though I have always loved literature and writing and have thought of myself as someone thoroughly embroiled in the written word, my studies of literature remained for a long time just that: studies. I may have swooned at the beauties of a novel, chewed over the characters in a short story, reached mightily for those ideas in the greatest poems that seemed just to elude me. But it was not until I felt my life falling apart that texts began glowing for me with the warmth of personal meaning.

I suppose the first classic I taught that seemed to resonate for me was D. H. Lawrence's "The Rocking-Horse Winner." I'd read it in early high school, and remembered it only dimly; I seemed to recall that the protagonist, a young boy named Paul, was able to go into some sort of trance on his rocking horse, which enabled him to pick the winners at the big horse races.

But I didn't remember, until I had reread it, what had driven him to develop such a skill. I didn't remember the bitter worries about money that ruled the house, the fact that the house itself seemed to whisper, "There *must* be more money!" Of course I didn't. The occult aspects of the story, which don't interest me at all today, will loom large in the mind of a teenager; the other stuff, the household economics, just seem like narrative setup. I didn't see the significance. I was the sort of teenager who never imagined he wouldn't have enough money. Growing up, all the families I knew, including my own, seemed solvent enough without breaking much of a sweat about it. But I wasn't privy to the whole story. I couldn't tell who had a good or bad job, who had wealthy parents, whose life was an unrelenting string of small, futile economies. I didn't know that having enough money was not life's default state, that having resources sufficient to navigate the shoals of life without anxiety takes some planning and doing.

The lack of tenderness in Paul's household in "The Rocking-Horse Winner" is heartbreaking, and money lies at the root of the problem. Paul is aware of the money issues swirling about— the walls and wainscoting fairly scream them out to him—and as I taught the story to a class for the first time I found my academic distance from the text shrinking. As I stood at the chalkboard, things seemed hopeless to me. Did my children understand why I was out working two and sometimes three nights a week? I would not let fatigue wear me down. I would not make my suffering apparent. I vowed to be, above all else, hearty. I returned from class each night full of vigor, and mischief, as though I had been out buying secret presents for everyone in the house, perhaps a shade too ebullient, rather more happy and empty-headed than actually I am, like a male incarnation of Sarah Ferguson, Duchess of York. But it worked. The children may have known that something was up, but they would never hear the smallest trickle of misery from my lips. I would not be short-tempered, or anguished, or desperate.

The truth dawned on me that I was in fact a very lucky man. I was not waiting tables, or working security, or tending bar, or stacking inventory in Wal-Mart. I was fortunate enough to be teaching school, an occupation about which I could be very upfront with the children. This was a world they understood completely, and they joined me in it.

I brought my work home joyously. I left my textbooks around for all to examine. Poetry and short stories bubbled up at the dinner table. My son has always been interested in mythology. And so together we read bits of Tennyson's "Ulysses," with its haunting valedictory on the dignity possible in middle age.

Though much is taken, much abides; and though
We are not now that strength which in old days
Moved earth and heaven, that which we are, we are—
One equal temper of heroic hearts,
Made weak by time and fate, but strong in will
To strive, to seek, to find, and not to yield.

These lines never fail to revive and hearten me, even as I return home exhausted, like one of the narcotized tars in "The Lotos-Eaters," from working and teaching. There is dignity possible for a hardworking man in the second half of his forties, and though the merest shell of myself, I will not yield—though tomorrow, I must ascend the ladder and clear the leaves from the gutters. When I am tired, I cannot resist the cruel conceit that I am engaged in the same work as Ulysses and Telemachus, only I bring the glories of literature to my rough and reluctant classes to "fulfill / This labor, by slow prudence to make mild / A rugged people. . . ." And then, as the family watches a documentary on the Kennedys, the tear-rattled voice of one brother eulogizing at another's funeral (I don't remember if it was Bobby at Jack's or Teddy at Bobby's) sounds through our home, saying the lines: "To strive, to seek, to find, and not to yield." The children squeal with the delight of recognition. We are in a house dripping with art and literature, the walls draped with British poetry, and Alfred, Lord Tennyson is as palpable a figure to us as Martha Stewart or Manny Ramirez. Poetry matters.

Other poems capture the household's imagination. William Carlos Williams's "This Is Just to Say" winds up transcribed onto a piece of loose-leaf and affixed as a joke, with a magnet, to the icebox.

I have eaten
the plums
that were in
the icebox

and which
you were probably
saving
for breakfast

Forgive me
they were delicious
so sweet
and so cold

We love this poem, but of course make lots of fun of it, and our own notes to one another start to be parodies of it. The poem opens us all up to the idea of plums, and we can't wait for them to come in season. They turn out to be something of a disappointment, or maybe we just never get a good one. The children are learning subliminal lessons about the need for civility in relationships, always; and the absolute requirement that we communicate. I love the idea of this polite little poem, this veiled ode to desire, the quenching of desire, and the regret that inevitably follows, burbling through our home like a Zen koan.

We also love Yeats's "An Irish Airman Foresees His Death." How timely, how contemporary seem these musings of the alienated aviator, who fights not because of "law" or "duty" or the exhortations of "public men" and "cheering crowds," but simply because of his profound love of flying. He has achieved the self-actualization we all strive for.

> *A lonely impulse of delight*
> *Drove to this tumult in the clouds . . .*

It is good for the children to imbibe a healthy dose of anti-jingoism, coupled with the marvelous evocation of all that man is capable of. Here is a man who has followed his dreams and freed himself, as nearly as one can, from the bonds and boundaries of the world. His passion may well lead to his doom, but following his heart is the means to achieve lasting happiness. I followed my heart and wrote my fiction, but my mistake was to abandon the dream and jump into real estate. I should have been content with my surroundings and written more; those reams of unpublished pages, in an odd way, were a key to satisfaction. I might never have succeeded as a writer, most likely wouldn't have, but my dreams at least kept my life grounded. It was only when I abandoned the dreams that I felt the gnawing, the nothingness, that I tried to fill with a house. I hope that my children have large dreams, and I hope they approach them more thoughtfully, with more self-awareness, than I did.

Other poems have come to be part of the shared language of the household. "It is better to produce one image in a lifetime than to produce voluminous works," wrote Ezra Pound; does any poet encapsulate this more than Robert Hayden? A great many poets never come with anything as devastatingly true and ringing as the money phrase from "Those Winter Sundays," his hit out of the ballpark: "love's austere and lonely offices." I joke around with the children about the phrase; making a peanut butter sandwich becomes one of life's austere and lonely offices; the phrase heartens me, and gives me the strength to proceed with my own evening offices. On the Little League field and the school basketball court, my wife and I watch with great fervor; there is no more total escape from workaday cares, as James Wright well knows, than youth sports. I see myself among the disappointed souls in his 1963 poem "Autumn Begins in Martins Ferry, Ohio," the "Polacks nursing long beers in Til-tonsville," the "ruptured night watchman of Wheeling Steel," the "proud fathers" who are "ashamed to go home." (Why? Are their mortgages too big?) And why do their wives "cluck like starved pullets, / Dying for love"? Have the cares of life extinguished all hope of sexual ardor? In the end, there is almost no joy to be had *but* the youth sports, and they take on a heft they would not have otherwise had: "Therefore, / Their sons grow suicidally beautiful / At the beginning of October, / And gallop terribly against each other's bodies." After the basketball game, we leave the hot gym and step into the freezing night; shivering in the quiet, our breath steaming, the still world somehow seems bereft, and I would give anything for the game to begin again.

From the abyss of despair comes the light of literature. Few things have been as comforting to me in the long middle of my life.

16

The Writing Workshop

WHEN I THINK OF MYSELF TEACHING, in my mind's eye I see a composite class of all the students I have taught. The faces looking out at me are not particularly eager. I see nursing students and EMTs, education students on the road to becoming teachers, midlife career changers, state and local government workers, military types and civilians who labor on military bases. I see a part-time high school coach looking to grab a certificate and get tenure. I see hopeful police officers, court officers, sheriffs, marshals, correctional officers, parole and probation officers—representatives in training, in short, from all stages of the criminal justice cycle, from pursuit to apprehension to release.

I can't say that I've been particularly successful as a writing instructor, but I teach in the way that comes most naturally to me. My goal is to demonstrate for my students the way a writer thinks.

I present myself to the class less as a writing instructor than as a writer. I emphasize what is, I believe, the greatest strength of the adjunct. As one writer has put it rather elegantly, adjuncts "possess something that regular, full-time faculty members essentially lack: authenticity." Adjuncts are, as the title of this article puts it, "emissaries from the world beyond."[1] I know the craft of writing. I tend to think of my students as apprentices.

I would pass on what I knew to them, like a stonemason or potter or auto mechanic. Writing is an art and a craft and a knack that can, with time and long effort—longer than we really have, unfortunately—be mastered.

I believe in the editing process, the procession and refining of draft after draft, but I also believe that students have to be shown exactly how to do it. It's all well and good to direct a student to edit a paper, to do a new draft—but what the hell does that mean? I tell my writing class on the first night: You'll hand in first drafts of every essay to me. But here is what won't happen. You won't get back your first draft covered by teacher hieroglyphics, *awk*s and *ill*s and *frag*s like the discordant cries of exotic birds, scrawled *???*s and arrows and circles like the tracks of those same birds, all followed by a small sermon at the end: *Your details are plentiful and your topic a novel one. The main problem is your thesis, which is underdeveloped. Your lack of topic sentences leads to wandering paragraphs and a loss of control. Watch capitalization and comma splices. Have a nice day.*

No one reads that stuff. I never did. It might as well be written in Sanskrit. No one reads anything but the grade on the last page. What we will do instead is pass out copies to everyone in class and edit the compositions together—we will workshop them.

I was a little nervous about this approach at first. I wondered if the workshop format was too intense for my tyro writers. I have been in many college classes, and the only ones in which people cried—and I mean broke down completely in huge, racking sobs—were the writing workshops. And these were English majors, who had asked for their misery! I wasn't sure my apprentices could hold up.

Students are capable of becoming good editors, but they must be taught how to go about it before they can work on someone else's paper. Anyone who wants to learn how to dismantle and clean a carburetor must watch it being done; writing works exactly the same way. To learn to write you must watch someone do it. Doesn't it stand to reason? Writing is the most private of arts. We are surrounded by the finished products, but the drafts are hidden from us, and we never get to live with the writer as he or she polishes, tunes, rejects, augments, agonizes, and generally reworks the thing. We talk volumes about the writing process and give the students no more than a few road signs—and those written in hieroglyphics—indicating how it actually works.

The idea is not complicated. For the first few classes, the students follow along with me as I edit their pieces on the chalkboard. Concept by concept, word by word, sentence by sentence, paragraph by paragraph, I edit out loud and on the fly. The class watches what I do, and listens to my thought process. Why do we need to expand this idea here? This paragraph seems rushed—can we slow it down? Why is this observation irrelevant? There seems to be a problem of logical structure here; D follows A—do we need to insert B and C? The author of the composition takes notes on what is to be done with his or her essay; the rest of the class follows along, seeing (one hopes) their own writing in the work of others, the same gaps in logic, the same sorts of confusion over and over again, the same infelicities—writing speed bumps—that slow the reader to a crawl.

This is all something of a high-wire act. This writing and rewriting and editing out loud can be risky. I am never sure how successfully it will go. This very book has moved smoothly and cooperatively on some days and crankily on others. Writing and editing well, being in a good zone of productivity, is as mysterious a process as hitting a baseball; who can say why on a given night the .300 hitter, facing mediocre pitching, goes 0 for 4? There are some nights when the student essays stump and defy, when the student writers seem to have done something magical: that is, created a Gordian knot of confused prose that cannot be undone, writing that cannot be improved. I feel like a jeweler who has dismantled a watch and forgotten how to put it back together: the wheels, the springs, the works lie about in disarray. My contribution to the student prose seems to add little more than a layer of rather high-blown confusion. When that happens, a cloud of deflation descends upon the room. Writing seems impossible—to the class, to me.

Those nights aren't completely wasted. The class gets to see just how difficult it can be to free one's prose from the weeds and brambles of composition. I am at least gratified that my students can see how torturous the process can be. They see it as I labor to edit and rewrite, standing at the board, staring in frustration, sweat glistening on my brow.

Oh, but on other nights the editing goes so sublimely well! Every emendation seems to tighten and strengthen and nourish and clarify the prose. The editing process seems magical. As a class, we read the original prose out loud, and then the rewrites. We savor the taste of good writing in our mouths. Even to a class that has never before given any thought to the business of writing, the results are impressive. And then comes that almost divine moment of clarity when a successful rewrite seems so achievable that the students, unbidden, join me in the process.

They, too, are writing out loud.

Their steps, at first, are tentative, their corrections elementary. They might note the sort of thing they have never noted before. Perhaps a clanging, empty sort of word like "particularly" appears three or four times in a paragraph ("I've never been particularly eager to buy a motorcycle. . . . The dealers I've spoken to have never been particularly convincing . . . There's something particularly dangerous about these vehicles."), catching our attention in as distracting a fashion as an oddly dressed movie extra who keeps passing by the camera in a crowd scene. I will ask them to compress a paragraph and they will do so by deleting words, which is a good start but only half the battle. The prose becomes oddly telegraphic and bare, like an old building whose gargoyles and pediment have been removed for safety reasons. And then finally, after long effort, a student will not just remove words but actually recast the writing, turning sentences around, substituting new and better verbs, and at that moment the writing teacher can bathe in the warmth and glow of learning.

We have made the first strides.

. . .

One of the tricks to this game is choosing the right essays to work on together. If a composition is too poor, our final product will differ too much from the original, and the students will suspect their instructor of trampling the piece to death for his own glory—entertaining, perhaps, like a magician who can transform a silk scarf into a dove but cannot convince the audience that the dove and the scarf don't remain separate entities. Essays that are too well written don't really work either. Light prose touch-up jobs, the mere ironing out of pronoun agreements and clipping of long sentences, give a distorted view of how much work a typical piece requires.

Very occasionally, a student will submit an excellent first draft, and I will present it to the class. A good piece of writing gives hope to all. The teaching of writing is unfortunately a negative business, with the vast majority of student essays illustrating many more don'ts than dos. Effective writing teachers must not let the smallest problem pass while, at the same time, remaining encouraging and upbeat. This might be the most difficult tightrope to walk in all of teaching. Students do not succeed just by writing a lot; they've got to be shown their errors for the work to be productive.

As I start to revise a piece in front of the class, I experience a moment of uncertainty. Will this actually help anyone? Isn't every sample of unskilled composition unique? The answer to the latter is no. The shortcomings of student writing fall into familiar and universal patterns. The thesis hasn't been sharpened to a point that guarantees a rigorous organization of thought. The paragraphs may start out with some unity, but after a bit the writer's attention wanders, and he leads the reader down a warren of back alleys and dead ends. The modifiers dangle. The prose may limp along in the passive voice, or, owing to a paucity of vocabulary, use ten dull words where three good ones would do.

The ideas in the essays are commonplace, when they exist at all, and the lack of ideas makes for a prose that churns in place. The writer metaphorically clears his or her throat, adjusts the microphone, fiddles with the lectern, consults notes, afraid to get to the point because really there is no point.

The writing is larded with clichés—not the ones listed in the writing texts, which really present no danger because no one actually uses them, like *more fun than a barrel of monkeys* and *sly as a fox* and *good as gold*. No, I'm talking about contemporary clichés, the ones we don't even notice as they float untethered around us: *she was there for me* and *I couldn't get past it* and *that was in my comfort zone* and *it is what it is*. The writing is deeply flawed, but as I work at the front of the room to peel away layers of verbiage, the class becomes eager to join in the process.

We discuss and justify every change. We're not in a hurry. We may get to only three compositions in a three-hour class. To wrestle with a piece of writing takes time—a scandalous amount of it. As we work, I direct the class's attention to the clock. Look, we've spent 40 minutes on the first paragraph.

Now it's 50. All of a sudden, it's an hour. To edit an essay effectively is sure to take several hours.

They are horrified, but that is the truth. It is what it is.

Writing clearly and well requires great effort, a level of effort which many of my students are not acquainted with. One of the comments I find myself making often about first drafts is that they appear to have been "hastily composed." Writing is unique in this way: 15 minutes at a computer and there exists something, a palpable chunk of writing, to be handed in; turning in such a piece of work is the equivalent of turning in, for an algebra assignment, random jottings of numbers and letters—gibberish, really—and hoping it passes muster. After a while, the students start to put more time into their assignments. They're afraid not to. That a crappy paper, even with the name of the author obscured, might find its way into the hands of the 22 other members of the class, all gleefully editing like crazy, is a real threat.

Threat? Did I say that? It's a crude teaching strategy but occasionally effective.

Writing, as we all know, isn't just a physical act, the clickety-clackety-clack of hands on a computer keyboard. Writing is thinking. Writing is saying something worthwhile. While we work on these compositions—editing, rewriting, tightening—I also spend a great deal of time on the front end: the conceptualization. I try to teach students how to do a better job, when they have the freedom, of selecting their topics. A great subject makes for better writing. My students think of their essays merely as exercises to be gotten through with as little exertion as possible. A subject with some depth, a topic about which they have some expertise, will generate livelier and—this is the intriguing part—more competent writing. My students are the protagonists of their own complex and fascinating lives. They view their own existence, as we all do, with a great deal of nuance, a fine and discriminating eye. They are capable of great wit. The hard part is to get them to channel all that marvelous stuff—all that life—onto the page.

Though sometimes enough life is too much life. I once made the mistake of editing with the class an essay written by a mother about her child's protracted death from leukemia. The essay dripped with grief; the child had died years ago, but she had obviously never gotten past it. We started working on tense agreement and chronological inconsistencies, but could build up no steam for the project. Our complaints about the essay's organization seemed carping and disrespectful. The sadness of the subject made the whole class question the worth of our larger endeavor. What did proper usage matter in such a world of tragedy? Writing seems powerless against the gods.

Personal subjects are a good start toward powerful writing. But part of college is a requirement that students write about subjects they know little about at first. Not every college essay can be about one's life. Sometimes, the essays have to be about things like wind turbines, and this is where the students really hit a brick wall. I recently asked my Pembrook students to write an essay comparing and contrasting Chief Justice John Roberts and Justice Sonia Sotomayor, based on a pair of biographical articles that appeared in the *New Yorker*. I thought they would enjoy the release from the oversaturation of possibility in the personal essay. These two articles were their complete universe. I thought, as I often do when I introduce these sorts of assignments, that I was doing the class a favor. How much would I have enjoyed a *New Yorker*–based assignment in college? Instead, my students found the task hopelessly onerous. They found the articles as difficult to get through as Kant's *Critique of Pure Reason*. The assignment overwhelmed them.

Michael Holden refers to the great "information void" of his students. He cites previous studies revealing some of their, ah, *misconceptions* (Heinrich Himmler invented the Heimlich maneuver; the Great Gatsby was a magician; Jefferson Davis played guitar for the Jefferson Airplane) and then cites the results of his own study. He administers the Information Subtest of the Weschler Adult Information Scale (WAIS-R) to his own students, and anyone who has ever listened to a Jay Leno monologue can tick off the results without my repeating them: 69 percent couldn't name the number of members of the United States Senate, 34 percent couldn't say how many weeks there are in a year, 66 percent couldn't name the person "usually associated with the theory of relativity."[2]

It is difficult if not impossible for a college student to compare two justices of the Supreme Court if he or she has never heard of such concepts as eminent domain or liberalism, and cannot rightly say just what it is a district attorney or appellate court does. The act of writing is difficult enough; to do so without a bedrock layer of hard knowledge with which you are intimately familiar and comfortable is just about impossible. So we go back, invariably, to the personal essay. The students must have free rein to write most often about themselves; otherwise, we would get nowhere.

. . .

A writing professor of mine once spoke of attending a fiction workshop led by Joseph Heller, author of *Catch-22*. Heller was a thoughtful and careful technician, said my professor, but he didn't concern himself with high-sounding obscurities. He spoke not of theme or texture. He lived in the world of what worked. "We've been waiting too long to hear some of this stuff down here," he would say in his gravelly voice, pointing to a flawed paragraph and seeming like a man about to disassemble a fuel pump. He was itching to get his hands dirty. "Chop some of it off and stick it in the intro. Move this description from the start to the finish, cut this part out, and turn this business right here around. And then I think you'll be good."

My professor was the one who gave me the fuel pump analogy. "It was sheer genius to watch," he said. "Every change he made was perfect. And the fuel pump ran a lot better when he was done with it."

We writing teachers could do a lot worse than to start turning out classes of skilled syntax mechanics, their hands soiled with the filth of discarded adjectives and the grease of potent verbs. My goal is that none of my students ever again experiences that desperate feeling of hopelessness that strikes the novice writer, that none will have to ask the despairing question "What should I do next?" Ideally, they will always be able to loosen a few bolts on a piece of prose and start checking fluid levels.

Once in a while, I experience a moment of writing triumph. Not often, mind you. That's why I remember them. One night, we were editing an essay about creating inexpensive Halloween costumes. The author of the piece, Chad, was right in the thick of things. In search of a transition and greater clarity, he had just inserted a three-sentence paragraph in the piece that seemed to cause more new problems than it solved. His sentence formation wasn't quite on point, and his diction was limp. The whole thing was fuzzy—so much so that I found myself at a loss for any specific suggestions. I suppose I was tired: his weak writing swirled around my head and left me temporarily speechless. I threw up my hands and said what exhausted editors have no doubt said since the dawn of the printed word:

"You've just got to make this better."

Chad nodded and bent over his notes. The class quieted. He considered what to do. He made all kinds of dissatisfied faces. He squinted. He looked toward the ceiling, only marginally aware that the rest of the class was watching him. He shifted in his seat and tugged at his baseball cap and groaned with what could have been appendicitis. The class laughed but the spell remained unbroken.

He was in the throes of some sort of agony. Was it writing agony? I was hopeful. He looked thoroughly miserable, which was a good sign. He wrote something, stopped, and wrote again.

"All right, listen to this," he said, and read aloud.

He had done it. He had tamed his prose. He had made the thing better. Chad's paragraph was shorter and crisper and fully—okay, 85 percent—logical. He had replaced a verb of being with one of action—"pierces," as I recall—and a fine, fine verb at that. He had abandoned my guidelines and done more than I asked. My little bird had ventured out of the nest and flown a little. Like a carpenter or roofer or auto mechanic or chef, he had a total picture of what the piece should be. He had taken the first step toward developing a *feel* for the writing.

17

Do Your Job, Professor!

O N VERY RARE OCCASIONS, I do have the classic, yearned-for teaching experience with a student who performs poorly but has potential and is willing to make the effort. I am sometimes able to spur them on. I remember one middle-aged mom named Gwen, a woman of Christmas sweaters and a tidy chin-length bob. She was initially suspicious of the class. "How are you supposed to do well in this if you're not a good writer?" she asked rhetorically, not exactly to me but to the gods in heaven, as she gathered her things at the conclusion of a class early in the semester.

She wrote a paper on the virtues of handwritten letters over e-mail. The paper really wasn't much good; it was vague and imprecise, filled with spongy half-formed thoughts served up like half-baked holiday cookies. She was inhabiting that alternate reality, the Land of Writing Assignments, that place so different from real life, where the object is not to amuse or enlighten or impart truth but just to fill the page with words, sentences of varying lengths that state the obvious in the most commonplace fashion. I saw that she wanted to do well, and I saw that she could, but she didn't know how. We talked after class. What was it that spurred her to write about this topic? For ten minutes, she danced around the issue. Letters were just more *interesting* than e-mail, she said. What more was there to say? She wouldn't get anywhere near the truth, but I interrogated her as though I were a cop, and finally wore her down. A truth emerged: she still had letters written to her by her dead mother, and she found herself reading them more and more frequently.

She told me about the letters. She started to well up. As her drill-sergeant and muse, I was delighted, for I knew we were approaching someplace good. But maybe we had overshot the mark. She was still more a daughter than a writer.

"Now we're getting somewhere," I said. "Let's not lose it. Give it to me on the page." And so she came back a week later, with a paper that hinged on the similarity of her mother's long and graceful hands to the long, graceful shapes of her looping cursive script.

Oh yes. Now we were cooking.

Moments like this do not happen often. Clearly I am not working miracles. I have great faith in my methods and what I am doing. But sometimes I do doubt myself. Who wouldn't?

When my original article "In the Basement of the Ivory Tower" appeared in the *Atlantic Monthly,* I received a good deal of negative mail. I was the embodiment of bad teaching and moral turpitude.

> The only kind of student with whom I've had little to no success is the one who shows zero interest in bettering himself . . . sort of like Professor X and his telltale lack of reflection on how he might improve his own practice.

> In short, this article serves to suggest that a large portion of the (working-class) population is unteachable—and this simply isn't true. . . . And there are a number of ways to teach such students to write coherent sentences. If one knows what one is doing, one can accomplish this with

most students in 15 weeks. Professor X should be giving himself—not his students—those failing grades.

I feel sorry for Professor X's students. He thinks his responsibility is to evaluate their results on his writing assignments. Good teachers know their responsibility is to help the student learn.

At my college, our class size is either 25 (pre-transfer) or 30 (transfer-level), and we consider it a failure if more than two students do not manage to pass. We do that by having individual meetings with each student, using collaborative learning to enhance active learning, and emphasizing multiple pathways toward learning.

Professor X is a white-collar criminal who couldn't qualify for the ivory tower and make it as a scholar, so he is employed to serve a screening function at the bottom of the system.

Instead of demonstrating his students' inability to succeed in academia, Professor X's jeremiad provides convincing evidence of his own weaknesses as an educator. While his gloomy blend of fatalism, guilt, cowardice, and low self-esteem is perhaps not unique, it should not be seen as representative of the mind-set of those who toil in the less prestigious strata of higher education. The image of the red-pen-wielding "button man" wringing his hands while handing out F's is as inaccurate as it is unfortunate.

Professor X bemoans admitting students to "classes they cannot possibly pass." But perhaps many of them could pass these courses if Professor X had the faintest clue as to how to teach them.

I hadn't been prepared for such a response. My mind reeled. Could it possibly be true that most students can be taught to write in 15 weeks? What were the multiple pathways? Tell me, please.

A white-collar criminal?

I was also the subject of numerous virulent dispatches from the blogosphere. This one is typical:

> I usually don't get that riled up by magazine articles, but after reading "In the Basement of the Ivory Tower" I was fuming. . . . Why am I so mad? I have spent most of my professional life in adult education and instructional design. . . . This is a GROSS failure of teaching and the man should be fired ON THE SPOT. . . . He has the students write a research paper as their first assignment. If your students have trouble writing coherent paragraphs, why are you starting with papers? Why not have them start with learning how to write a grammatical sentence. (Play Mad Libs to learn the parts of speech) Then teach them how to write a good paragraph. Then teach your students to outline. Then have them write a five-paragraph essay. THEN move to a "college" paper. Once they have the fundamentals of writing they can write anything but you will never create good writers our [sic] of them if you do not teach the fundamentals.[1]

Mad Libs. In college? Hadn't thought of that.

Then the academics started to weigh in. One English professor at Eastern Michigan University said, on his blog:

> There was quite a bit of discussion about this piece on one of the professional mailing lists that I'm on, and the basic conclusion was that Professor X doesn't really know what

he's doing as a teacher and/or doesn't know what he's talking about.[2]

. . . [T]he course he was teaching sounded just horrible to
me—not at all close to the "best practices" in the teaching
of writing, and no where [*sic*] near the progressive program
we have at EMU.[3]

And then the most wounding of all, a post by the director
of first-year writing at the University of Mississippi. He was
knocking not just me but my students as well, though I don't
think he really meant to:

[Professor X] landed in these classrooms in exactly the
same way his students did: out of inertia; out of laziness;
out of a sense that it was too much trouble to go farther
afield.[4]

Comments like these worried me. Maybe I wasn't as prepared as I should be. Maybe I should look into the science of
rhetoric and composition, verse myself in pedagogy. And so I
did. I immersed myself in theories and practices. I read lots of
scholarly writing, digested lots of different opinions, philoso-
phies, strategies.

I went in search of enlightenment. I even went to the online catalogue for the first-year writing program at the University of Mississippi, which sent me to the Council of Writing
Program Administrators and their WPA Outcomes Statement
for First-Year Composition. I ran to the thing, hoping for a set
of guideposts to help me in my own instruction. I went right
to the *Processes* section of the course outline. I couldn't get
there fast enough. "By the end of first-year composition, stu-

dents should . . ." Okay, here it was: the Holy Grail in seven points. Here were the outcomes of the teaching processes:
Students should:

Be aware that it usually takes multiple drafts to create and complete a successful text

Develop flexible strategies for generating, revising, editing, and proof-reading

Understand writing as an open process that permits writers to use later invention and re-thinking to revise their work

Understand the collaborative and social aspects of writing processes

Learn to critique their own and others' works

Learn to balance the advantages of relying on others with the responsibility of doing their part

Use a variety of technologies to address a range of audiences[5]

I started to think about the seven points. English 101 consists of 15 classes. So I supposed I had two classes for each point, which would leave me a week to administer a final exam.

Let's look at the first one, the one about multiple drafts. Now, surely this is something that has been drilled into even the most indifferent student since first or second grade. It was difficult for me to imagine how this particular fact would be taught in any fashion other than by standing up at the front of the room and saying, "All right, students. Be aware. It takes multiple drafts to create a successful text." The students may be underprepared, but they aren't idiots. I could make short work of that one.

Number one was mere introduction. Number two had

more meat to it. As far as I can tell, "generating" means think-ing of what to write, and it's hard to imagine what those strate-gies would be aside from (a) thinking, and thinking quite hard, about what would make a suitably complex and compelling topic, and (b) rejecting those topics which are too simplistic to provide the writer with anything but the most rudimentary starting point. The student must be willing to put in the time and the sweat and the sheer misery that comes with thinking of compelling topics to write about.

Next, the student must revise the work, and revision has one especially troublesome demand: a skilled writer must have read, possibly over the course of 15 or 20 years, enough good quality expository writing so that the patterns of complex thought and syntax used by skilled writers are thoroughly ingrained in his or her mind. Revision then has an aim: to bring the writing closer in quality and depth to that which all would consider good writ-ing. What is the point of revision if the student does not have an archetype in his or her mind? Archetypes cannot be provided by instructors in 15 weeks. Some of the college students I teach, I venture to say, have not read ten books in a lifetime.

Which brings me to the strategies for "editing and proof-reading." Some of the educational bloggers who knocked me speculated that I hadn't even read Mina Shaughnessy. They were right; I hadn't. So I did. I went to her book *Errors and Expectations: A Guide for the Teacher of Basic Writing.* Shaugh-nessy is one of the goddesses of writing instruction. She was present at the creation; her book is a reaction to the academic fallout stemming from the decision, in 1970, by the City Uni-versity of New York to move to an open admissions policy, which admitted

a wider range of students than any college had probably ever admitted or thought of admitting to its campus—academic winners and losers from the best and worst high schools in the country, the children of the lettered and the illiterate, the blue-collared, the white-collared, and the unemployed, some who could barely afford the subway fare to school and a few who came in the new cars their parents had given them as a reward for staying in New York to go to college; in short, the sons and daughters of New Yorkers, reflecting that city's intense, troubled version of America.[6]

What had been called in the past remedial or developmental writing Shaughnessy labels Basic Writing (BW). She has no illusions about the students' level of skills, commenting that "the pile-up of errors that characterizes BW papers reflects more difficulty with written English than the term 'error' is likely to imply."

Shaughnessy believes that every student can improve his or her writing. I agree with her, of course; the question is whether there is enough time and money for this to happen when so many students have made it through high school without mastering the building blocks. Her work has been embraced by some educators who seem to feel that the belief that writing should be error-free is fascistic. Shaughnessy, it should be noted, doesn't think that way herself. She bemoans errors in writing, calling them "unprofitable intrusions upon the consciousness of the reader. . . . They demand energy without giving any return in meaning. . . ." She understands the motivation of those who would like to think only about content:

> Some [teachers] rebel against the idea of error itself. All linguistic forms, they argue, are finally arbitrary. The spelling of a word, the inflectional systems that carry or reinforce certain kinds of information in sentences—these

are merely conventions that differ from language to language and from dialect to dialect. And because the forms of language are arbitrary, the reasoning goes, they are not obligatory. . . .

When one considers the damage that has been done to students in the name of correct writing, this effort to redefine error so as to exclude most of the forms that give students trouble in school and to assert the legitimacy of other kinds of English is understandable.

Nonetheless, she says, errors in writing must be dealt with. We've got to understand what the student is trying to say.

To try to persuade a student who makes these errors that the problems with his writing are all on the outside, or that he has no problems, may well be to perpetuate his confusion. . . . In any event, students themselves are uneasy about encouragements to ignore the problem of error, often interpreting them as evasions of the hard work that lies before teachers and students if the craft of writing is ever to be mastered.

I was no closer to the holy truth: how does one teach fledgling writers to make their writing understandable? I went to Mina Shaughnessy's section on "Suggestions for Reducing Error." It was right there in chapter 4, on page 128. It seemed a little late in the book to embark on the subject, but I was eager to learn.

We come finally to the question of how to help students reduce their errors to a level that is tolerable to their readers. . . .

I grew excited. She was going to give me knowledge from the mountaintop.

> . . . and here the individual talents and training of teachers, the learning styles of students, the time allowed in a writing program or department for the mastery of grammatical forms, and a variety of other considerations preclude my recommending The Way or The Book or The Grammar.

My heart sank. Can't you always tell when a writer, before ostensibly telling you something, cautions you that she won't actually be telling you anything?

Here are her suggestions. First,

> When the intent is to spot and correct errors, grammar (which is used here to mean any effort to focus upon the formal properties of sentences) provides a useful way of looking at sentences.

How right she is. The point seems blisteringly obvious. In what other language can we talk about sentence structure and logic than the language of grammar? The problem, of course, is that the teaching of grammar has become an enormous taboo in American public education. I taught in public school back in the late eighties; grammar lessons were exchanged surreptitiously among the English faculty, like Soviet-era samizdat, and it was well known that to be caught teaching the stuff was, for a new teacher without a permanent appointment, the quickest road to dismissal.

Few of my students at Pembrook and Huron State know the first thing about grammar. Forget about predicate nominatives. Forget about case and mood. They don't know how to find the subject of a sentence. So on those occasions when the class is completely lost as to how to repair a particular sentence, or even why the sentence is wrong in the first place, we need to do an emergency grammar lesson. Things get very muddied very quickly because the class and I don't share a language. I can't use the term "subject," because that would confuse and frighten them. I must refer to it as "what the sentence is about." Verbs they kind of understand on a basic level but then we arrive at agreement between subjects and verbs and the class is quickly lost and discouraged. The language of grammar seems a hopeless tangle—as does any language if you don't know it. Many of my students have never been taught the rules of English; I might as well be asking them to write in Latin.

Shaughnessy makes an excellent point about grammar instruction:

> The grammar students study for the purpose of reducing error should accomplish two objectives: introduce them to several key grammatical concepts that underlie many of their difficulties with formal English and equip them with a number of practical strategies for checking their own writing.

"Key grammatical concepts"—that's what teachers are supposed to impart, as though you can teach a few biggies, the greatest hits, David Letterman's Top Ten list, and get their writing in pretty good shape. This is a misconception, as Shaughnessy goes on to explain.

> This is not easy advice to follow, however, because grammar itself is a web, not a list, of explanations, and often a seemingly simple feature of instruction will be located at the interstices of several grammatical concepts.

To decide whether a subject agrees with a predicate, Shaughnessy says, the student must be familiar with no fewer than five concepts: what the term "agreement" means, what a subject and a predicate are, whether the subject is singular or plural, how that is indicated in the noun's form, and how the number of a verb is indicated.

Students must understand that a sentence is a "structure" rather than a mere string of words; Shaughnessy calls this "the most important insight a student can gain from the study of grammar, an insight that is likely to influence him not only as a proofreader but as a writer."

I was looking for some magic, for a tool kit—to use a currently hot educational term—for showing novice writers how to repair their prose. And what did I get? Essentially, a recommendation that poor writers need a grounding in grammar.

The college-writing machine would have you believe that skilled teachers can teach any student, no matter what his or her level of preparation, and that is simply not true. There are no easy answers or magic bullets, whatever cliché suits you.

18

Grading the Teacher

A FTER A SCHOOL has grown comfortable with an adjunct instructor, he or she will start to seem indispensable. Often, scheduling of classes taught by adjuncts is done not by deans or department chairs but by harried secretaries, who become tempted to use the more dependable and money-hungry adjuncts to fill in holes in the schedule. In the process, the adjunct's credentials may start to lessen in importance, his or her actual areas of expertise growing a bit blurry around the edges.

I was hired to teach English 101 and 102, but was eventually tapped by Pembrook to instruct some journalism classes and a business class, Business Communication. The last was a disaster. To this day, I don't exactly know what business communication consists of, which is perhaps a tip-off that I shouldn't have been teaching it. The course had something to do with business correspondence, something to do with memos, and something to do with corporate hierarchies. The textbook veered from abstruse complexity *(Stryker and Statham posit an integrative theoretical latticework called structural symbolic interactionism [SSI] . . .)* to that which was comically self-evident: *(All forms of communication involve a sender and a receiver).*

Not being an expert in the subject—not even being minimally versed in the subject—I couldn't fathom what information might possibly lie outside the contours of the textbook. I couldn't possibly have answered any questions posed by the students, but fortunately my teaching was so uninspired that none were raised. My methodology consisted of going through the textbook with the class, summarizing (as best I could) and restating the main points of each little section.

The experience was torture for both the sender and the receivers. Class time stretched hopelessly before me. All the while I taught, my heart raced with anxiety as I waited for a student to raise his hand and ask, "Why the fuck are we coming here every week and wasting our time?" This is exactly the sort of question I couldn't have answered. When things got particularly desperate I screened movies that had some remote connection to the business world. *Roger and Me. Working Girl. The Bonfire of the Vanities.* I figured the class would be open to watching any movie I popped into the VCR, but *Bonfire* was so bad that the students actually asked me to stop it about halfway through. When a class goes bad, *everything* goes bad.

I gave everybody an A and wrote the whole experience off as a mistake. I vowed never to teach out of my comfort zone again.

The next time I ran into my department chair, the subject of Business Communication came up. She told me how disappointed she was that I didn't want to teach it again.

"It's really a shame," she said. "You did a great job in there."

I don't want to make too much of her pleasant and offhand comment, but what she said caught my attention. How on Earth could she have the smallest idea of how I did in there? She never saw me teach. She wasn't even on campus at night, when the class was offered; she never happened to walk by the room and catch the smallest snatch of the proceedings. Good thing. The truth was that I did horribly in there. I absolutely *died* in that room. The jokes sputtered and the silence was deafening. Feet scraped, ballpoint pens clicked, and resentment hung in the air like a woolen blanket, stifling the life out of us. If my Business Communication class had been a comedy club, I would not have been invited back. Ever. The trouble was, I was booked for a 15-week minimum.

Teachers are rated and graded, lionized and slandered all the time. Administrators at every level can tell you the names of their strongest and weakest instructors. That teachers at all levels vary wildly in quality is a universally accepted truth. The best schools, of course, are blessed with great teachers, dedicated teachers, effective teachers, selfless teachers, youthful and enthusiastic teachers, seasoned teachers, inspirational teachers, teachers of the year, teachers for whom 40 hours is just the beginning of the workweek. Inner-city public schools are said to be filled with burned-out teachers, lazy teachers, indifferent teachers, inept teachers, and, most damning of all, teachers just putting in their time for a paycheck. As a reaction to these terrible teachers, sometimes special academies are chartered, and the goal, of course, is to staff them with teachers great, dedicated, effective, selfless, youthful and enthusiastic, etc.

I have one question. How on Earth does anybody know anything about anybody's teaching?

The last time I looked, nobody was watching anything that goes on in the classroom.

I have worked as an adjunct instructor now for a decade. I have been observed twice, once by each school. My department chair at Pembrook observed me on the second night of my adjuncting career. I was teaching English 102. She stayed for 20 minutes and took off, which seemed to me a fair amount. She was just making sure that my hiring was, in broad strokes, in the realm of the reasonable: that I knew what it meant to analyze literature, that my hygiene was good and I didn't advocate the violent overthrow of the United States government, and that I could address a class from the front of the room and didn't suffer from hysterical dysphonia or anything like that. She winked and gave me a thumbs-up on her way out of the room.

Instruction is of necessity a private enterprise. Virtually no one, except for the students, ever sees it being done.

This is as it should be, for the sake of the students. Learning is one of the first things we start doing after birth. It is a primal human act. It requires a near-total surrender of will, a reversion to an earlier state of being: the adult's baggage of pride and skepticism, his measured consciousness, do little but get in the way. The beautiful agony of learning can be a brutal and messy business, and intruders have no place in the classroom. The presence of any outsider disturbs what is a delicate mechanism.

Learning is a struggle and a battle; it can no more be done in public than I can wrestle publicly with a piece of prose. As I write this, my wife would like me to sit in the wing chair in her office with her while she reads the Sunday *New York Times* on the Internet. But I can't fight with words in her presence. Writing uses some of the same muscles as learning, and a bad session of it can be as humbling as losing a bar fight. At some point, my verbs and modifiers and half-formed ideas will get the better of me and start pummeling. I can't let my wife see me get the shit beaten out of me.

. . .

In the fall, my busy season as an adjunct, I spend many weekends watching my son play basketball in various leagues. Sitting in the bleachers, I often have a folder of compositions on my lap to work on at halftime; as I grade them, I sometimes become aware that I am being watched. My seatmates stare at me with fascination—and it must be plenty fascinating to distract them from their own kids' dribbling and shooting—as I scrawl grades and transfer the numbers to my ledger. Invariably, I get comments: some rueful, some marveling, some a little chastising. There is a sense that I am performing, in public, a forbidden and private act. One man said to me, "I just didn't picture that's how it was done." I don't know what he pictured: the reading room of the British Museum, perhaps; the faint strains of Mozart in the background.

Teaching is a mysterious profession. I have worked in offices, warrens of cubicles, and have always been able to judge the status of my colleagues—who's up and who's down—from their body language. I could always tell who worked diligently and who didn't, who was on a roll and who couldn't even get started because every new task seemed to be going so badly. I cannot judge the performance of my fellow teachers with anything like the same certainty. At Pembrook College, I work with the same crew of adjuncts year after year: the business teacher who favors pastel suits and matching high heels, the ex-priest who talks like a tough guy and teaches religion and philosophy, the retired executive who specializes in the history of the Middle East and the history of Islam. We teach in the same classrooms leading off the same hallway semester after semester, but it would be the height of absurdity for me to make the smallest inference about how competently they are conducting their classes.

Every school has its coterie of "great teachers," but of course few have ever actually witnessed them doing any teaching. Their performances are the stuff of legend, like those of Laurette Taylor, the tragic, alcoholic actress who first played Amanda in *The Glass Menagerie*. Taylor died in 1946 and left behind virtually no filmed work: a couple of silent films and a brief screen test. Few who actually saw her in *Menagerie* are still alive to talk about it, yet her name continues to be spoken with hushed reverence. Some in the know persist in calling her America's greatest actress on the basis of no evidence whatsoever. I suppose there is something comforting about such romantic legend making. The problems of education are knotty and thorny—impossibly complex—involving students' background and home life and motivation. How comforting is the myth of the great teacher! *If only we had a few more of those, we'd be in good shape.*

But I'm not so sure. No one sees what goes on except the students, and their judgments are fallible. It's difficult even to know if perfect competence as a teacher inspires perfect learning. Is the teacher who explains things thoroughly, completely, and clearly actually necessarily better for the students than one who doesn't? Could the teacher who forces the students to complete the job on their own actually be better for some learners? Absolutely. Could the instructor who spells everything out; who covers every possible circumstance, exception, and quirk of a subject; whose approach seems in short a model of clarity, actually foster a more haphazard approach in some students? Absolutely.

There are many ways to get results. The magic of teaching is vastly overstated, mostly by teachers, and by those who staff programs that have an economic interest in teaching prospective teachers how to teach. In the general dumbing-down of second-tier-college academics—the transformation of college into years five, six, seven, and eight of high school—a wafting, smoky presence has come to obscure the atmosphere in college classrooms. College instructors never used to worry about their teaching; expertise was enough, and the assumption was that a college student would be able to extract meaning from any course, no matter how uninspired the professor—the professor becomes, sometimes, beside the point. The fog of pedagogy, once the province solely of schools of education, has settled on the college campus. I call it a fog, but in truth it sometimes grows as thick as a stew: a stew of jargon, gobbledygook, and theorizing. It has been brewed of necessity. Rather than facing squarely the painful issue of whether unqualified students are being admitted to college programs, administrators have obscured the question with the fog that comes between the expert at the front of the room and the end-users in the desks.

The act of teaching has become separate and distinct from subject-matter expertise. If the students cannot satisfy the requirements of the college curriculum, it is not necessary to assume that they do not possess the requisite skills. Let us instead say that the teacher's pedagogy was faulty, that he did not teach well enough.

I think I know about writing and literature. I have been writing all my life, wrestling and tinkering with prose, beating it like bread dough, sometimes in delight and often in utter frustration. I have been reading and analyzing literature all my life. I can spot foreshadowing at fifty paces. You want a theme? An epiphany, perhaps? I've got a million of them. Analyzing literature has never paid me very well, and has never seemed all that useful a skill. A rather dull party trick, really. But I know how to do it, and motivated students locked in with me for 15 weeks will take baby steps toward knowing how to do it as well.

My department chair was dead wrong. I didn't do a good job teaching Business Communication, because I didn't know the subject. It wouldn't have mattered what sort of gyrations I did in there. I could have pulled a Jaime Escalante and taught in the helmet of a bicycle messenger. I still wouldn't have known what I was doing, and you don't have to be in the classroom with me, indeed even anywhere near the classroom with me, to recognize this as a recipe for disaster.

19

On Borrowing Liberally
from Other People's Work

A T ABOUT 10:30 ONE NIGHT I sat with a student in a classroom in the Pembrook Arts and Sciences building. Class
was over for the night. We were alone. Between us, on my
desk, like something neither one of us wanted to touch, was
the research paper he had handed in.

"This seems to be plagiarized," I said.

I've seen plagiarism before, usually about once per class.
Cowering at the thought of having to do the research paper,
some students leave it until the last minute, and, thoroughly
overwhelmed and in a panic, copy out stuff from some corner
of the Web. The plagiarists don't even use the research databases. They don't copy from legitimate academic journals.
They just take the first thing that Google belches up. I've seen
large chunks of papers plagiarized from course outlines and
syllabi from other colleges. Two students over the years have
plagiarized from the same Wicca / Magic / Herbalism / Tarot
Card Web site that glancingly mentions one of the assigned
poems and turns up near the top of the search results in
Google's magical algorithm. One student lifted a large swath
of his paper on conflicts between Christians and Muslims in
Nigeria—and I mean three or four pages—directly from the

transcript of a segment from National Public Radio's *All Things Considered.*

Plagiarism is always simple to spot. My students' writing skills are so rudimentary that the bits lifted from other writers gleam like gold nuggets in a prospector's pan. Obviously, I grow suspicious when I read, from a student who can't even identify first-person narration, the rather smug observation that such-and-such a work remains one of the poet's most anthologized works, but that its dominative romanticism gives little hint of the more practiced verse to come. One writer talks about *Death of a Salesman* in the most childish manner imaginable, and then opines that the play offers a postwar American reading of personal tragedy. Oh, does it? The writer also notes, in another casually piercing insight, that the play romanticizes the rural-agrarian dream but keeps it, tantalizingly, just out of Willy's grasp.

Another writer, analyzing a poem about a marriage ceremony, writes about those who are observing the wedding. She says that the poet ascribes to the gathering feelings of tenderness for the newlywed pair. The overwhelming majority of my students are not capable, on their own, of using "ascribes," "tenderness," or even "newlywed."

When I lecture on *Hamlet,* I sometimes tell the students how editors must decide among the different approaches of the First Folio, the First Quarto, and the Second Quarto, and how scholars have gone so far as to identify different typesetters because of the characteristic errors they have made. All of this seems highly irrelevant to most of my students, but I am involved in much the same sort of detective work when I read their papers.

The research paper before us was, however, unlike anything I had encountered. Next to it on the desk I placed a paper I had downloaded off the Internet. The papers were identical, down

to the eccentric line spacing and typos, and the quirk of thinking that Flannery O'Connor was a man.

"I found this on Cheathouse.com," I said.

He studied the two papers. He was in his thirties, my student, angular and lean, with a hard body and a large head. He
wore old-fashioned black horn-rimmed glasses—the sort you
see in 1950s high school yearbooks.

The building was deathly quiet. Classes had dismissed for
the night. No stray custodian passed by. No security guard.
Downstairs, I knew, the ice cream vending machines were
doing that weird thing they do when it gets late, filling with
steam as they defrosted their coils for the night. There is no
other time to meet with students. Adjuncts don't have offices
or office hours, and meetings before class aren't practical for
anyone. Some students can barely get to the start of class on
time; some know that they can't but take the class anyway.

My student licked his lips. "So what are you saying?"

"This paper is not your work."

"So there's no credit for it?"

"Well, no," I said, a bit irked by the question. "There's a bit
more to it than that. I have to report you. The administration
could conceivably toss you out for academic dishonesty. If the
charges are sustained, of course."

His expression darkened. A small feeling of cold dread swept
over me. Again, I listened for footsteps in the stairwells. I sipped
the dregs of my cold, dead coffee, the one that had been sitting
untouched on my desk since early that evening.

My student was a criminal. A small-time criminal, yes, but
a criminal nonetheless. His eyeglasses, which seemed designed
to impart a look of seriousness, started to look sinister. He told
me that he worked—for a school, in fact, as some sort of classroom aide—but who knew whether that was even true? A
teacher would be on a faculty list somewhere, and could be

Googled, but not an aide. And he didn't even carry a backpack, the way most students did; he carried three loose textbooks, like teenagers on *Leave It to Beaver.*

He rose from his chair and started pacing back and forth across the front of the classroom. His jaw was set and his eyes unfocused. He was clearly enraged. I asked him to sit down. "I have to keep moving," he said. "If I don't keep moving I'll throw something." A chair, I thought? His instructor? I really wanted to call security, but had made no provisions to do so. There was no telephone in the classroom. I do not carry a cell phone, which at that moment seemed the apogee of folly. I didn't know security's number anyway.

We were alone, and I had leveled my damning accusation, one that could get him booted out of the school. Why had I chosen this moment? Hadn't I seen this situation countless times in movies and mysteries? Wasn't the hero always confronting the villain alone—stupidly, I thought—as the story built to a climax?

"I'm very disappointed," he said. "Very disappointed."

I said nothing.

"I'm going to be truthful with you," he said.

The villain always comes clean in the end.

"I bought that paper," he said. "I admit it. I bought it off a friend of mine. I paid him to write it for me. But I didn't pay for some old piece of junk that was out there, floating around on the Internet."

Suddenly everything about him, his tale, his situation, his ineptitude, seemed sad. I felt sorry for him. He nodded at me, picked up his paper, and shuffled away. I listened to his footsteps fading down the stairwell.

When I got home that night, I checked my life insurance policies. The old cliché about the workingman was true: I was worth a lot more dead than alive. The thought empowered me.

All fear of death vanished. I have not a trace of it to this day. I walk around weirdly cocky for a middle-aged man. Maybe all middle-aged men feel this way. I feel pumped up and energetic, as though I've been eating well and working out. I walk the streets practically looking for violent street crime in which I can intervene.

Death be not proud, though some have called thee mighty and dreadful, for thou art not so.

The life insurance is a good start, but my wife would need more.

I asked her, "Do you know where I was tonight?"

"Teaching, of course."

"No. Where? Which school?"

I've often got classes going on in both schools at once. My wife has her own busy life and can't always keep my schedule straight. "Huron State?"

"No, Pembrook," I said. "It's crucial for you to know where I am on any given night, because when some dissatisfied student kills me, I want you to sue the right place. I don't want any Perry Mason endings with some registrar revealing that I wasn't even teaching at his college on the night in question."

"Whatever," she said.

"But don't worry," I said. "If anyone kills me, you can be sure I'll take them with me."

. . .

The whole enterprise of teaching in college sometimes looks dark to me. My students and I are in an impossible situation. Some of them move across campus as though in a fog: confused, always a little frightened, sometimes despairing, never sure at any moment what the next development will be, hoping against hope that they will pass.

My students and I are trapped in a tense and unnatural relationship. To do poorly in a course can really throw a monkey wrench into their life plans. If I have to lower the hammer, my students resent it mightily. Why wouldn't they? And when I leave campus for the night, my footsteps echoing as I pass the closed bookstore and shuttered coffee stands, I often question myself. *Wouldn't it be easier if I gave them all A's? What would it matter? Who would know? Who would care?*

Late at night, in an empty, soiled classroom, with seemingly not another living soul on campus, grade disputes start to seem very personal. The administration isn't around; the students can't go vent to a dean or ask an academic adviser for intervention. Late at night, it's as though the administration doesn't exist. Lack of academic success seems my doing, and my doing alone.

Do I really think that a disgruntled student might pull out a gun and shoot me? I don't live in fear of it, but neither do I rule out the possibility. I am informed by the lessons of Northern Illinois University and Virginia Tech and the University of Arkansas. Remember that one?

FAYETTEVILLE, ARKANSAS—A graduate student shot to death a professor of English and himself on the first day of fall classes at the University of Arkansas yesterday, police and campus officials said.

Associate professor John R. Locke, 67, died around noon in his second floor office in Kimpel Hall, which houses the English, journalism, and foreign language departments.

University chancellor John A. White identified the graduate student as James Easton Kelly of Marianna, Ark., who had been a doctoral degree candidate at the school for 10 years and was dismissed last week from the Ph.D. program in comparative literature.

Locke was Kelly's faculty advisor, White said last night.[1]

The participants in a student-teacher conference at 10:00 P.M. have both put in a full workday, about twelve hours' worth. Tempers will grow short. There are no metal detectors on these campuses. No full-body scanners. Who knows who's packing heat? Much of my clientele consists of people who are, in one way or another, up against it. I wonder if it is only a matter of time before one of them crosses a line with me.

I love my life in the classroom. I love the three hours discussing ideas. But I have few illusions about the daunting nature of our task, and sometimes there seems to me a somewhat grimmer reality just beneath the surface.

20

The College Bubble

FOR ALL OF MY BELIEF THAT reading good literature leads to spaciousness of mind, largeness of spirit, and generosity, I sometimes seem to myself a most small-minded and spiritually bereft person. Christ, I seem at times so awfully *cramped*.

For a long time, I wasn't completely happy. I was less and less comfortable in my home and my village. I indulged in a new fondness for pornography. Not sexual pornography. Apartment pornography. I gazed longingly at the seedy rental condos on the outskirts of my village, at the base of the hills, the same rental condos at which I once sneered, despairing of their effect on my property values. Now they seemed a nice place to set up shop. I liked the little terraces. I watched reruns of *Seinfeld,* and noted that Jerry had a very nice apartment. It looked cozy and well heated. I started reading Paul Auster novels. His protagonists always lived in snug apartments on the edges of New York City. The life seemed attractive, especially since Auster never mentioned cockroaches or bedbugs.

Mine is a prosperous little village of picket fences and tidy flowerbeds. The French bakery serves lovely, bracing coffee. There is a warm and homey little diner for bacon and eggs, a drugstore with a pressed-tin ceiling, and a barbershop. I walk around my village on a Saturday morning, feeling too strapped to spring for a plate of bacon and eggs—though I will have a coffee! I must! Is life worth living without coffee from a French press? I see lots of people whom I know: neighbors, parents of my children's school friends, Little League coaches, an attractively pregnant bank teller. An attorney parks his Mercedes outside the diner. I purchase caulk from the hardware store. The youngest volunteer in the firehouse hoses down the hook and ladder. The rawboned woman who homeschools her brood cycles by.

I thought I was spiritually generous, but it turns out that I am not. Such is the smallness of my spirit that I rank my position in the universe against everyone I encounter. I never used to do this; now it is a tic that I cannot stop. Mostly I rank us all monetarily: income, assets, newness of vehicle, home equity, size of 401(k), and the like. Many in the village seem to have me beat. Their clothes are newer, their cars newer and bigger, their appliances (I've been inside some of their houses) shinier, their kitchen stoves all slick and flat-topped and digital. Nothing about them seems shabby.

The pink-cheeked, gentle old woman with the nimbus of cottony white hair and green garden clogs—she has me slammed to the floor, her clog on my throat. I triumph over only a few. I think I've got the bank teller beat. I don't think she wants to be on her feet this Saturday morning; the strain shows around her eyes. I'm also ahead of the barista who French-presses my coffee, and the barbers who speak no English.

There are several inhabitants of the village who seem right at my economic level, and so I perform a series of secondary calculations in my mind to evaluate our positions. How attractive is the wife? How much vacation time does he get? Does his health care coverage carry into retirement? I think about some of the local wealthy childless couples. I assume that they are tortured and miserable. I have to assume that for my own sanity. I feel like one of the townspeople in "The Lottery," one of the locals who looks at the wealthy and powerful Mr. Summers and "is sorry for him, because he had no children and his wife was a scold."

Walking my town is an exhausting endeavor. I cannot stop my mental gymnastics. Too bad I can't seem to exercise my body as vigorously as I do my mind—I'd be a lot thinner.

. . .

Some years ago, notices of foreclosure began to be put up in the post office, which became suddenly a lot more interesting a place to visit, a place not just of mail and stamps and Christmas parcels and stacks of tax forms but of the official record of shattered lives. Our post office is dark and cool, seemingly unchanged from the days of the New Deal. Above the parcel post window a cast-iron American eagle watches over all. On the wall hang display sheets of commemorative stamps and plaques honoring local dead in foreign wars. Week after week, the sheaf of foreclosure postings on the clipboard grows thicker. I don't know many of the names. Most of the houses are in the new developments outside the village, off in the hills, as I think of them. I recognize one woman's name. I believe that she works in the kitchen of a nursing home. Her 3,200-square-foot house, built in 2006, is in foreclosure. She seems like a very nice person. She lived in a mansion. I used to wonder, occasionally, how she and her husband did it.

It turns out they didn't.

They, too, are the victims of the postmodern impulse. It seemed the right thing to do to improve their narrative, to install them in a mansion that they couldn't really afford. "The development of lax lending standards, both by banks and by Fannie Mae and Freddie Mac," according to Thomas Sowell, resulted from a series of government policies "directed toward the politically popular goal of more 'home ownership' through 'affordable housing,' especially for low-income home buyers. These lax lending standards were the foundation for a house of cards that was ready to collapse with a relatively small nudge."[1]

President George W. Bush said it back in 2002, back when I was buying my house. "We can put light where there's darkness, and hope where there's despondency in this country. And part of it is working together as a nation to encourage folks to own their own home."[2] *Encourage* them—as though it were something that had slipped their mind, or that they hadn't gotten around to.

I took a shallow breath. I still walked a tightrope. Money was always tight, but things no longer seemed desperate. I hoped that enrollments at my schools would stay up. Teach my usual load of classes every year, and I'd be all right. And then, wonder of wonders, as the recession deepened, I heard for the first time Barack Obama saying words I never thought I would hear him say. Community college, he said. What? Yes, that was where his hope was. Community college. He had a notion to give $12 billion to community colleges over the next decade. I went to the White House Web site and read the description of the American Graduation Initiative:

> In an increasingly competitive world economy, America's economic strength depends upon the education and skills of its workers. In the coming years, jobs requiring at least an associate degree are projected to grow twice as fast as those requiring no college experience. To meet this economic imperative, President Barack Obama asks every American to commit to at least one year or more of higher education. . . .[3]

The sound of the thing was familiar. President Obama desired, by administrative fiat, to redefine exactly who among the populace qualifies as a college student. The good news is that everyone qualifies. Everyone is a winner! Now where have we heard that before? Perhaps from the lips of the Bush administration, which had similar ideas about broadening the base of homeownership.

Just because we call someone a college student, just because we enroll him or her and sit them down at a desk, doesn't make it all on the up and up. Granting a mortgage to someone doesn't confer the status of a solvent homeowner, either.

My adjuncting work has been crucial to keeping me financially sound for all these years. I persevere in my middle-class status. I am not in any danger of foreclosure, but I don't blame the poor souls who are. We all overspent for these damn houses.

The surface of a housing bubble is opaque, and when you're trapped inside, seeing outside to the real world is impossible. Our impulses were not bad, not greedy, not evil. We were naïve, yes, and credulous, and the argument could be made that we were, in rather a poignant sense, patriotic. All we wanted, for ourselves and for our children—mostly for our children—was a sliver of the American promise of prosperity. We believed that diving into as much real estate as we could was the bedrock foundation of that prosperity. We believed because we saw it. We saw who lived in the old, spacious houses in town, the ones with the turrets and the hammocks and gliders on their wraparound porches, the ones that every spring had their gardens overhauled with fresh applications of sod that was tall but airy, like sponge cake. Just like my writing students, we in the housing market got cause and effect a little mixed up: the houses are an integral part of the wealth, but they don't exactly cause it. Buying a house in 1930 was a good move; buying the same house in 2002, not so much. The market was mature and then, when the bubble burst, beyond mature, and perhaps beyond repair.

When everyone owns a house, the economic benefits of homeownership diminish. The college market is equally mature. My students sit before me in their desks because they understand that college is the path to a better life, which they want for themselves but, even more, for their children. College is the crucial first step—some sort of college credit is nonnegotiable in the job market—but no one has mentioned one salient detail: there are no guarantees. Unprepared college students and unprepared homebuyers are both very much at risk. Markets tumble, houses enter foreclosure, students fail.

. . .

I have been teaching as many courses as I can—for the money, yes, but at some point I discovered how happy I was walking the quads and arranging the desks in my classroom. To paraphrase the song from *A Chorus Line*, everything was beautiful at the college. I had grown to be a respected figure, a veteran teacher, a Mr. Chips–like venerable old institution—if you forgot that I was an adjunct, and could disappear tomorrow, leaving no trace, no memory save, perhaps, that of my long coat. Only occasionally would I be reminded of my second-class status. I once attended a plagiarism hearing for a student who had turned in a paper larded with stuff off the Internet. Like cops called to a domestic dispute in a slum, the full-time English professors on the panel treated both the student and me with thinly veiled distaste. The whole affair struck them as sordid, I know, and I could almost read their thoughts: Can't you crazy losers work this stuff out yourselves?

There are times when the campus can be a wonderful place of escape. I have lost myself in the stacks in the subbasement of the college library. I've watched baseball games, and basketball games. I've wandered the aisles of the campus bookstore as the new semester began, and admired the shelves of pens and racks of school hoodies and stacks of textbooks with not-yet-cracked spines and felt that old sense, dormant in many of us, of the endless possibilities of the school year. I've gone to staged readings of new plays by English department faculty. I've taken my English 102 students to hear visiting authors speak. I've come out of the classroom, after a great night, as satisfied as I have ever been in my life, filled with the uncommon bliss of a sense of true purpose. I may not be the best teacher in the world, but I'm probably not the worst. Teaching these classes is what I was put here to do, I think. The road of life seems torturous and twisting, and we can't make sense of it, but it is all for some purpose. Our ends are shaped, rough-hew them how we will. I have attended the faculty barbecues, and been invited to join a chorus of professors as they gathered around a piano and sang the rousing college song. The college song! I didn't know the college song, of course, which was a little bit of a bummer, but I hoisted my stein of beer and joined in as best I could.

But as the years pass, and the stack of archived grade books and attendance sheets grows taller in my attic, the colleges have lost their power to distract me. I can't get it out of my mind: the same societal urges that lowered the bar for homeownership have lowered the bar for higher education, and the similarity haunts me. I am at the nexus of it all, for I, who fell victim to the original pyramid scheme of real estate, the constant expansion of the base of buyers to keep demand and prices up, have used the educational pyramid scheme, the redefining of who college students are, for my own salvation.

Last week, I visited the campus library. I found I could hardly work because of the noise. I was tempted to go out and write in my car. Some of the students were working hard, but most weren't. Most were just bullshitting. We sat in an area next to a sign: MODIFIED QUIET STUDY AREA: QUIET CONVERSATIONS ONLY. I really don't know what that means. What is modified quiet? Is it possible really to have quiet if there are any sorts of conversations going on, even quiet ones? Why can't the library just be unambiguously quiet? I thought back to my own college days. Were the libraries quiet? The MODIFIED QUIET STUDY AREA: QUIET CONVERSATIONS ONLY sign started to depress me. It seemed to indicate, in rather a cynical fashion, a surrender of institutional will. The library administration has called for a sort-of quiet study area—no one can say that it hasn't—but the rule has no teeth, no one enforces the regulation, no one cares. The students don't care to be quiet and the librarians don't care to compel them to be. Even the library, that sanctuary I love, seemed at that moment rather a cynical place.

My household finances have improved. They would have anyway, without all the adjuncting, but I continue to teach as many courses as I can. It's a part of who I am. So long as there are potential firemen required to learn the MLA format for the research paper, I will have work. Teaching has helped me to stay afloat. My old cracked wallpaper is up. My boiler seems peeved at having to work past its retirement age. I've got loose sconces and a driveway in need of resealing, lawns in need of reseeding, a kitchen in need of updating. But what I don't have is the old terror. Adjuncting helped rescue me. My mortgage is still annoyingly large each month, but the balance does dip, slowly, slowly.

In the course of time, something like peace returned to our home and our marriage. The one thing throwing our life off-kilter, the box in which we resided, faded in our minds as the rest of life expanded, mostly as the children grew and blossomed and their lives, so rich with possibility, seemed to fill the space. Our fears diminished. The house began to recede in our consciousness, becoming more like the ideal expressed by Le Corbusier: a machine for living in. We took less notice of its demands. More and more, my wife and I found ourselves inhabiting our old world. Worries gradually lifted—most worries, anyway, on most days. The general cloud of concern that dimmed our vision and made our eyes teary finally seemed to disperse. After a while, the house still seemed an error, but perhaps not a fatal one.

The writer composes a draft, puts it away in a drawer for a week, and upon reexamining it, discovers its flaws to be shockingly apparent. All the defects, the gaps in logic, the ideas not fully thought out and certainly not fully explained, stand out in brilliant high relief, as though someone else had written the thing—which, in a way, is the case. The prose has captured the writer's essence at the moment of composition; the writer, now older and more experienced by just a single week, nonetheless is a different person. Time passing creates critical distance. That fellow from ten years ago, the one who bought the house in the village, who gave up on literature and craved leaded glass windows—he's just a rather slipshod draft of myself. His errors stand out in their own brilliant high relief. I live with the havoc he has wrought, but at least it doesn't frighten and mystify and debilitate me anymore. His mistakes seem, after all this time, rather comic. I feel well able to cope with his screwups.

My wife and I remain attuned to the fragility of our existence together. We are careful. I hope we are careful enough. I have great faith in both of us—more in her than me.

Fall has arrived, but we won't take the air conditioner out

of the boys' window. A family of sparrows has built a nest beneath it. I don't want to evict or upset them. Let them have their shelter as long as they need it. If it's a little colder in the room, we'll just crank up the heat a bit. Let the birds enjoy our house and our village. There are many worse places to be.

21

Nobody Move

I HOLD A GUN ON YOU. You hold a gun on me. Who will surrender first? Who will even flinch? We are trapped in that narrative trope so beloved by America's high priest of violent movies, Quentin Tarantino. We are locked in a Mexican standoff.

Five groups point weapons at one another: the adjunct instructors, the colleges, the students, industry, and the American people in the person of the new sheriff in town, Barack Obama. Guns drawn, we are frozen. Nobody can move. How long can this go on? Our arms are getting pretty tired.

The adjunct instructors. We are hired to teach college to the unprepared. We are expected to maintain standards. We fail a good many students, and we pass some, and we wonder, as we place the C-minus or D-plus on the transcript, exactly what such a bad grade is worth to anyone: to the student, to an employer, to another college. At times, the whole process seems a terrible waste of time. Some of these students will never pass. They are not, to use the quaint and politically incorrect phrase, college material. But the question remains: do they need to be? Does the registered nurse who tends to me in the emergency room need to understand the ebb and flow of Molly Bloom's soliloquy? But then I can't help thinking: maybe the better nurse, the one who will make better clinical decisions, is the one who can appreciate Molly's cry of affirmation. *Your heart is going like mad yes but you're not having a heart attack don't worry yes you're only hyperventilating yes I will take care of you yes I said yes I will Yes.*

Better students would be less harrowing. Better students would eliminate fundamental inconsistencies, but better students would also eliminate the need for adjunct instructors, who are really only necessary so long as we keep expanding the parameters of what jobs require college and who exactly needs to go. So we instructors in search of a paycheck persevere with the students we have. We enjoy what we do and we like the students and we provide a valuable service to college and students both. But we look at those stacks of essays that need to be graded and realize, over and over, the challenges that we face.

The colleges. We think of them as institutions with goodness in their hearts, and they may very well be that, but in the end they are businesses, and like all businesses, they are happiest while expanding. Stasis, even a happy and fulfilling stasis, can never be a permanent state. College presidents love to put on mortarboards and attend commencement exercises, but what they love even more is slapping on a hardhat and grabbing a shovel for a groundbreaking ceremony. They want to serve as many students as possible, for reasons of mission and philosophy and the bottom line.

The big schools have big dreams. The University of Delaware announced in 2009 that it was planning the largest expansion of its campus in the school's history.[1] Yale is building two new residential colleges that are planned to open by 2013, which will enable it to expand its undergraduate enrollment from about 5,250 to 6,000, an increase of approximately 15 percent.[2] In New York City, both Fordham University and New York University are in the early stages of large-scale 25-year expansions. Fordham has spent $900,000 since 2006 in lobbying fees to try to get the project approved.[3] NYU is doing battle with preservationists, who oppose the building of a new 40-story tower in Greenwich Village, and community groups, who hand out flyers bearing the slogan "Overbuild, Oversaturate, Overwhelm."[4] Columbia University is expanding, too, north into West Harlem, at a cost of more than $6 billion. The university's Web site sounds a bit defensive as it justifies the plan in tortured prose not worthy of the Ivy League: "As new fields of knowledge emerge, the nation's universities are growing to pursue the expanding missions of teaching, research, public service, and patient care. With only a fraction of the space enjoyed by our leading peers across the country, Columbia has had to face an especially critical need for space in a dense urban environment."[5]

The community colleges are right there with their more upscale brothers, launching expansion projects both grand and modest. Work has begun on a $31 million expansion of Community College of Philadelphia; a pet project of Senator Arlen Specter, the new Northeast Regional Center is billed as the first certified "green" facility in the area.[6] In Texas, Austin Community College is preparing to open its eighth and largest campus in the fall of 2010.[7] In Michigan, Kalamazoo Valley Community College has begun taking bids for its $12 million expansion.[8] On April 8, 2010, ribbon was cut at a new facility at Bucks County Community College, a $15 million 28,000-square-foot facility—"green," of course—housing a library, café, student commons, classrooms, and outdoor amphitheater.[9] Ivy Tech Community College plans to expand into downtown Muncie, Indiana, taking over the former offices of the Muncie *Star Press*.[10]

Some of the cannier institutions are using the recession to their own advantage, picking up real estate on the cheap. The aforementioned University of Delaware has centered its expansion plans on the acquisition of a closed-down Chrysler automobile plant. Arizona State University wants to acquire a couple of office buildings and vacant computer-chip plants that became available when the manufacturing moved overseas. The University of Pennsylvania is looking at picking up a real bargain, a "stillborn condominium development."[11] St. Louis Community College–Florissant Valley wants to expand into the vacant Circuit City building next door.[12]

The economic downturn has done nothing but help community colleges. Even without President Obama's American Graduation Initiative, the price of community college tuition is highly attractive during a recession. A late-2009 cover story in *Community College Week,* "Bursting at the Seams: Study Finds Colleges Struggling With Unprecedented Demand," talks about surging enrollments fed by the recession. College administrators would no doubt say that they are merely trying to satisfy a demand that already exists, and that is true. But every new facility, every expanded student union, every additional classroom wing, commits colleges to maintaining enrollments high enough to justify their expense. That infrastructure will never go away. A college such as Yale may be able to increase its enrollments 15 percent without dropping its standards. There are many elite students who do not get in. It is not as clear to me that an institution such as Huron State, which has done its own expansion in years past, can do the same.

The students. Even the worst-performing students, who have scant hope of graduating, may use government-sponsored financial aid, or get themselves buried under mountains of debt in the form of student loans. And for what? For something that is very important in our culture: to try to participate, successfully or not, in what Bryan Caplan, associate professor of economics at George Mason University, calls a "signaling game":

> Most college courses teach few useful job skills; their main function is to signal to employers that students are smart, hard-working, and conformist. The upshot: Going to college is a lot like standing up at a concert to see better. Selfishly speaking, it works, but from a social point of view, we shouldn't encourage it.[13]

The students understand the signaling game, and the necessity of their playing it. They feel compelled to attend and succeed at college. They pay their money, or sign the aid forms, and they expect to thrive, no matter what level they start from. They see everybody participating, so it seems that everyone should be able to succeed; the sheer universality of college attendance makes for an odd sense of entitlement among the students. The students understand that they need a college degree to get a good job, and even though attending college might never have been their fondest wish, what choice do they have? But a more inefficient system can not have been devised by man. For a certain percentage of students, college attendance is an emotional, spiritual, and financial drain, with the expected financial rewards only tangentially a result of all the effort and expense. Until the core job-training components are separated from the rest of the college curriculum, students less inclined toward an academic track will suffer.

Industry. A college diploma means higher earning power—no one denies that. But the number of jobs calling for college has become artificially inflated. In much the same way that the country spent the first decade of the 2000s redefining what it meant to be a homeowner (to disastrous effect), so too we have reclassified which jobs require a college degree of some sort. Industry, including the civil service, wants its workers to be as credentialed as possible.

The Bureau of Labor Statistics has published a list of the 30 fastest growing occupations covered in the 2008–2009 Occupational Outlook Handbook. One requires a professional degree: veterinarian. Five normally require a master's degree: mental health counselors, mental health and substance abuse social workers, marriage and family therapists, physical therapists, and physician assistants. Nine normally require a bachelor's degree: network systems and data communications specialists, computer software engineers (applications), personal financial advisers, substance abuse and behavioral disorder counselors, financial analysts, forensic science technicians, computer systems analysts, database administrators, and computer software engineers (systems). Four normally require an associate's degree: veterinary techs, physical therapist assistants, dental hygienists, and environmental science and protection technicians. Three normally call for nothing beyond postsecondary vocational education: theatrical makeup artists, skin care specialists, and manicurists. The rest call for just on-the-job training: home care aides, home health aides, medical assistants, social and human service assistants, pharmacy techs, and dental assistants.

I am not impugning anyone's career, but it seems apparent that the bachelor's or even the associate's degree required for some of these professions is an inflated credential. Surely a vocational certificate coupled with on-the-job experience would be sufficient for a substance abuse counselor or forensic tech. Why does a dental hygienist require 60 credits of college? Why would a computer software engineer require a full four-year degree? Five of the nine professions requiring a bachelor's degree, in fact, involve computer systems, networks, or software, and it seems particularly challenging to connect the technical aspects of the computer science program with the remaining requirements of the bachelor's degree, the hallmark of which is a breadth of learning much at odds with vocational training.

Let's look at the requirements of one school at random, a nice prestigious college: the University of Pittsburgh. For a Bachelor of Science degree from the Department of Computer Science, the student is required to take 8 core courses for 25 credits and electives for 15 credits, making for 40 credits. Additionally, 2 math courses and a statistics course are required, bringing the total to 52 credits or thereabouts, which is less than half of the 120 credits needed to graduate. Industry wants the bachelor's degree for all that it signifies about a candidate. The larger question is: what is the value of those additional 68 credits, those 22 or 23 courses, in terms of computer expertise? Couldn't the computer degree be compressed into a smaller, shorter, cheaper, more efficient certificate?

I suppose if we don't want nineteen- or twenty-year-olds horsing around the corridors of industry, or causing trouble in the streets, four-year colleges are the best place to warehouse them. But the burden of debt a baccalaureate degree imposes on many students is cruel. The latest available figures state that 66 percent of students graduating with a bachelor's degree find themselves saddled with debt. The top 10 percent of those with student debt owed $44,500 or more on graduation; 50 percent owed at least $20,000. Almost as many graduates of certificate programs, 63 percent, graduated with the debt, but that debt was smaller by half. The top 10 percent of certificate recipients with student debt owed $22,300 or more; 50 percent owed at least $9,000. Credential inflation has ensured that earnings for certificate holders are smaller, but this really doesn't need to be the case.[14]

Credential inflation can be insidious. After a while it starts to seem that a particular occupation requires a degree, when it simply may not be the case. Consider the illustration of nursing. Currently, approximately 60 percent of nurses graduate with a three-year associate's degree, but that wasn't always true. Although a few baccalaureate programs in nursing began in the late nineteenth century, they never provided more than 15 percent of the new nurses each year; most nurses originally came from diploma programs affiliated directly with the hospitals. The model was that of an apprenticeship; the nursing students were essentially employees. The discovery of antibiotics expanded the need for health care services, and by the end of World War II the United States faced a serious shortage of nurses. Tasked by the Carnegie Foundation to study the problem, a sociologist named Dr. Esther Lucille Brown recommended a game change: that nurses be educated in colleges and universities, an idea that suited many of the young women entering the profession as well as the hospitals, which had begun to find their nursing programs burdensome. Meanwhile, President Truman's Commission on Higher Education urged large-scale expansion of the community college system, and soon the two-year colleges had moved into nursing education.[15]

The Associate Degree in Nursing, originally a two-year program, has grown to three years. And now the Carnegie Foundation, once again seemingly in the forefront of credential inflation, has put in its two cents: a new study from their Foundation for the Advancement of Teaching recommends that a Bachelor of Science in Nursing, a four-year program, be a prerequisite for all those seeking to work as nurses.

Kim Tinsley, a member of the National Organization for Associate Degree Nursing's Board of Directors, raises her objection to the recommendation. "[The nursing students] cannot afford to attend four years of B.S.N. classes and not work. The A.D.N. student does take up to four years to complete their degree, but it is due to the fact that they are working (sometimes full time) and have a family to support. The average age of our student is 27. The majority of our students are either married with a family or are a single parent. They cannot afford the time nor resources to attend a four-year program."[16]

Soon, they'll need a master's degree.

Sheriff Obama. President Obama is a cheerleader for universal education. Perhaps because of his own unusual biography, a multiplicity of individual narratives rings in his ears. He is an educationist: a believer that "schooling will guarantee the creative growth of cultural systems" and tends to influence "positively the development of an individual's potential."[17]

"We need to put a college education within reach of every American," says President Obama, and I can hear his inspiring cadences. "That's the best investment we can make in our future."[18]

It seems to me we've done that already.

The schools, the teachers, the students, industry, and the sheriff hold their weapons aloft. No one will back down. For any movement to occur, someone has to move first, and no one will. Mexican standoff.

. . .

I have had no choice but to recognize that many of my students have no business being in college. Putting an end to their participation without sentencing them to a life in the aisles of Wal-Mart would require that Americans relinquish their ill-thought-out love affair with higher education. Which would require an abandonment of the cockeyed optimism that has taken over our educational discourse. Which would require an embracing, again, of simple job training. Which would involve an acceptance on the part of human resource gatekeepers that college is far from essential in many professions. Which would require the colleges, particularly the lower-tier and community colleges, to rethink whom they are enrolling, whom they are serving, what the purpose of the whole rigmarole is. Which might lead to some streamlining, and the elimination of my job.

None of which I see happening. Undeniably, it is a societal ill for a poor student, financially poor and academically unskilled, to get lots of aid and go off to college where the likelihood is that he will not even finish the degree. But no student wants to be the first to forsake going to college for the good of society. No employer wants to be the first to admit that his job may not require college skills. No college wants to sacrifice enrollments. No senator wants to cut educational funding. No president of the United States wants to grab the podium and call, in bell-like tones, for fewer enrollments in the coming years, for more blue-collar workers who are skilled at what they do and make a good buck but don't have a clue about Bloom's Taxonomy. And the American people, bless their hearts, have no stomach for limiting anyone's options.

Here is Daniel Yankelovich, founder and chairman of Viewpoint Learning, Inc., who believes that anyone who can should go to college:

Most advanced industrial democracies distinguish more sharply than we do between higher education in the sense of a four-year college education and apprenticeship training. Theirs is a test-based meritocratic system. Our system of four-year and two-year colleges is more flexible, allowing greater opportunity for highly motivated students. Our democracy tips the balance, in keeping with our social norm of equality of opportunity. I am not arguing that our system is superior to that of other countries, but simply that it is a core American tradition that fits our culture and history—a bastion of stability in an unstable world. We should do everything we can to safeguard it.[19]

Part of American culture and tradition, yes, but as outmoded a tradition as the ritual stoning in "The Lottery."

Here is the bitter reality, as spoken by Marty Nemko, a career counselor who is subjected to a steady diet of college aspirations from people who in all likelihood will not succeed:

> I have a hard time telling such people the killer statistic: Among high-school students who graduated in the bottom 40 percent of their classes, and whose first institutions were four-year colleges, two-thirds had not earned diplomas eight and a half years later. . . . Yet four-year colleges admit and take money from hundreds of thousands of such students each year![20]

The United States of America does a few things extremely well. It is unmatched at completing a certain species of task requiring a relentless approach. John Kennedy knew this when he promised America would land a man on the moon by 1970. For us, that was kid's stuff. We're not the best at figuring out why we're doing any particular task, but we are a people who can get the stuff done. Is there a bathroom in America without a handicapped-access toilet, or a parking lot without a couple of special-needs spaces? Is there a residence abutting a highway that has not been discreetly separated from the noxious flow of traffic by one of those decorative noise-absorbing walls? The Hurricane Katrina debacle was particularly upsetting, I think, because the tasks at which we failed, the rescue and cleanup, the airlifting and people-moving and retrofitting of levees, are of the sort usually right in our wheelhouse.

We are, if nothing else, thorough.

Years ago, it seemed a noble goal (if you didn't think about it too carefully) to get as many students as possible into some sort of postsecondary education. And we have done that. God, have we succeeded. We have done too good a job. We haven't figured out why all these people are going to college, and we haven't figured out a way to get them to graduate, and the colleges haven't come up with a good grip on their new identities as vocational schools on steroids, but we've got those people enrolled. Every high school student in America who understands even dimly the concept of higher education can be whipped into a desk in an ivy-covered lecture hall so fast his head spins.

To automatically reclassify every high school graduate as college material just to conform to a national philosophy or as a shortcut for human resource departments is not a very precise approach. We have to adjust our thinking, and reject our sense of the primacy of the bachelor's and even the associate's degree. The old model of the vocational school is not a bad one. For everyone's good, industry should take a hard look at the value of those college degrees it persists in requiring. Let's reboot the civil service at the federal, state, and local levels by eliminating the college requirement for jobs that clearly do not need it. The list is longer than we think. Let's start devising human resource qualifications that actually reflect an ability to do the job, and not an applicant's skill at coming up with a certificate of dubious relevance. Let's start judging based on skills and experience and talent, and save failing students from a mountain of unnecessary debt.

But, meanwhile, I keep my weapon raised. I press on. I teach my classes. And I know that all the usual stuff will happen.

I will teach college students for whom college is a fairly

meaningless exercise. I will give them a questionnaire at the beginning of the course and ask: have you ever taken college English before? Yes, two years ago, someone will respond, but won't remember specific details. Did you write essays? I will ask. Don't remember. Did you do a research paper? Not sure. Two years ago! I can remember details of college classes I took 35 years ago. Their answers will suggest that they have suffered a profound head injury in the interim. They don't need me; they need Oliver Sacks.

They will write argumentation papers, and I won't know which side of the argument they are on. I may have to ask: are you fur it, or agin' it?

I will continue to attempt to fairly evaluate students in an introductory literature class who have spent their lives avoiding all mention of the subject.

I will teach off-campus, as I occasionally do, at the satellite locations set up to serve those who, for whatever reason, cannot rouse themselves to get to the main campus. This will put me in an actual high school classroom. There will be nasty messages left for us on the blackboard, reminders not to touch certain books or equipment, not to use up all the chalk, not to change the arrangement of desks and chairs. The high school teachers will post DO NOT ERASE signs and leave every blackboard in the classroom filled with writing. The behavior of my students will sink to a high school level. Some of my underperforming students will be sitting in one of the very same classrooms in which they underperformed as high school students. Our class will meet while varsity athletic teams condition themselves by running up and down the stairs. We will study Shakespeare with the faint buzz in our ears of *Oklahoma!*, which is being staged in the auditorium. One of my students will ask me, plaintively, can we go to the play? Wouldn't that be good for an English class? And I will be sorely tempted.

I will give tests with matching columns, and the students will leave three or four answers blank, as though the effort of guessing were simply too much for them. If I tell them before the test that each matching column letter is used just once, they will get all skeptical on me, and use "M," say, three times.

They will tell me interesting things about Flannery O'Connor's characters in answers to questions about "The Dead." They will think that Edward Said is a literary technique, and "allusion" the author of *Ulysses*.

We will spend hours on "The Lottery." They will take copious notes. And when the exam rolls around, a student or two or three will think that the massive autobiographical novel unpublished in James Joyce's lifetime is called *The Lottery*. They will think that the word, repeatedly incanted in "A Clean, Well Lighted Place," that embodies life's great yawning nothingness, is "Hemingway." Whose ghost keeps appearing in *Hamlet*? I will ask on a reading quiz. The last time I did, someone answered "Shakespeare." I had to think about that for a minute. Who would possibly give that as an answer? Who would confuse the author with his creation? Perhaps the student was simply acknowledging the tradition that Shakespeare played the ghost at the Globe. Perhaps she was conflating—no, no, there was no conflating going on.

Likewise, when they spell it "Shaksper," it is not because they want to be historically faithful to the author's autograph.

They will manage to find new and endlessly innovative ways to flummox me, my students. But I don't care. Years of teaching have left their marks on me; I feel scarred, nicked, marked up, chipped, bearing the signs of life lived as vividly as the old wallpaper in my bedroom. But I wouldn't dream of stopping. Ever. It's too good, in its own singular way. Adjuncting used to be something I struggled to fit into my world; now, years hence, I've come to see how much it anchors and enriches that world—how much it actually is my world. Without English 101 and English 102, I think I might well be bereft. Doesn't that seem odd? It does to me.

. . .

"We need a thesis sentence," I tell the class, for perhaps the five-hundredth time. I search for fresh words to convey what I mean. "We need an overarching statement. We need a great utterance that our writing endeavors to support. What are we trying to prove?" I throw out my arms dramatically. "Why are we writing at all? Why are we even here?"

"We have to be," says a youthful wiseguy. We all laugh. "No, just kidding," he assures me. "We love it here."

I bring my hands together, the way a priest would. Experience has left me with a surfeit of hard-won wisdom, life's consolation prize. I dispense a nugget. "Having to be here will not lead to profundity. Wanting deeply and seriously comes first. Rebelling against our circumstances will get us nowhere. Acceptance of where we are—knowing the shape of one's life—is the first small step in giving shape to one's writing. Let's all have something to say. And while we're at it, very important: subject-verb agreement. Always."

While you watch *American Idol* and *Dancing with the Stars,* we're gathering for another semester in the basement of the ivory tower. Students and teacher alike share flickerings of wonderment and uncertainty. How did we all get here? The classroom surroundings are familiar, even cozy: there's a comfort to sitting in rows, and the desks wrap around the students protectively. The textbooks seem compendia of all the world's knowledge. Who among us wouldn't think: we can do great things in this room! What happens in a classroom can be of such great consequence, but for that to be true, the work done there must be worthwhile, suitably complex, challenging, even daunting. In the classroom there must always be much at stake, which doesn't necessarily lead to ease of mind, and thus classrooms are not always the welcoming places they may seem at first. Important work is very often done in anguishing circumstances. A few students will thrive; many will wither.

We are, all of us there gathered, trembling with fright, short of breath, sick at heart, but perhaps hopeful. That our senses are so alive is thrilling. The whiteboard markers give off a vaguely medicinal smell. The edges of posters from semesters past curl away from the wall. Motes of dust bob in the light from the overhead projector. The old heating unit comes on with a shudder. There seems a meaning in all this mundanity that lies just beyond our grasp. Every new assignment, at least, starts us all thinking.

Notes

Preface

1. Sandy Baum and Patricia Steele. "Who Borrows Most? Bachelor's Degree Recipients with High Levels of Student Debt." *College Board Advocacy and Policy Center—Trends in Higher Education Series*, 2010.
2. Monitor's Editorial Board. "Raise the Community College Graduation Rate." *Christian Science Monitor*, 26 Apr. 2010.
3. Eric P. Bettinger and Bridget Terry Long. "Does Cheaper Mean Better? The Impact of Using Adjunct Instructors on Student Outcomes." *Review of Economics and Statistics*. In press.
4. Census Questionnaire Content, 1990 CQC-13. United States Census Bureau, Sept. 1994.
5. *Statistical Abstract of the United States, 2008*. Section 4, Education. United States Census Bureau.

1. The Adjunct

1. "Ensuring the Quality of Undergraduate Programs in English and Foreign Languages: MLA Recommendations on Staffing." Modern Language Association, 2002.
2. Michael Murphy. "Adjuncts Should Not Just Be Visitors in the Academic Promised Land." *Chronicle of Higher Education* 48.29 (2002): B14–15.
3. Jeffrey R. Young. "Seton Hall Adjunct Professor Lashes Out at Students in E-mail Message." *Chronicle of Higher Education* 49.27 (2003): A12.
4. Jeffrey J. Selingo. "An Administrator Takes Up the Cause of Adjuncts." *Chronicle of Higher Education* 55.9 (2008): A4.
5. American Federation of Teachers. *American Academic: The State of the Higher Education Workforce 1997–2007*, Feb. 2009.
6. Alexa Sasanow. "Some Departments Seeing Rise in Number of Adjunct Professors." *Tufts Daily*, 27 Apr. 2010.

7. DI Editorial Board. "Sharp Rise in Adjunct Professors Has Obvious Downsides." *Daily Iowan,* 29 Mar. 2010.

2. Writing Hell

1. Richard Peabody and Lucinda Ebersole, eds. *Conversations with Gore Vidal.* Jackson: University Press of Mississippi, 2005.
2. E. B. White. *Letters of E. B. White.* Ed. Dorothy Lobrano Guth. New York: Harper & Row, 1976.

4. Compare and Contrast

1. Shirley Dickson. "Integrating Reading and Writing to Teach Compare-Contrast Text Structure: A Research-Based Methodology." *Reading & Writing Quarterly* 14 (1999): 49–79.
2. Mark Richardson. "Writing Is Not Just a Basic Skill." *Chronicle of Higher Education* 55.11 (2008): A47–8.
3. Jennifer I. Berne. "Teaching the Writing Process: Four Constructs to Consider." *New England Reading Association Journal* 40.1 (2004): 42–6.
4. Alex Reid. "Atlantic Monthly Offers Clichés of Writing Pedagogy." Digital Digs. Weblog. www.alex-reid.net/2008/05/atlantic-monthl .html. 17 May 2008.
5. Mike Rose. "Teaching Remedial Writing." Mike Rose's Blog. Weblog. mikerosebooks.blogspot.com/2008/07/teaching-remedial-writing .html. 8 July 2008.

6. Community College

1. American Association of Community Colleges, Commission on the Future of the Community Colleges. *Building Communities: A Vision for a New Century.* Washington, D.C.: American Association of Community Colleges, 1998. Quoted in Henry D. Shannon and Ronald C. Smith. "A Case for the Community College's Open Access Mission." *New Directions for Community Colleges* 136 (2006): 15–21.
2. Becky Orr. "Education Secretary Duncan Pitches Community Colleges." WyomingNews.com. 19 Sept. 2009.
3. "Bill Cosby Back in Detroit to Help Schools." Click On Detroit. 13 Sept. 2009.
4. Barack Obama. Remarks by the President on the American Graduation Initiative. Macomb Community College, Warren, Michigan, 14 July 2009. Transcribed on www.whitehouse.gov/the_press_office/ Remarks-by-the-President-on-the-American-Graduation-Initiative-in-Warren-MI/.
5. Susan K. Grimes and David C. Kelly. "Underprepared Community College Students: Implications of Attitudinal and Experiential Differences." *Community College Review* 27.2 (1999): 73–92.

6. John Rouse. "The Politics of Composition." *College English* 41.1 (1979): 1–12.
7. David Bartholomae. "The Study of Error." *College Composition and Communication* 31.3 (1980): 253–68.
8. Barack Obama. Remarks by the President on Innovation and Sustainable Growth. Hudson Valley Community College, Troy, New York, 21 Sept. 2009. Transcribed on www.whitehouse.gov/the_press_office/ Remarks-by-the-President-on-Innovation-and-Sustainable-Growth-at-Hudson-Valley-Community-College/.

7. Remediation

1. Thomas Bailey. "Challenge and Opportunity: Rethinking the Role and Function of Developmental Education in Community College." *New Directions for Community Colleges* 145 (2009): 11–30.
2. Craig Hadden. "The Ironies of Mandatory Placement." *Community College Journal of Research and Practice* 24 (2000): 823–38.
3. Dolores Perin. "Can Community Colleges Protect Both Access and Standards? The Problem of Remediation." *Teachers College Record* 108.3 (2006): 339–73.
4. Ibid.
5. Ibid.
6. Ibid.
7. Bailey. "Challenge and Opportunity."
8. Eric P. Bettinger and Bridget Terry Long. "Remediation at the Community College: Student Participation and Outcomes." *New Directions for Community Colleges* 129 (2005): 17–26.
9. David Mazella. "Blessings and Curses." Long Eighteenth. Weblog. http://long18th.wordpress.com. 26 May 2008.

9. The Pain

1. Michael Holden. "Baseless Assumptions About Students' Basic Knowledge—What Students Know (a Survey): What Can the Informationally Challenged Write Beyond Personal Narratives?" *Contemporary Education* 68 (1996): 64–66.
2. Thomas Bailey. "Challenge and Opportunity: Rethinking the Role and Function of Developmental Education in Community College." *New Directions for Community Colleges* 145 (2009): 11–30.

10. College as Eden

1. Kim Barto. "Speaker Encourages Students: Carver Grad Stresses Education." *Martinsville Bulletin,* 6 Nov. 2009.
2. Abby Luby. "Bronx Teens Get a Taste of Upstate Life for a Month in Ritzy Chappaqua." *Daily News* [New York], 29 Aug. 2009.

3. Robert Delaney. "Detroit Tigers MVP Magglio Ordóñez Funds New Scholarship for Area's Young People." *Catholic Online*, 15 Feb. 2008.

4. Michael Scherer and Nancy Gibbs. "Interview with the First Lady." *Time*, 21 May 2009.

5. "Estrella Mountain Community College Gives 50 Kindergartners College Experience." *US Fed News*, 15 Oct. 2009.

6. "Parents Enroll Newborns in State Prepaid Tuition Plan at Record Rate." *US States News*, 11 Feb. 2008.

7. Jennifer L. Berghom. "Texas State University President Talks About Importance of College to Memorial High Students." TheMonitor.com. 13 Feb. 2008.

8. Linda Saslow. "Suffolk County College is Raising Tuition." *New York Times*, 26 April 2009, Section LI: 2.

9. Beata Mostafavi. "MCC Eyes 11.7% Hike in Tuition." *Flint Journal*, 17 June 2010: A3.

10. David Slade and Diane Knich. "Why Is College Tuition So High? In South Carolina, Costs Have Nearly Tripled in a Decade." *The Post and Courier* [Charleston, SC], 8 Aug. 2010: A1.

11. Scott Carlson. "The $50K Club: 58 Private Colleges Pass a Pricing Milestone." *Chronicle of Higher Education*, 1 Nov. 2009.

12. Abby Goodnough. "New Meaning for Night Class at 2-Year Colleges." NYTimes.com. 28 Oct. 2009.

13. Sandra Block. "In a Recession, Is College Worth It? Fear of Debt Changes Plans." USAToday.com. 31 Aug. 2009.

14. "College Education Is About More Than Money." Letters to the Editor. *USA Today*, 3 Sept. 2009, final ed.: 10A.

15. Tamara Draut. "Debt-for-Diploma System: Student-loan Debt Saddles College Grads Long After They Earn Degrees." *New England Journal of Higher Education*, Winter 2009: 31–32.

16. Mark C. Taylor. "Academic Bankruptcy." NYTimes.com. 14 Aug. 2010.

17. Brunner v. N.Y. St. Higher Educ. Servs. Corp., 831 F.2d 395 (2d Cir. 1987).

18. Charles Booker. "The Undue Hardship of Education." *Journal of Law & Education* 39.2, April 2010: 273–79.

19. Jon Gertner. "Forgive Us Our Student Debts." *New York Times Magazine*, 11 June 2006.

20. Jeffrey Selingo and Eric Hoover. "U.S. Public's Confidence in Colleges Remains High." *Chronicle of Higher Education* 50.35 (2004): A1+.

21. "College Enrollment and Work Activity of 2008 High School Graduates." *News: Bureau of Labor Statistics*, 28 April 2009.

22. "U.S. Census Bureau: College Enrollment Up 17 Percent Since 2000." *Education Business Weekly*, 1 Oct. 2008: 19.

23. "Are Too Many Students Going to College?" *Chronicle Review: The Chronicle of Higher Education*, 8 Nov. 2009.

24. Stephen J. McNamee and Robert K. Miller Jr. *The Meritocracy Myth*. Lanham, MD: Rowman & Littlefield, 2004.

25. Timothy F. Geithner. Remarks at the White House Task Force on Middle-Class Families Meeting on College Access and Affordability. Syracuse University, Syracuse, New York, 9 Sept. 2009.

26. "Excerpts of the President's Remarks in Warren, Michigan, Today and a Fact Sheet on the American Graduation Initiative." White House—Office of the Press Secretary, www.whitehouse.gov. 14 July 2009.

27. Community colleges have long contended that such statistics as graduation rate, which they are required by the federal Student Right-to-Know Act to report to the National Center for Education Statistics in order for their students to receive federal financial aid, are flawed. The schools claim that the numbers ignore the transfer mission of community colleges: students who transfer before graduation are counted as dropouts, and the transferring school is penalized in the rankings. However, Thomas Bailey, Peter M. Crosta, and Davis Jenkins, in their study of graduation rates at Florida's community colleges, conclude that although the SRK rates do "yield a biased and potentially misleading picture of individual community college student outcomes," when adjustments were made for varying student and institutional characteristics, "college rankings were still fairly stable." Correcting for transfers using a database that tracks students across multiple institutions, the researchers found that the "SRK graduation rates do not present a significantly more negative picture of community college performance than rates that could follow individual students across transfers." See "What Can Student Right-to-Know Graduation Rates Tell Us About Community College Performance?" *CCRC Working Paper No. 6.* Community College Resource Center. Teacher's College, Columbia University, Aug. 2006.

28. James Vaznis. "Hub Grads Come Up Short in College: Most from Class of 2000 Have Failed to Earn Degrees." *Boston Globe,* 17 Nov. 2008. Also, "Getting In Isn't Enough." Editorial. *Boston Globe,* 17 Nov. 2008.

11. Grade Inflation Temptation

1. Phil Primack. "Doesn't Anybody Get a C Anymore?" *Boston Globe Sunday Magazine,* 5 Oct. 2008.

2. Jillian K. Kushner. "College Admits Record-Low 7 Percent." *Harvard Crimson,* 31 March 2009.

3. Brenda S. Sonner. "A Is for Adjunct: Examining Grade Inflation in Higher Education." *Journal of Education for Business* 76.1 (2000): 5–8.

4. Ronald C. McArthur. "A Comparison of Grading Patterns Between Full- and Part-Time Humanities Faculty: A Preliminary Study." *Community College Review* 27.3 (1999): 65–76. I can't help but get a

little fed up at the constant demonizing of adjuncts. On the one hand, we're letting the students skate through the system with vastly inflated grades. On the other, "community colleges with the largest proportion of part-time instructors have the worst student-graduation rates." See the Jacoby study cited in "Study Sees Link Between Part-Time Instructors and Graduation Rates." *Chronicle of Higher Education* 53.10 (2006): A10. Jacoby thinks the problem is mainly due to adjuncts' lack of office hours. "They [adjuncts] don't have offices, and some schools don't even list part-time faculty in their directory. . . . People don't even know how to find them." Either we adjuncts are goosing them through the system or we're not; one can't have it both ways.

5. These things are all over the Internet, if that's your idea of Web-surfing entertainment. I got this one at http://webpages.yosemite .cc.ca.us/keriotisd/Handouts/101_Rubric.pdf.

6. Ian Marshall. "'I am he as you are he as you are me and we are all together': Bakhtin and the Beatles." In *Reading the Beatles: Cultural Studies, Literary Criticism, and the Fab Four.* Kenneth Womack and Todd F. Davis, eds. Albany: State University of New York Press, 2006, 9–35. This work is the exact contemporary equivalent of *The Beatles Book* to which I referred earlier: I am a sucker for pointy-headed academics rocking out—if talking about the Beatles can still be considered rocking out.

7. Barbara H. Wooten. "Gender Differences in Occupational Employment." *Bureau of Labor Statistics—Monthly Labor Review,* April 1997. Also "Labor Force Statistics from the Current Population Survey. Table 11: Household Data—Annual Averages: Employed Persons by Detailed Industry, Sex, Race, and Hispanic or Latino Ethnicity." *Bureau of Labor Statistics,* Jan. 2010.

12. The Textbooks

1. "PhD Program in English: Ira Shor." Graduate Center, CUNY Web Page. City University of New York.

2. Ira Shor. "Why Teach About Social Class?" *Teaching English in the Two-Year College* 33.2 (2005): 161–71.

13. An Introduction to the Research Paper

1. Betsy Barefoot. "Bridging the Chasm: First-Year Students and the Library." *Chronicle of Higher Education* 20 Jan. 2006 supp.: B16.

16. The Writing Workshop

1. Bruce E. R. Thompson. "Emissaries from the World Beyond: The Authenticity of Adjuncts." *Chronicle of Higher Education* 47.46 (2001): B16.

2. Michael Holden. "Baseless Assumptions About Students' Basic Knowledge—What Students Know (a Survey): What Can the Informationally Challenged Write Beyond Personal Narratives?" *Contemporary Education* 68 (1996): 64–66.

17. Do Your Job, Professor!

1. "I Spout Off . . ." Itinerant Oak—A Family Journey. Weblog. http://itinerant-oak.blogspot.com/2008/06/i-spout-off.html. 9 June 2008.
2. Steven D. Krause. "Yet Another Topic to Discuss: 'In the Basement of the Ivory Tower.'" emutalk.org. Weblog. 24 May 2008.
3. Krause, Reply. 24 May 2008.
4. Doug Robinson. "Like Students, Like Professor." Comspot: The First-Year Writing Program at the University of Mississippi. Weblog. http://www.olemiss.edu/depts/English/blog/2008/05/like-students-like-professor.html. 16 May 2008. This blog seems to have been taken down.
5. "WPA Outcomes Statement for First-Year Composition." Council of Writing Program Administrators. wpacouncil.org. n.d.
6. Mina P. Shaughnessy. *Errors and Expectations: A Guide for the Teacher of Basic Writing.* New York: Oxford University Press, 1977.

19. On Borrowing Liberally from Other People's Work

1. "Student Kills Arkansas Professor, Himself." *Philadelphia Inquirer,* SF Edition, 29 Aug. 2000: A04.

20. The College Bubble

1. Thomas Sowell. *The Housing Boom and Bust.* New York: Basic Books, 2009.
2. Jo Becker, Sheryl Gay Stolberg, and Stephan Labaton. "Bush Drive for Home Ownership Fueled Housing Bubble." NYTimes.com. 20 Dec. 2008.
3. "Excerpts of the President's Remarks in Warren, Michigan, Today and a Fact Sheet on the American Graduation Initiative." White House—Office of the Press Secretary. www.whitehouse.gov. 14 July 2009.

21. Nobody Move

1. Susan Snyder. "U. Delaware Planning Big Expansion." *Philadelphia Inquirer,* City-C Edition, 27 Oct. 2009: B01.
2. Tamar Lewin. "Yale to Raise Enrollment by 15 Percent." *New York Times,* Late Edition—Final, 8 June 2008: A37.
3. Frank Lombardi. "Fordham Growin' Up: Expansion of Lincoln Cen-

ter Campus Likely Will Be Approved After Key Vote." *Daily News* (New York), Sports Final Edition—Suburban, 11 June 2009: 46.

4. Lisa W. Foderaro. "Critics Turn Out at Open House on N.Y.U. Expansion." *New York Times,* Late Edition—Final, Metropolitan Desk, 15 April 2010: A21.

5. "Columbia University in the City of New York: Manhattanville in West Harlem." Manhattanville Planning Updates. www.columbia .edu.

6. "Community College of Philadelphia; Community College of Philadelphia to Break Ground on Multimillion Dollar Expansions in Philadelphia." *Biotech Business Week,* 20 Oct. 2008. Expanded Reporting: 1390.

7. Ralph K. M. Haurwitz. "Trustee Candidates Aspire to AAC Board at Time of Growth." Statesman.com. 2 May 2010.

8. Sean McHugh. "Kalamazoo Valley Community College to Start $12 Million Expansion." Mlive.com. 3 Sept. 2009.

9. "Officials Cut Ribbon at Expanded Upper Bucks Campus." News release. www.bucks.edu.

10. "Ivy Tech Unveils Major Muncie Campus Expansion." www.ins ideindianabusiness.com. 3 Sept. 2009.

11. Goldie Bluemenstyk. "Expansion in Mind, Colleges Snap Up Real Estate in Buyers' Markets." *Chronicle of Higher Education* 56.19 (2010): A14.

12. Curtis Daniels. "Florissant Valley Seeks Campus Expansion." www .meramecmontage.com. 24 Feb. 2010.

13. "Are Too Many Students Going to College?" *Chronicle Review: The Chronicle of Higher Education,* 8 Nov. 2009.

14. Sandy Baum and Patricia Steele. "Who Borrows Most? Bachelor's Degree Recipients with High Levels of Student Debt." *College Board Advocacy and Policy Center—Trends in Higher Education Series,* 2010.

15. Liana Orsolini-Hain, Ph.D., R.N.; and Verle Waters, M.A., R.N. "Education Evolution: A Historical Perspective of Associate Degree Nursing." *Journal of Nursing Education* 48.5 (2009): 266–71.

16. "Nursing Tug of War." *Inside Higher Ed,* 7 Jan. 2010.

17. Normand R. Bernier and Jack E. Williams. *Beyond Beliefs: Ideological Foundations of American Education.* Englewood Cliffs, N.J.: Prentice Hall, 1973.

18. Barack Obama. "Reclaiming the American Dream Speech." Bettendorf, IA, 7 Nov. 2007. Quoted in "Barack Obama and Joe Biden: Making College Affordable for Everyone." www.barackobama.com.

19. "Are Too Many Students Going to College?" *Chronicle Review: The Chronicle of Higher Education,* 8 Nov. 2009.

20. Marty Nemko. "America's Most Overrated Product: the Bachelor's Degree." *Chronicle of Higher Education* 54.34 (2008): B17–18.